RAJA RAMMOHUN ROY

THE FATHER OF MODERN INDIA

RAMPRAKASH SINGH PAVAIYA

TRUE SIGN
PUBLISHING HOUSE

Published by True Sign Publishing House

Address: SY. No. 21/2 & 21/3, Sonnenahalli,

Krishnarajapura, Bengaluru,

Karnataka - 560049 India

E-mail: truesignbooks@gmail.com

Website: www.truesign.in

Copyright © 2023 by True Sign

Raja Rammohun Roy: The Father of Modern India

Author: Ramprakash Singh Pavaiya

ISBN: 978-93-5805-059-2

First Edition: 2023

All Rights Reserved. No part of this publication may be reproduced, stored in a retrieval system, or transmitted, in any form, or by any means, electronic, mechanical, photocopying, recording or otherwise, without the prior permission of the publishers.

This book is dedicated to
my parents
(Sunita Beerval Singh Pavaiya)
who always inspired me
to move forward.
I hope to write books
on the lives of great men
and present them as a
good writer in the
future as well.

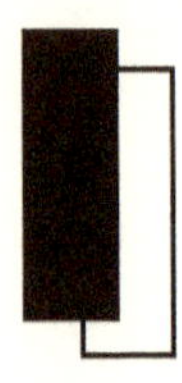

Preface

Raja Rammohun Roy, the father of modern Indian education can undoubtedly be called a great man. He contributed in removing those evils prevailing in Indian society which took our society into darkness.

The creator of modern India, the founder of one of the biggest socio-religious reform movements, the Brahmo Samaj, Raja Rammohun Roy played an important role in eradicating social evils like the Sati system. He also advocated various changes in the Indian society popularizing the study of English, modern medical technology and science.

Rammohun Roy worked tirelessly to support various social reforms like education of women, widow remarriage, inter-caste marriage, property rights for women and he fought against social evils like female infanticide, child marriage, polygamy and sati.

Through this book the readers will understand the life of Rammohun Roy more closely. It is the effort of the author and our publication to provide you more information about such great men which is not generally available.

CONTENTS

1. The Spirit of Raja Rammohun Roy 7

2. The National and Universal in Raja Rammohun Roy 12

3. Rammohun Roy - The Father of Political Regeneration
   of India 15

4. Raja Rammohun Roy A Man of Letters 17

5. Rammohun Roy - A Jurist and a Politician 20

6. Searching for Truth (1772-1803) 22

7. Throwing Down the Gauntlet (1803 -1814) 29

8. Spiritual Theism versus Idolatry and Suttee (1814-1820) 40

9. Regular and Irregular Campaigns against Trinitarian
   Orthodoxy (1820 -1824) 65

10. Journalistic and Educational Pioneer-work (1821 -1826) 94

11. Founding the Brahmo Samaj (1826 -1828) 115

12. The Abolition of Suttee (1828 -1830) 131

13. Embassy to Europe (1830-1833) 154

14. Autobiographical Image of Rammohan Roy 207

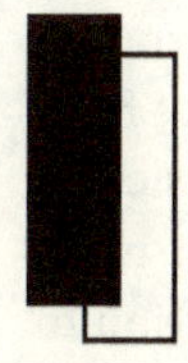

The Spirit of Raja Rammohun Roy

To my mind, Rammohun Roy is distinctly different from the other great men of India. He is the father of a new race of Indian heroes. He heralds a new epoch in Indian History. His illustrious predecessors - mighty souls that have so richly endowed India with truth and goodness by their holy careers - were mostly sages, a few philanthropists, some patriots. But he was the first and (let me add) the greatest nation-builder that India has produced. His spirit ramified into diverse branches covering the whole area of national life. In his career is illustrated the harmonious play of that cycle of forces which, by their conjoint operation evolve and shape out a modern nation. In range of vision, in reach of sympathy, in versatility of powers, in variety of activities, in coordination of interests and in coalescence of ideals - in fine, as realizing an all-round, all-receptive life in its manifold fullness, Rammohun Roy is a unique figure in the history of India, if not, in the annals of the race. I may attempt to illustrate this by a reference to this, our National Week. Here is the national life, as it were attracted to and centred in the metropolis. Here is a round of gatherings - Congress and Conferences - calculated by their deliberations and sub-sequent working to foster the growth of a sound, steady, complete nation. In the whole hierarchy of Indian worthies, is there another name that evinces equal fitness with that of Raja Rammohun Roy to be the ruling spirit of this great week, the presiding genius of all these gatherings? Is not their very mutual appreciation an emblem of his spirit? Verily, he is the Father of Modern India; he is the rishi of the modern age.

Rammohun was essentially a religious genius. He knew that human growth was endogenous from the soul outwards. He was sure that out of the heart were all the issues of life. His faith in the saving, regenerating power of the Spirit was unbounded. To him a being not illumined by belief and trust in God, a progress not impelled by a religious force, was worse than inconceivable - it was degenerating, degrading. To the myriad ills of India the sovereign remedy was a living faith in a wise and living God - neither a cloistered faith that scorns and shuns the world, nor a busy careworn faith that assigns the leisure hour to a hurried worship, nor the prudent faith that imports a god to watch a truant world, nor yet a speculative faith that prefixes a creator to a law-governed universe. It was a direct vision of an indwelling Glory, a personal communion with an immanent Spirit, an implicit trust in an all regulating Providence, a wholehearted devotion to an all-controlling Purpose, a cheerful obedience to an all-governing Will, a conscious participation in an all-saving Grace, a rapturous delight in an all-entrancing Beauty. It was a faith to which the universe was a consecrated temple, the soul a holy shrine, conscience a sacred oracle, duty a divine ordinance, truth the imperishable gospel, love the perfect rule, life a progressive pilgrimage, humanity an abounding grace. It was a faith that interpreted law as the method, force as the will, and matter as the localized potency of God: it was a faith that esteemed the world as a reflection, the soul as a vision, and history as a panoramic presentation of the nature and the purpose of the Deity. With Rammohun Roy the man this faith - this sublime invigorative theism - was a passion, a power and a joy, that made of him a hero and a prophet. To Rammohun Roy the nation-builder this vital, fertile faith - a faith lofty as the love of God and ample as the wants of man - furnished alike the enduring basis and the cementing strength, the ample range and the towering greatness of a united and vigorous nation.

This spirit of a deep and broad faith proceeded to apply to, and realize in, the national life. The work of Rammohun Roy, as of every great nation-builder, was four-fold: to reassess the national heritage, to replenish the national resources, to infuse a new quickening and harmonizing spirit, and to use the awakened energies for the new national wants and demands.

The hope and assurance of a reviving nation springs largely from its "storied past." Therein lies the evidence of national possibilities, the guarantee of national solvency and in a large measure the impetus to national endeavour. The inspira tion of the ancestral example is the cheering outlook of the dutiful successor, the acquisition of the sturdy sire, the starting capital of the ambitious son; the glory of past national achievement, the load-star-the light on the path of the advancing generations. India's wealth, her richest acquisition, and her highest achievement, is the sublime consciousness, the vision, of the all-permeating and all-transfiguring, all-embracing and all-fulfilling, all-absorbing and all-transcending spirit. Limitations - nay, aberrations - there might be; but the distinguishing mark, the predominant note, the prime concern, of blessed Bharatavarsha is God-consciousness. The central principle, the master passion, 'the driving power,' of her accredited worthies is God-vision. To trace the lineaments and study the ways, to follow the footsteps and bow to the will, to imitate the purposes and reproduce the nature - in a word, to realize and fulfil oneself as a projected emblem - of the divine spirit, is the one prevailing national ideal, surviving all vicissitudes; and to have saved from oblivion, purified from accretions, and readjusted for modern needs - this indwelling spirit of India, was the Raja's high service to the nation. His translations of the 'Upanishads,' his elucidation of the 'Vedanta,' his exposition of the 'Gayatri,' his defence of 'Hindu Theism,' his advocacy of spiritual worship, his passionate pleading for a devout life as incomparably superior to the most engrossing ceremonializm - all these were suggested and sustained by that patriotic and nation-building purpose of re-instating a living liberal faith amidst clogging symbolism and enervating superstition. He re-directed the national intellect to the teachings of the ancient national scriptures, and reopened the national soul to the inspiration of the most honoured national seers.

To the keen gaze of his soul there lay bare, amidst the puzzling heap of national scripture, a fund of eternal truth and inexpressible joy which, sympathetically studied, judiciously adopted, intelligently imparted, and reverently received, might form the pabulum - the staple food - for his and many a coming generation of eager seekers after God. In this spirit (as Max Muller has thoughtfully pointed out), not of a prudent adherence to mere antiquity, but of an honest search for and a grateful appreciation of the seeds of imperishable truth, that he sought to lay down the Vedanta of the Upanishads, stripped of its strange and disguising coverings, as the basis of the new national life. There he rejoiced to meet the seers of ancient wisdom - types of Emerson's "teachers from within"- proclaiming (to adopt the happy language of the same sage) a God, not of tradition, not of rhetoric, not even of inferential conviction, but of direct sight - a vision and an ecstasy - that circled the world with a halo of celestial glory and transported the soul with the raptures of Heaven. There he was grateful to find a revelation of God's truth that for loftiness of conception, depth of insight, serenity of contemplation, fervour of devotion, austerity of discipline, perfection of disinterestedness, and intensity of beatitude, would ever remain unsurpassed, if at all equalled, in the history of the world.

Rammohun Roy, the ardent restorer of the Upanishadic Vedanta as the deepest insight of the Hindu (the Eastern) genius, was likewise the gifted interpreter of the richest expression of the Semitic (the Western) genius - the heart of Jesus. The India of the rishis, rich and blessed in the wealth of the soul, was, however, not - could not be - the India of Rammohun Roy. Alike external pressure and internal throb were all along modifying and recasting the national ideals and replenishing and redirecting the national energies.

Heaven had ordained India to be the spiritual Prayag of the world - the sacred spot of the congruent confluence of the mighty world - currents of East and West - of the joy and the strength that come of a lasting, vital harmony of intellect and will, knowledge and power. A vaster and more comprehensive synthesis than had hitherto been realized - had hitherto been, perhaps, possible -- had to be attempted: a reverent garnering of "the wisdom of the East and the West," a holy communion of sage and prophet in truth and goodness. In this devout spirit of genuine yet thoughtful enthusiasm Rammohun Roy submitted his "Precepts of Jesus, the guide to peace and happiness" to the world, as a spiritual and ethical code calculated powerfully to conduce to the elevation of "men's ideas to high and liberal notions of God" and to "the maintenance of the peace and harmony of mankind at large." To bring home to the "business and bosom" of India the serene godliness, the self-sacrificing love, the ethical vigour and the winning grace of Jesus, and thus to enshrine the Heaven-appointed author of the Christ - and life and civilization of the west in the heart of the nation, was the avowed object of this remarkable publication.

The warm controversy led to perhaps, the indirect testimony to its worth and its necessity. Now with the lapse of nearly three generations all the personal and occasional element in that tough fight for truth had ceased to disturb the vision, the work may justly be valued as the prophetic forecast of that great reconciliation - that organic federation - of East and West, through which every faithful and progressive nation will realize the fullness of its potency in a universal humanity. The future of India is rich with a promise almost baffling present estimation, even because it appears to be that eternal capital of the Spirit-empire, whither pilgrim souls from all quarters, with their heart-offerings of ideals, aspirations, endeavours and achievements, are drawn to the shrine of immortal Love, and whence will issue forth a Light radiant as the glory of the Lord and a Peace passing all mere human understanding. That this ancient land, thus high-honoured of Heaven, may fulfil this lofty destiny, depends undoubtedly on her readiness to imbibe this catholic-liberal and reverent-spirit of Rammohun Roy - a spirit inspired by the faith and active in the hope that it is with the sublime soul-contributions and the loving heart-tributes of all worthy people that God will at last make "the pile complete." This spirit, now fairly familiar, at any rate in theory, was the unique distinction of Rammohun Roy to have inaugurated; and here is one further proof that he is the builder of modern Indian nation, the father of new India.

It is very cheering to note that this gradual commingling of the best in the East and in the West for the ultimate perfection of both, and, of the whole humanity, as being Heaven's own method, is realized in an increasing degree on all hands.

This was an intuitive perception of Rammohun Roy; who was, not only (to use Prof. Sir M. Williams's language) "the first earnest-minded investigator of the science of com- parative religion that the world has produced," but also (as Prof. Max Muller put it) the first to complete a connected life - current between the East and the West - the inspired engineer in the world of faith that cut the channel of communication, the spiritual Suez, between sea and sea landlocked in the rigid sectarianism of exclusive revelation, and set their separate surges of national life into one mighty world-current of universal humanity.

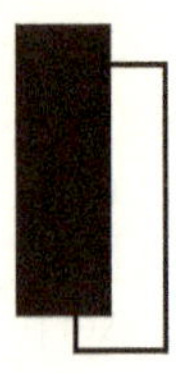

The National and Universal in Raja Rammohun Roy

For a right understanding and estimate of the Raja's thought and utterance, it is necessary to bear in mind the two essentially distinct but equally indispensable parts which the Raja played on the historic stage. There was Raja Rammohun Roy, the cosmopolite, the rationalist thinker, the representative man with a universal outlook on human civilization and its historic march; a Brahmin of the Brahmins, and hierophant moralizing from the commanding height of some Eiffel Tower on the far seen vistas and outstretched prospects of the world's civilization, Jeremy Bentham's admired and dearly loved collaborator in the service of mankind; the peer of the Humes, the Gibbons, the Voltaires, the Volneys, the Diderots or any free-thinker or rationalist of them all. For him all idols were broken, and the parent of all illusions, authority, had been hacked to pieces. He, the cosmopolite, was daunted by no speculative doubts, discouraged by no craven fears. For him the veil of Isis was torn; the Temple had been rent in twain and the Holy of Holies lay bare to his gaze! For he had had his disillusionment, was indeed a thorough roue of the monde (or demimonde) intellectual. Calmly fearlessly, truthfully, he probed, fathomed, dissected. And by deep meditation and brooding, he had won a glimpse of the Truth.

But there was another and equally characteristic part played by the Raja - the part of the Nationalist reformer, the constructive practical social legislator, the renovator of National Scriptures and Revelations. For the Raja was cast in Nature's regal mould. His was the work of half a dozen giants. His name was Legion. Hindu Pandit, Zabur-dasht Moulvie, Christian Padree, the Rishi of a new Manwan-tara or Yuga, the Imam or Mahdi of a new tradition, the Prophet or Nabi of a New Dispensation - by what name shall I call this man?

Yes, the Raja carried on single-handed the work of Nationalist Reform and Scripture Renovation and Interpretation for three such different cultures and civilizations as the Hindu, the Christian and the Mohammedan. Unfortunately, the Manezaratul Adiyan and other Arabic and Persian works in which the Raja developed his scheme of Moslem religious or socio-religious restoration are lost. But his later writings dealing with the Hindu and Christian scriptures remain and are an endless mine of the most precious material to the student of comparative religion, sociology and ethnology.

The Raja was no doctrinaire. He had a wholesome historical instinct, a love of concrete embodiments and institutions, such as characterize the born religious and social reformer. A rationalist and universalist in every pulse of his being, he was no believer in the cult of the worship of Reason, of naked logical Abstractions. The universal guiding principle of the Love of God and man he sought and found in the scriptures of the nations, and rose from the barren religion of Nature or theo-philanthropy of his eighteenth century predecessors to a liberal interpretation and acceptance of the Historic Revelation and scriptures, not indeed in any supernatural sense, but as embodiments of the collective sense, of races of mankind, and as concentrating and focusing that principle of Authority which, in this mundane state, is an indispensable cement and foundation, an elementary factor of communal life, whether in the social, the political or the religious sphere.

"I have often lamented," says the Raja, "that in our general researches into theological truth, we are subject to the conflict of so many obstacles. When we look to the traditions of ancient nations, we often find them at variance with each other; and when discouraged by this circumstance we appeal to reason as a surer guide, we soon find how incompetent it is alone to conduct us to the object of our pursuit. We often find that instead of facilitating our endeavours or clearing up our perplexities, it only serves to generate an universal doubt incompatible with principles on which our comfort and happiness mainly depend. The best method perhaps is neither to give ourselves up exclusively to the guidance of the one or the other, but by a proper use of the lights furnished by both endeavour to improve our intellectual and moral faculties."

This has the ring of the "large utterance of the early gods," and its sanity, its balance, its nice mental equipoise, is beyond the reach of the Voltaires and Volneys of the world. This rationalistic Raja has verily been the founder and father of the nineteenth century conception of the scriptures which discards supernaturalism and miracle-mongering, and yet retains and reassures for the race those precious treasures, those storehouses of moral and spiritual force, and of living authority. The Raja's method of interpretation was at once a marvellous 'Novum Organum' applied to the scriptures of the world, and a sure instinct anticipating the historic and evolutionary method of modern sociology. The essential and vital principles held in solution in the Hindu and Christian cultures and civilizations precipitated themselves. The spirit of reason and universalism was breathed into those ancient bodies for giving them an immortality of youth and fresh national vigour.

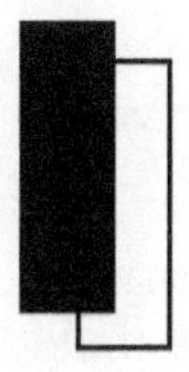

Rammohun Roy - The Father of Political Regeneration of India

This day, 71 years ago, Raja Rammohun Roy died in the suburbs of Bristol in the beautiful mansion of Miss Castle, amid the tears and regrets of his English friends. In the estimation, however, of his own countrymen, he died an outcast - our fathers would not eat and drink or associate with him - his very touch was pollution to them. Today, he is the adored hero of our race - indisputably the mightiest product of English Education -the pioneer of all those public movements, which have in them the rich promises of an abundant harvest of good - to whom we offer the spontaneous tribute of our hearts, leavened with the sad reflection that one so good, so true, so noble, should have been so dealt with. But that has always been the way of humanity. We bite the hand that feeds us and spurn the good that contains in it the messages of our salvation. We torture and crucify the blessed redeemer of mankind. The chariot-wheel of human progress is smeared with the blood of our martyrs and bedewed with the tears of their sufferings. Error revenges itself upon truth by persecution and posterity makes amends by tears and pains. We are here tonight assembled round the yet unextinguished ashes of Rammohun Roy not merely to atone for the errors of the past and perform a great act of national penance but derive from him the inspiration and guidance for our work in the future.

Amid the gathering difficulties of our situation, let us sit at the feet of Rammohun Roy and hold communion with his Master-spirit. The light breaks in upon our spirit. The light breaks in upon us across the vista of years from him, who in this, as in other matters, has been to us the source of our illumination and of inspiration. For let it be remembered that Rammohun Roy was not only the founder of the Brahmo Samaj and the pioneer of all social reform in Bengal, but he was also the father of constitutional agitation in India. He started a newspaper, strenuonsly agitated - for the emancipation of the press and the abolition of Sati; he pressed for the separation of judicial and executive functions in the administration of criminal justice, and protested against men who are too young being appointed as members of the covenanted Civil Service. It is remarkable how he anticipated us in some of the great political problems which are the problems of today, of which one at least remains unsolved.

But the Raja was not only the Father of political agitation, his fame was even greater as a social and religious reformer. His activities were co-extensive with the entire range of our being. Everything that could conduce to our welfare, no matter to what department of human activity it belonged, was the theme of his incessant efforts. For he recognized the truth that to improve man in one direction is to stimulate his improvement in all directions. In the matter of social reform, sympathy for woman was the keynote of his creed. That too was the guiding principle of Vidyasagar's efforts. It was sympathy for women that led Vidyasagar to agitate for the remarriage of Hindu widows. It was sympathy for women that led Rammohun Roy to agitate for the abolition of Sati.

Rammohun Roy's great effort was to make the Hindu system conform to its environments. His work has not been completed, though his spirit endures; and I trust that spirit, in its own good time and operating under happier and more auspicious circumstances, will lead to a transformation of Hindu society, suited to the requirements of the age. conceive of no more solemn obligation resting upon our countrymen than that they should recognize the changed circumstances under which they live and adapt themselves to those circumstances.

Sitting at the feet of Rammohun Roy, let us be imbued with his lofty spirit - his love of country, his devotion to truth, his enthusiasm for progress, let us be regenerated by the touch of his great example, and we shall then have acquired the impulse which will carry us on to and will help us to secure for ourselves a place among the progressive nations of the earth and to accomplish those high destinies which, I fully believe, are reserved for us in the decrees of Providence.

Raja Rammohun Roy A Man of Letters

Forms of expression, though important, do not afford by themselves, an adequate criterion for judging a literary or generally an artistic character. Technique is great, but the idea underlying the subject is greater. Rammohun Roy's culture was so many-sided, his scholarship so wide and profound, his natural gifts so rare, that anxious thought and close study are needed for a proper appreciation of his position as a man of letters.

Considering the varied character of his writings, one is struck by his sturdy faith in his art as an engine of human progress. 'Primers of Grammar and Geography' and abstruse 'Treatise on Law,' 'Politics and Theology' are alike members of his literary family. From popular songs to unpopular science, his literary hospitality is extended. His love of knowledge in its multiform aspects, beams out of his writings with equal radiance. As witness, his letter on English Education addressed to Lord Amherst. His motto may well have been the words of Goethe, "Licht meir Licht,"- light more light.

His controversial writings are instinct with a singular love of truth and a reverence for freedom of thought. In form they are the productions of a scholar and a gentleman. Not a word, not a syllable has he written for mere effect or to hurt an antagonist's feelings. His method was justified by the result-conversion by controversy. Ramchandra Vidyabagish and Dr. Adam were the fruits of his labours in his fields. Read his Appeals to the Christian Public and Judge. The filial piety of Mr. Marshman finds an apology for his father; but Rammohun Roy has never needed one. "With the exception of this deviation from liberality (on the part of Dr. Marshman)," remarks Dr. Rees in his preface to the American Edition of the precepts of Jesus, "the controversy on both sides has been throughout conducted with a spirit of Christian candour and fairness." The following words of Rammohun himself indicate the spirit of his controversial writings better than anything. One might say, "I hope it will not be presumed that I intend to establish the preference of my faith over that of other men. The result of controversy on such a subject however multiplied must be ever unsatis factory for the reasoning faculty, which leads them to certainty in things within its reach, produces no effect on questions beyond its comprehension."

Sincerity, according to Carlyle, is the test of heroism. A prominent quality of Rammohun Roy's writings is his transparent sincerity, which indeed is but the outward mani- festation of his love of truth. He has not said a word that he did not feel to be true. In religion he discarded esotericism in every form and did not believe in deceiving the multitude for their own good. "By taking the path which conscience and sincerity direct," he says, "I, born a Brahmin, have exposed myself to the complainings and reproaches even of some of my relations whose prejudices are strong and whose temporal advantage depends on the present system. But however accumulated I can bear them tranquilly, trusting that a day will arrive when my humble endeavours will be viewed with justice, perhaps acknowledged with gratitude." However severe may be the tests applied, his literary honesty will come out the purer and brighter from the fire. He never misrepresents or misunderstands his antagonists. The whole of his writings will be scanned in vain for a single instance of imputing to his adversary an opinion for the sole glory of demolishing it. He takes his opponents at their best. Scriptural texts, cited or relied on by him, are never mutilated, wrenched from context or divorced from their authorized meaning. Who will say, with the experience of our own days, that such honesty, which ought to be ordinary, is not deserving of extraordinary praise? Rammohun Roy has never allowed rhetoric to master logic or passion sobriety. The 'Tuhfatul Muwahhiddin,' in so far as one can judge to whom the original is inaccessible, is a model of close logical reasoning. His highest praise is this, that there is not a line of fine writing in all his works.

In the political writings of Rammohun Roy, one is impressed by the dutiful care with which he avoids making a statement not resting on his own experience or legitimate inference arising from it. In concluding his answers to questions on the Judicial System of India, he says, "In preparing my replies to these queries I have not been biased by the opinions of any individual nor have I consulted with any person or men or referred to any work on the subject of India. I have, for the facts, consulted only my own recollections and in regard to the opinions expressed, I have been guided only by my conscience."

An attentive student of the writings of Rammohun Roy finds on every page the stamps of thoroughness, sobriety, straight-forwardness and modesty. His conscientiousness and sympathy cannot fail to impress the open mind.

The conditions under which this imperfect sketch has been prepared prevents any attempt at adequate treatment of Rammohun Roy's form and expression.

But the form is worthy of the substance. The stately and dignified prose of his English works calls to mind the masters who adorned English literature in the latter period of the last century and the early years of the present. Since his time many of his countrymen have achieved eminence as writers of English prose but few have attained such a style of classical purity as Rammohun. His expressions may at times offend against the rules of Grammar, but never against the rules of style or taste. Bentham's appreciation of Rammohun Roy's English style is too well-known to need reproduction.

Rammohun Roy - A Jurist and a Politician

It is a remarkable proof of the Raja's versatility that such of his writings, as it has been possible to trace, on subjects connected with law and politics, exhibit deep research, acccu- ate knowledge, clearness of conception, and a firm grasp of principles. His paper, entitled 'Brief Remarks regarding Modern Encroachments on the Ancient Rights of Females according to the Hindoo Law of Inheritance,' may be cited as an illustration. Here the writer comes to the conclusion, as the result of his researches, that under the old Hindu Law, women enjoyed rights which have been presented in a very much narrower form by modern commentators. "These restraints on female inheritance," the writer is shrewd enough to observe, "encourage, in a great degree, polygamy, a frequent source of the greatest misery in native families; a grand object of Hindus being to secure a provision for their male offspring, the Law which relieves them from the necessity of giving an equal portion to their wives, removes a principal restraint on the indulgence of their inclinations in respect to the number they marry."

Within the present limits it is not possible to refer in detail to the evidence cited by the writer or to dwell on the keenness of the insight he exhibits into the causes of a social evil. His Essay on the 'Rights of Hindoos over Ancestral Property' according to the Law of Bengal, would do credit to any trained and professional lawyer deeply versed in the history of the Hindoo Law. One of his conclusions in this paper is that in following those expositions which best reconcile law with reason, the author of the Bengal system is warranted by the highest sacred authority as well as by the example of the most revered of his predecessors, the author of the 'Mitaksara.'

The Rule and Ordinance that was passed on 14th March 1823, by Mr. Adam, Officiating Governor-General, curtailing the freedom of the press elicited a Memorial to the Supreme Court which had to register the Regulation. The Memorial, which was signed by several leading gentlemen of the town, was presumably drawn up by the Raja, who was one of its signatories. This proved unsuccessful, and a Petition of Appeal was addressed to His Majesty the King (George IV) in Council. This Petition also appears to have been the Raja's handiwork. The two documents are remarkable productions. For cogency of argument, accuracy of fact, and appreciation of principle, they could not be surpassed. No writer of the present day could put the case for liberty more effectively than the Raja has done. Space will not permit the making of any extracts, specially where a selection is difficult from among paragraphs almost every one of which is gem rich and rare. The writings on Suttee, which one might imagine to be so warm and vehement as to be devoid of balance, are themselves an illustration of the Raja's unfailing sobriety and clearness of vision.

Nowhere does he plead that every practice which is morally wrong has to be repressed by penal legislation. The issue he sets forth is clear and definite. He abstains, as far as possible, from the enunciation of abstract doctrines of sweeping generality, confines himself to the consideration of practical evils, material wrongs, and argues in effect that a practice which is not merely immoral, but criminal, must be treated as a crime. Whatever is productive of injury to the individual, and, through the individual, to the society, is criminal, and should be dealt with as such, all usage to the contrary notwithstanding.

That appears to be the substance of the Raja's contention, and it will hardly be resisted by the most fastidious philosopher of the laissez faire type. The breadth of the Raja's knowledge of the administration of the country, the accuracy of his insight, and the soundness of his opinions on many questions of Government, are well illustrated by his answers to the numerous questions put to him by the Select Committee of the House of Commons. It was certainly no ordinary person that could show as complete and masterly a knowledge of the practical operation of the Judicial and Revenue Systems of India, and of the general character and condition of its native inhabitants, as he undoubtedly possessed of the Upanishads and of the Precepts of Jesus:

Searching for Truth (1772-1803)

Rammohun Roy was born in the village of Radhanagar, near Krishnanagar, in the zilla of Hooghli, on the 22nd of May,1772.

(* Much uncertainty has existed as to the year of Rammohun's birth. The date most frequently accepted is that given on his tombstone, viz., 1774; but I give the earlier date in the text on the following authorities :- The Rev. C. H. A. Dall, in a letter to the Sunday Mirror of Jan. 18, 1880, reported that Rammohun's younger son Rama Prasad Roy, said in 1858 before a circle of friends and clients in Calcutta,"My father was born at Radhanagar, near Krishnanagar, in the month of May, 1772; or according to the Bengali era, in the month of Jyaishtha, 1179." Mr. Dall asked for the day of birth, but Rama Prasad was unable to give this. The fact has since, however, been supplied by another lineal descendant of Rammohun, Babu Lalit Mohun Chatterji, who has stated that "Rammohun Roy was born in the year 1772, on the 22nd day of May." For this and other details, I am indebted to the kindness of Babu Phani Bhusan Mukherji, of Rajshahee College, who learnt them from Babu Rabindra Nath Tagore, to whom Babu L. M. Chatterji had given the information.)

His pedigree has been preserved up to a very early date, but we need not trace it in detail beyond his great grandfather, (1) Krishna Chandra Banerjee, who entered the service of the Nawab of Bengal, and received from him the title of "Roy Roy" afterwards contracted into Roy, which has ever since remained the designation of the family. This occurred during the reign of the Emperor Aurangzeb (1619-1707.)

Krishna Chandra is said to have been an acute and able man, and a zealous member of the Vaishnava sect. He had three sons; Hari Prasad, Amar Chandra, and Brajabinode. Brajabinode Roy was wealthy and philanthropic and devotedly attached to his gods. He was employed under the Nawab Siraj-ud-Dowla in some honourable position at Murshidabad, but on account of some ill treatment, he quitted that employment, and spent the rest of his life at home. His fifth son, Rama Kanta Roy, was the father of our hero. But Rammohun's maternal ancestors belonged to the rival sect of the

Saktas, of which his mother's father was a priest, a curious conjuncture of antecedents for the future reformer of Hinduism. How this came to pass is thus narrated :- As Brajabinode Roy lay dying on the banks of the Ganges, a man named Shyama Bhattacharya, of Chatra near Serampore, came to him requesting a boon. He was of honourable parentage, and his family were well known as the priests of the locality. The kind-hearted Brajabinode readily consented, and swore by the Ganges to grant the boon; whereupon Shyama Bhattacharya asked permission to bestow his daughter in marriage upon one of Brajabinode's sons. Now as he was not only the priest of a rival sect, but a (2) Bhanga Kulin, the dying man felt as if he had been trapped, but having sworn by the Ganges, he could not break his word. So he called his seven sons and requested them, one by one, to make good his promise. All refused except the fifth son, Rama Kanta, who readily accepted the unwelcome bride, and in due course married her. They had three children the eldest was a daughter (name not recorded); the second and third were sons, Jaganmohun and Rammohun. The daughter married one Sridhar Mukherji, said to have been a clever man (whose father is reported to have lived to his 125th year), and her son, Gurudas Mukerji, was much attached to his uncle Rammohun, and is said to have been the latter's first convert in his own family.

Sources

[1]

[According to Pandit Mahendranath Vidyanidhi, who made careful investigations, it was the great great grandfather of Rammohun Roy, Parasuram Banerjee, who first accepted office under the Mohammadan rulers and was rewarded with the title of Roy-Roy.]

[2]

[A Bhanga (or broken) Kulin is a Kulin who has broken his kul or caste.]

Rama Kanta Roy had also another wife, of whom nothing is known except that she had a son named Ramlochan, of whom but little is recorded. But it is quite evident that Rammohun's mother was the mistress of the household. Her name was Tarini, but she was always called Phulthakurani, i.e., "the fifth son's wife." She was a woman of strong character and of fine understanding, and appears to have had considerable influence over her husband.*

(*She was evidently a remarkable woman both for the firmness of her will and her piety. After the death of her eldest son she took the management of the family property in her own hands and conducted the intricate affairs of the estate satisfactorily. Her treatment to her great son does not seem to have been always kind. When Rammohun Roy left the ancestral house at the age of about sixteen she was, as natural, deeply affected. But afterwards she was very harsh to him for his heterodox religious views. It is even said that Rammohon Roy was compelled to leave the ancestral home and his native village on account of her hostility. Mr. Adam at a public meeting in London soon after the death of Rammohun Roy, said that she had brought a suit against Rammohun Roy in the Supreme Court to disinherit him. Yet Rammohun Roy was invariably respectful and affectionate towards her, and is said to have won her to his views. In her old age she is reported to have said to Rammohun Roy that he was right, but she was too old to change her views. Like many Hindu ladies she was very devout. In her old age she made a pilgrimage to the shrine of Jagannath at Puri. Though sufficiently rich, out of regard for the deity, she walked all the distance of about 300 or 400 miles); this for a respectable Hindu lady, who never before walked out of the precincts of her home, was a remarkable feat. At Puri she used to sweep the yard of the temple daily for a year, as a devout service to the presiding god.)

All that is recorded of Rama Kanta Roy shows him to have been an upright and estimable man. He, like his father, served for a time (as a Sarkar) under Siraj-ud-Dowla, but subsequently retired to Radhanagar. Here he rented some villages from the Raja of Burdwan, which seems to have been the first beginning of a long series of disputes between the Raja and the Roy family. Judging from the full report of a lawsuit brought against Rammohun Roy many years later by this Raja, he appears to have been so unscrupulous a man that we may fairly conclude him to have been in the wrong in his early conflicts with Rama Kanta Roy, who was often so disgusted with the treatment he received that he would neglect his affairs for a while, and retire to meditate and tell his Harinam beads in a garden of sacred Tulsi plants. He was very devout, and a staunch believer in Vishnu as the Supreme God, and in Rama as the last incarnation but one of Vishnu. Fortunately for his domestic peace, his Sakta wife was soon led to adopt his beliefs, which she did so heartily as to occasion some slight friction with her father, if legend speaks truly.

*(According to the investigations of Pandit Mahendranath Vidyanidhi, Krishna Chandra Banerjee, the great grandfather of Rammohun Roy, and not his father or grandfather, migrated to, and settled at Radhanagar.

Krishna Chandra Banerjee, at the recommendation of an official in the service of the Nawab of Murshidabad, was engaged and sent by the Raja of Burdwan to settle accounts with and realize the arrears of rent from Anantaram Chaudhuri of Khanakul. Krishna Chandra accordingly had to come to Khanakul and stay there for some time. He was pleased with the locality and settled there permanently, selecting a site on the left bank of the river Darakeswar opposite Krishnanagar.)

Such was the home into which Rammohun Roy was born. His father spared no expense in his education; and local traditions assert that he showed great intelligence at an early age, and possessed a remarkably tenacious memory, never forgetting anything which he had once heard or read. After completing his school course of Bengali education, he took up the study of Persian (then the Court language throughout India), and soon became fascinated by the mystic poetry and philosophy of the Persian Sufis, for which he retained an ardent attachment throughout his life. He was next sent to Patna to learn Arabic, and (it is said, by his mother's desire) to Benares to learn Sanskrit. At Patna, his masters set him to study Arabic translations from Euclid and Aristotle, and he then also made acquaintance with the Koran. All these influences, especially the last, tended inevitably towards the disintegration of his earliest religious beliefs, which had been very fervent. His friend, William Adam, wrote of him in 1826:- "He seems to have been religiously disposed from his early youth, having proposed to seclude himself from the world as a sannyasi, or devotee, at the age of fourteen, from which he was only dissuaded by the entreaties of his mother." It is said that his reverence for Vishnu was at one time so great that he would not even take a drop of water without first reciting a chapter of the 'Bhagavat Puran.' The boundless veneration which he is said to have entertained for his father's household deities, is still more characteristically illustrated by the story that he could not bear to witness the performance of the Yatra (or popular play) of Manbhanjan, in which god Krishna weeps clasping the feet of his fair Radhika, and his peacock head-gear and green clothes are seen rolling in the dust.

Another anecdote is reported of his Hindu period, that "for the attainment of knowledge and wisdom," he had, at great expense, a certain ceremony performed for him 22 times, called purashcharan, consisting in a repetition of the name of a deity, accompanied with burnt offerings.

But Rammohun was not to pass out of this early phase without one mark of Hinduism which remained to colour his whole life. While yet a mere child, his father married him three times. The first bride died " at a very early age" and after her death, as we learn from William Adam's letters, "his father, when he was only about nine years of age, married him within an interval of less than a twelve month to two different wives. This was in perfect conformity with the usage of his caste [the Kulin Brahman] and was done when he was incapable of judging for himself."*

(* The first of these two wives was the mother of his children. She died in 1824. The second wife survived him.)

At last came the inevitable break. All accounts agree that it was preceded by much theological discussion between Rammohun and his father, and it is probably to this period that we should refer the following reminiscences of Mr. Adam, given in his Memorandum of 1879.

"It is not often that we get an insight into Hindu family life, but his [Rama Kanta Roy's] son gave me a slight glance at least in referring to the amicable differences that arose between himself and his father on this subject. I inferred from what R. R. said that he always left it to his father, as the head and most venerable member of the family, to open the question which he thought fit to moot, and when he had finished his immediate argument, he was generally willing to listen to his son with patience, which sometimes, however, forsook him. The son's response after the necessary preliminary admissions, usually began with the adversative particle 'But' (Kintu). But notwithstanding all this, the orthodox conclusion you aim at does not follow.' The father complained of this, and on one occasion, at least, burst out in the tone of remonstrance, as of an injured party: Whatever argument I adduce you have always your Kintu, your counter-statement, your counter-argument, your counter-conclusion to oppose to me.' The son recounted this to me with half a smile on his lips and a touch of humour in his voice, but without any expression of disrespect to his father.

What follows may best be told in the words of Dr. Lant Carpenter:

"Without disputing the authority of his father, he often sought from him information as to the reasons of his faith; he obtained no satisfaction; and he at last determined at the early age of 15, to leave the paternal home, and sojourn for a time in Tibet, that he might see another form of religious faith.* He spent two or three years in that country, and often excited the angers of the worshippers of the Lama by his rejection of their doctrine that this pretended deity - a living man - was the creator and preserver of the world. In these circumstances he experienced the soothing kindness of the female part of the family; and his gentle, feeling heart lately dwelt with deep interest, at the distance of more than forty years, on the recollections of that period which, he said, had made him always feel respect and gratitude towards the female sex."

(* Review of the Labours, Opinions, and Character of Rammohun Roy, 1833, pp. 101-102. Dr. Carpenter adds in a footnote: "The statement made in the preceding [i.e., the above] sentence, I heard from the Rajah himself in London, and again at Stapleton Grove [Bristol]." This testimony is important as distinctly contravening the story that Rammohun left home on account of a family disagreement caused by his having "when about the age of sixteen composed a manuscript calling in question the validity of the idolatrous system of the Hindus; a story which, although repeated by all Rammohun's biographers, was never heard of till after his death, and rests upon no authority whatever, except the spurious "autobiographical letter" published by Sandford Arnot in the Athenæum of Oct. 5, 1833.)

The precise extent and duration of his travels is not known; † but they appear to have lasted about three or four years, and to have been terminated by a message of recall from his father, who is said to have grieved much at his absence, and to have shown him great kindness on his return.

† (Rammohun Roy wrote a few articles about his early travels in the 'Sambad Kaumudi,' but unfortunately no copies of that magazine could be found.)

But all accounts agree that he did not remain long under the family roof, the incompatibility being too great. Our only actual knowledge as to his next step is derived from his own evidence in the Burdwan lawsuit already referred to, in which he states that "so far from inheriting the property of his deceased father, he had, during his lifetime, separated from him and the rest of the family, in consequence of his altered habits of life and change of opinions, which did not permit their living together." Whither he betook himself none of his biographers seem to have known; but happily the missing fact is supplied in the letters of his friend, William Adam, who wrote in 1826 that Rammohun, after relinquishing idolatry, "was obliged to reside for ten or twelve years at Benares, at a distance from all his friends and relatives, who lived on the family estate at Burdwan, in Bengal." Referring to this period, another friend has testified as follows:- 'So strongly were his feelings wrought upon by the alienation which then commenced, that through life, under the pressure of dejection or disease, the frowning features of his father would rise unbidden on his imagination."

Probably he fixed his residence at Benares on account of the facilities afforded by that sacred city for the study of Sanskrit; and if so, we may conclude that it was chiefly at this period that he acquired his extensive knowledge of the Hindu Shastras. Certainly it was not till then that he began family life on his own account, for his eldest son, Radha Prasad, was born in the year 1800, when Rammohun must have been about twenty-eight years old, apparently seven years after his return from travel. On what resources he then subsisted does not appear. The only lucrative occupation in which he is ever known to have been engaged was his work in the Civil Service under the East India Company; but that must certainly be referred to a later date, as he only began to learn English in 1796, and had not obtained much proficiency in it by 1801. Probably, however, in such a seat of Hindu learning as Benares he might have obtained employment by copying manuscripts. In any case, he seems to have remained there until his father's death in 1803. It is a relief to know that after all their differences, the father and son were together at the last. This we learn from Mr. Adam, who reports as follows in his Memorandum:

"R. Roy, in conversation, mentioned to me with much feeling that he had stood by the deathbed of his father, who with his expiring breath continued to invoke his God - Ram! Ram! with a strength of faith and a fervour of pious devotion which it was impossible not to respect although the son had then ceased to cherish any religious veneration for the family deity."

Rama Kanta Roy was succeeded in his estate by his son Jaganmohun. Rammohun inherited no portion of his father's property. *

* In Rammohun's evidence on the Burdwan law-suit, he describes his own position as that of "a son separating himself from his father during his lifetime, and by his own exertion acquiring property unconnected with his father, and after his father's death inheriting no portion of his father's property,"

Throwing Down the Gauntlet (1803-1814)

Relieved from the fear of paining his father, Rammohun soon began to make his heresies known to the world. He moved to Murshidabad, the old Moghul capital of Bengal, and there he published his first work, a treatise in Persian (with an Arabic preface), entitled 'Tuhfatul Muwahhidin' or Gift to the Monotheists. This was a bold protest against the idolatrous element in all established religions,* the drift of the treatise being that while all religions are based on one common foundation, viz., the belief-justified by the facts,- - in One Supreme Being who has created and sustained the whole universe, they all differ in the details of the super-structure erected thereupon, these superstructures being all equally unjustified by any basis of fact, and arising solely from the imagination of men working in vacuum. The treatise bears many traces of Rammohun's Patna training, being written in an abstruse style, and abounding with Arabic logical and philosophical terms. Its arrangement is, however, quite unsystematic, and the whole is merely a series of descriptive sketches; but these show much acuteness of observation and reasoning, and are pervaded by a strong tinge of that bitter earnestness which results from the long suppression of intense feeling. The author writes as though he had been obliged to stand by and witness a number of priestly impositions which he could not hinder and was prevented from exposing; and no doubt this had really been the case. The treatise is important as the earliest available expression of his mind, and as showing his eagerness to bear witness against established error but it is too immature to be worth reproducing as a whole. A few passages only are worth quoting as indications of what he was at this early period.

* (By a very natural mistake, the subject of this treatise was long supposed, in England, to form its actual title, and the essay was always designated by the name "Against the Idolatry of all Religions." No translation of this treatise appears to have been made until quite recently, when it was rendered into English by a learned and enthusiastic Mohammedan. The full title of his pamphlet is as follows:- 'Tuhfatul Muwahhidin' (Gift to the

Monotheists)s, by the late Raja Rammohun Roy, translated into English by Moulavi Obaidullah El Obaide, Superintendent of the Dacca Government Madrassa, and published under the auspices of the Adi Brahmo Samaj, Calcutta, 1884.)

It may be seen that the followers of certain religions believe that the Creator has made mankind for the performance of the duties bearing on our present and future life by observing the precepts of that particular religion; and that the followers of other religions who differ from them are liable to punishment and torment in the future life. And as the members of each particular sect defer the good results of their own acts and the bad results of their rival acts to the life after death none of them can refute the dogmas of others in this life. Consequently, they sow the seeds of prejudice and disunion in the hearts of each other and condemn each other to the deprivation of eternal blessings -whereas it is quite evident that all of them are living in the equal enjoyment of the external blessings of heaven, such as the light of the stars, the pleasure of the season of spring, the fall of rain, health of body, external and internal good, and other pleasures of life; and that all are equally liable to suffer from inconveniences and pains, such as gloomy darkness, severe cold, mental disease, narrow circumstances and other outward and inward evils, without any distinction, although following different religions.

The Brahmins have a tradition that they have strict orders from God to observe their ceremonies and hold their faith for ever. There are many injunctions to this effect in the Sanskrit language, and I, the humblest creature of God, having been born among them, have learnt the language and got those injunctions by heart; and this nation having confidence therein cannot give them up, although they have been subjected to many troubles and persecutions, and were threatened with death by the followers of Islam. The followers of Islam, on the other hand, according to the purport of the holy verse of the Koran - 'Kill the idolators wherever you find them, and capture the unbelievers in holy war, and after doing so either set them free by way of obligation to them or by taking ransom,' quote authority from God that killing idolators and persecuting them in every case are obligatory by divine command. Among those idolators the Brahmins, according to the Moslem belief, are the worst. Therefore the followers of Islam, excited by religious zeal, desirous to carry out the orders of God, have done their utmost to kill and persecute the polytheists and unbelievers in the prophetic mission of the Seal of Prophets [Mohammed], and the blessing to the present and future worlds (may the divine benediction rest on him and his disciples). Now are these contradictory precepts or orders consistent with the wisdom and mercy of the great, generous, and disinterested Creator, or are these the fabrications of the followers of religion? I think a sound mind will not hesitate to prefer the latter alternative.

There is a saying which is often heard from teachers of different religions as an authority for their several creeds. Each of them says that his religion, which gives information about future reward or punishment after death, is either true or false. In the second case, i.e., if it be false, and there be no future reward or punishment, there is no harm in believing it to be true; while in the first case, i.e., its being true, there is a great danger for unbelievers. The poor people who follow these expounders of religion, holding this saying to be a conclusive argument, always boast of it. The fact is that habit and training make men blind and deaf in spite of their own eyes and ears. The above saying is fallacious in two respects. Firstly, their saying that in the second case there is no harm in believing it to be true, is not to be admitted. For to believe in the real existence of anything after obtaining proofs of such existence is possible to every individual man; but to put faith in the existence of such things as are remote from experience and repugnant to reason is not in the power of a sensible man. Secondly, the entertaining belief in these things may become the source of various mischief and immoral practices, owing to gross ignorance, want of experience, bigotry, deceit, etc. And if this argument were valid, the truth of all forms of religion might be proved therefrom; for the same arguments may equally be advanced by all. Hence, there would be great perplexity for a man. He must either believe all religions to be true, or adopt one and reject the others. But as the first alternative is impossible, consequently the second must be adopted and in this case he has again to make inquiries into truth and falsehood of various religions, and this is the chief object of my discourse.

The followers of different religions, seeing the paucity of the number of monotheists in the world, sometimes boast that they are on the side of the majority. But it may be seen that the truth of a saying does not depend upon the multitude of sayers, and the non-reliability of a narration cannot result from the small numbers of its narrators. For it is admitted by the seekers of truth, that truth is to be followed although it is against the majority of the people. Moreover, to accept the proposition that the small number of the sayers leads to the invalidity of a saying, seems to be a dangerous blow to all forms of religion. For in the beginning of every religion it had a very few supporters, viz, its founder and a few sincere followers of his, ... while the belief in only one Almighty God is the fundamental principle of every religion.

In short, men may be divided into four classes in reference to this subject.

1st. - Deceivers who in order to attract the people to themselves, consciously invent doctrines of religious faith and cause disunion and trouble among men.

2nd. - Deceived persons who,without inquiring into the facts, follow others.

3rd. - Persons who are at the same time deceivers and deceived; having themselves faith in the sayings of another, they induce others to follow his doctrines.

4th. - Those who by the help of Almighty God are neither deceivers nor deceived.

These few short and useful sentences expressing the opinion of this humble creature of God, have been written without any regard to men of prejudice and bigotry, in the hope that persons of sound mind will look thereon with eyes of justice. I have left the details to another work of mine entitled 'Manazarutul Adyann, Discussions on Various Religions.'

P.S. In order to avoid any future change in this book by copyists, I have had these few pages printed just after composition. Let it be known that the benediction pronounced in this book after the mention of prophets is merely done in imitation of the usual custom of the authors of Arabia and Ajan.

The Discussions on Various Religions above alluded to are, unhappily, no longer procurable. I conclude then it must have been in one of these that Rammohun made some rather sarcastic remarks on Mahomet, to which reference is made by several of his biographers as having excited an amount of anger against him among the Mohammedans which was a chief cause of his removing to Calcutta. In Mr. Leonard's 'History of the Brahmo Samaj', these sarcastic remarks are said (p. 27) to occur in the Tuhfat, but certainly no such passage is to be found there. On the other hand, it is indubitable that Rammohun always retained a large amount of sympathy with Islam for the sake of its cardinal doctrine of the Unity of God, and that he warmly appreciated the good which had thence resulted in counteracting Hindu idolatry. Mr. Adam says that Rammohun "seemed always pleased to have an opportunity of defending the character and teaching of Maho- met," of whom indeed he began to write a biography which was unhappily never finished.

It must have been at this period that Rammohun Roy entered the Civil Service under the East India Company. The exact date of his doing so I have not been able to ascertain but (for several reasons) it can scarcely have been before his father's death, and it must have occurred not long after that event. Our only contemporary information on the subject comes from Mr. John Digby, an English gentleman who was for several years Rammohun's superior officer in the Bengal Civil Service, and who during a visit to England, edited a reprint of Rammohun's translations of the Kena Upanishad and Abridgment of the Vedanta (London, 1817) to which he prefixed an interesting account of the translator. In this he said:

Rammohun Roy is by birth a Brahmin of very respectable origin, in the province of Bengal, about forty-three years of age. His acquirements are considerable: to a thorough knowledge of the Sanskrit (the language of the Brahminical Scriptures) he has added Persian and Arabic; and possessing an acute understanding, he early conceived a contempt for the religious prejudices and absurd superstitions of his caste. At the age of twenty-two [really twenty-four, i. e., in 1796] he commenced the study of the English language, which not pursuing with application, he, five years afterwards [1801], when I became acquainted with him, could merely speak it well enough to be understood upon the most common topics of discourse, but could not write it with any degree of correctness. He was afterwards employed as Diwan, or principal native officer, in the collection of revenues, in the district of which I was for five years Collector, in the East India Company's Civil Service. By perusing all my public correspondence with diligence and attention, as well as by corresponding and conversing with European gentlemen, he acquired so correct a knowledge of the English language as to be enabled to write and speak it with considerable accuracy. He was also in the constant habit of reading the English newspapers, of which the Continental politics chiefly interested him and from thence he formed a high admiration of the talents and prowess of the late ruler of France, and was so dazzled with the splendour of his achievements as to become sceptical as to the commission, if not blind to the atrocity of his crimes, and could not help deeply lamenting his downfall, notwithstanding the profound respect he ever professed for the English nation; but when the first transports of his sorrow had subsided, he considered that part of his political conduct which led to his abdication to have been so weak, and so madly ambitious, that he declared his future detestation of Bonaparte would be proportionate to his former admiration.

From a paper furnished to me by the courtesy of the India Office, I learn that Mr. Digby was never so long as five years at any station except that of Rungpur, where he served from October 20 1809, to December1814, when he returned to England for a few years. Now it is at Rungpur that popular tradition chiefly connects the name of Rammohun Roy with Mr. Digby; but as Mr. Digby was previously at Ramgurh (1805 to 1808) and Bhagalpur (1808 to 1809), and as Rammohun mentions in his evidence on the Burdwan law-suit having resided at "Ramgarh, Bhagalpur, and Rungpur," it is highly probable that he was working under Mr. Digby in the two former localities before he went to Rungpur; although we have no details as to the successive posts which he then occupied.

It is usually stated by Rammohun's biographers that "a written agreement was signed by Mr. Digby to the effect that Rammohun should never be kept standing (a custom enforced by European Civil Servants towards natives of the highest rank) in the presence of the Collector, and that no order should be issued to him as a mere Hindu functionary." So far as I can trace, this statement first appeared in a letter by Mr. R. Montgomery Martin (in whose words I have quoted it) in the Court Journal of October 5, 1833, just after Rammohun's death. So many statements in that letter are undoubtedly erroneous that I can feel no assurance as to the fact of this written agreement. There can, however, be no doubt that Mr. Digby held Rammohun in high regard, and that a sincere friendship existed between them, honourable alike to both.

Mr. G. S. Leonard in his 'History of the Brahmo Samaj,' based on a MS. work by a highly respected member of the Adi Brahmo Samaj, makes the following statement :-

The Permanent Settlement of zemindaries under Lord Cornwallis in 1793, and its ratification by the Court of Directors some three years after, required a general survey and assessment of all lands in Bengal under European collectors, some of whom were empowered with the settlement of several districts at once. Mr. Digby had the charge of settling the districts of Rungpur, Dinajpur and Purnea, a work which kept him employed for three years, and in the execution of which he gained a lasting renown in the memory of the people for justice and probity, a result which is mainly due to the exertions of his diwán.

Pandit Siva Nath Sastri mentions in his excellent, but unfortunately unpublished, 'History of the Brahmo Samaj,' that the state of things in the above mentioned districts of North- ern Bengal was especially complicated. Here there were many powerful landlords who had a large number of unsettled disputes. In many individual case of settlement involved the examination of a variety of records and documents and the consideration of conflicting claims. cases there were no documents whatever to substantiate the claims of actual owners of land, and they required personal attendance and local inquiry from the settlement officer. In settlement work in those days, the trusted native Sheristadars were, as a rule, the chief agents employed by the Collectors, who were guided to a large extent by their decisions and counsels.

Mr. Leonard enumerates Rammohun's special qualifications for this work, his "proficiency in zemindary accounts and land surveying"; "his acquaintance with all the cunning and dishonest devices of the Amins and Amlahs in furnishing false accounts and statements"; and also "the practical reforms he suggested regarding the ascertaining of rightful ownerships and descriptions of land, etc." I have not been able to procure any original documents of this period which could fix dates and events; but the above summaries come from reliable sources and may be accepted as genuine.

From all accounts, it was during his residence in Rungpur that Rammohun first began to assemble his friends together for evening discussions on religious subjects, especially on the untenableness and absurdities of idolatry. Rungpur was then a place of considerable resort, and among its inhabitants were a good many merchants from Marwar in Rajputana, Jainas by faith. Some of these Marwaris used to attend Rammohun's meetings, and Mr. Leonard says that "he had to learn on their

account the Kalpa Sutra, and other books appertaining to the Jaina religion," and adds:-

He met, however, with much opposition from a counter party headed by Gauri Kanta Bhattacharya, a learned Persian and Sanskrit scholar, who challenged him in a Bengali book entitled the 'Gyan Chandrika.' This man was a Diwan in the Judge's Court at Rungpur, and his influence enabled him to gather a large body of men about whom he hounded on to Rammohun Roy, but without any success.

A far more serious hostility was that of his mother. As already mentioned, the family estate passed after (Rama Kanta Roy's death in 1803) into the hands of his eldest son, Jaganmohun. He died in 1811. To whom it then passed, I have sought in vain to discover. Certainly it did not go to Rammohun Roy; yet a few years later we find him in possession of it, and his mother bringing suits against him to deprive him of the property on the ground of his dissent from the current religion. I have not succeeded hitherto in obtaining any published report of these suits, but the following passage from William Adam leaves no doubt as to their reality.

When the death of Rammohun Roy's elder brother made him the head of the family, she [his mother] instituted suits against her son both in the King's and Company's Courts, with a view to disinherit him as an apostate and infidel, which according to strict Hindu law, excludes from the present and disqualifies for the future, possession of any ancestral property, or even according to many authorities, of any property that is self-acquired.

In this attempt she was defeated; but for many years he had much to suffer from her persecution. In his great grandson's anecdotes there is a story of his going to see her on returning from Rungpur, and being harshly repulsed from her embrace, when she is reported to have said, "If you would touch me, you must first go and bow down before my Radha and Govinda" whereupon, it is added, "Rammohun, who so loved his mother, submitted and went to the house of the gods and said, "I bow down before my mother's god and goddess." If this be true, it can scarcely have been done so as to impose seriously on his mother, for he never relaxed in his public attitude towards idolatry. But the anecdote may stand as a half-mythical illustration of the great reluctance with which he opposed his parents' faith. Another of these anecdotes tells of his mother's anger because, when in bad health, he had by his doctor's advice, taken some broth made from goat's flesh. On this occasion, it is said, she raised a great disturbance, and adjured the family thus:- "Be careful! Rammohun has turned Christian, and has begun to eat forbidden things. Let us all unite and drive him from my ground; wholesale ruin has begun!" This would seem to imply that he still held some footing in Burdwan, and did not reside entirely at Rungpur during the whole of Mr. Digby's five years there (1809 to 1814). Probably his family still remained in the ancestral neighbourhood. At any rate, it is clear that owing to his mother's hostility, he had to remove them. But the whole of Krishnanagar belonged to her, and she would not let him have any land there for his own. He therefore took up his quarters on a large burning-ground at the village of Raghunathpur not far off, and there he built a house for himself.

It must have been during this period that one of his hostile neighbours, named Ramjay Batabyal, an inhabitant of the village of Ramnagar near Krishnanagar, resorted to a curi- ous mode of persecution. He collected a number of men who used to go to Rammohun's house early in the morning and imitate the crowing of cocks, and again at nightfall to throw cow-bones into the house. These proceedings greatly annoyed and disturbed Rammohun's womankind, but he himself took it with perfect coolness, and made no retort whatever; which enraged his persecutors all the more. At last, however, finding him hopelessly impervious, they wearied of their attacks and desisted therefrom.

* (His adversaries soon adopted more serious measures to trouble and humiliate him. They tried to excommunicate him. At the time of the marriage of his eldest son, they endeavoured to persuade people not to give any girl in marriage to him on account of the father's religious views. There was a great commotion in the community, but the designs of his enemies were frustrated. A respectable gentleman of Irpara in the district of Hugli gave his daughter in marriage to the son of Rammohun Roy.)

With respect to the family estate, which probably passed at the death of Jaganmohun Roy to his son, Govinda Prasad Roy, it has been suggested to me by one of Rammohun's descendants that Govinda Prasad may have failed to continue the payment of the land tax, in which case the estate would have been thrown into the market; and that Rammohun, who had by that time saved money in Government Service, may have bought it in. Certainly he came into possession of it while his mother still lived. It would appear, however, that after he had established his right to the property, he did not at once take possession of it, from reluctance to pain his relatives, and that "for sometime everything remained as before in the hands of his mother. She taking up the superintendence of the land under her own care, managed the affairs most successfully... It is said that Phulthakurani used to place before her all her numerous gods and godesses while superintending the management of her landed property."*

It is always stated by Rammohun's biographers that in his ten years' Government Service he saved enough money to enable him to become a zemindar or landowner, with an annual income of Rs. 10,000 (about £1,000). Commenting on this fact, Babu Kishory Chand Mitra, in a long and elaborate sketch of Rammohun which appeared in the Calcutta Review of December, 1845, insinuates that such gains raise the suspicion that he "sold justice." "If", he says, "Rammohun Roy did keep his hands clean, and abstain- ed, as in the absence of all positive evidence to the contrary we are bound to suppose, from defeating the ends of justice for a consideration - he must have been a splendid exception." Mr. Leonard, in his 'History of the Brahmo Samaj,' refutes these unworthy suspicions by pointing out that "if Kishory Chand had possessed any knowledge of the duties of a diwan in those early days, and the legal perquisites appertaining to the office recognized by Government," he would not have been entitled to wonder at Rammohun Roy's gains. " It is no great achievement to amass by frugality and thrift a lakh of rupees after ten years' service, the value of a dependent taluk of Rs. 10,000, when others have been known by a service of half or a quarter that time, to have made a provision of ten times that amount." Mr. Leonard also remarks that "had Mr. Digby's diwan been so corrupt as he is suspected to have been, Mr. Digby himself would never have obtained renown for justice and probity." But the insinuations of K. C. Mitra, though admittedly made "in the absence of all positive evidence," have unhappily been repeated from the early memoir by later writers, and were reproduced so lately as 1888 in the Saturday Review. So difficult is it to rectify a false impression once given.

Mr. Digby left Rungpur for England at the end of 1814; and in the course of that year Rammohun took up his residence in Calcutta.* But previous to doing so, he seems to have been living for a short interval at his house on the burning-ground at Raghunathpur. In front of this house he erected a mancha or pulpit, for the purpose of worship and engraved upon each of its sides three mottos from the Upanishads. (1) "Om" (aum) - The most venerable and solemn designation of the Hindu Trinity; (2) "Tat Sat," That [i .e, He] is Truth; and (3) "Ekamevadvitiyam,"- The One without a second. Here he offered his prayers thrice a day; and on going home, and on again returning to Calcutta, he would first walk round this mancha, said to be still standing. It was in reference to this mancha that his youngest wife, Uma, is said to have asked him which religion was the best and highest? Rammohun is said to have replied: "Cows are of different colours, but the colour of the milk they give is the same. Different teachers have different opinions, but the essence of every religion is to adopt the true path,"- i.e., to live a faithful life.

* (Rammohun Roy seems to have made up his mind to settle in Calcutta and the house at Maniktala where he began to live on his removal to

Calcutta had been purposely built under the superintendence of his step-brother Ramlochan Roy.)

One other family event in this preparatory period of Rammohun's life must be chronicled here. At the death of his eldest brother Jaganmohun in 1811, the widow became a suttee. It is said that Rammohun had endeavoured to persuade her beforehand against this terrible step, but in vain. When, however, she felt the flames she tried to get up and escape from the pile; but her orthodox relations and the priests forced her down with bamboo poles, and kept her there to die, while drums and brazen instruments were loudly sounded to drown her shrieks. Rammohun*, unable to save her, and filled with unspeakable indignation and pity, vowed within himself, then and there, that he would never rest until the atrocious custom was rooted out. And he kept his vow. Before 19 years had fully elapsed, that pledge was redeemed by the Government decree abolishing suttee, Dec. 4, 1829.

* (There is evidently some confusion here. Rammohun was at Rungpur at the time of his brother's death. The incident narrated here must have happened on some other occasion.)

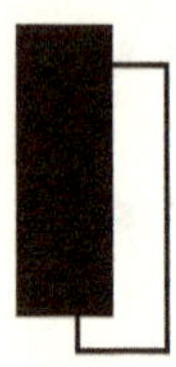

Spiritual Theism *versus* Idolatry and Suttee (1814-1820)

At last, in the year 1814, at the age of forty-two, Rammohun Roy emerged from provincial obscurity, and took up his abode in the capital of British India. He was now in the prime of manhood; a majestic looking man, nearly six feet in height, and remarkable for his dignity of bearing and grace of manner, as well as for his countenance and speaking eyes. He seems to have owned two houses in Calcutta, but that of which we chiefly hear was his garden house at Maniktala, which he furnished in the English style. Babu Rakhal Das Haldar says that Rammohun's Calcutta house was built for him by his half brother (whom Babu Rakhal calls Ramtanu Roy, though he is usually known as Ramlochan). Here then Rammohun settled himself, and took up his life's work in thorough earnest.

How formidable that work was, can with difficulty be realised in present day. Thick clouds of ignorance and superstition hung over all the land; the native Bengali public had few books, and no newspapers. Idolatry was universal, and was often of a most revolting character; polygamy and infanticide were widely prevalent, and the lot of Bengali women was too often a tissue of ceaseless oppressions and miseries, while as the crowning horror, the flames of the suttee were lighted with almost incredible frequency even in the immediate vicinity of Calcutta. The official returns of the years immediately following Rammohun's removal thither, give the number of suttees in the suburbs of Calcutta alone as twenty-five in 1815, forty in 1816, thirty-nine in 1817, and forty-three in 1818, the ages of these victims ranging from 80, 90, and 100, down to 18, 16, and even 15. All these inhumanities deeply afflicted the heart of Rammohun Roy. An ardent lover of his country, he longed to deliver her from her degradations, and to set her feet on safe paths, and to that end he devoted his whole energies from this time forth. He did not, however, confine his activity to one or two subjects. His alert and eager mind ranged with keen interest over the whole field of contemporary life, and in almost every branch thereof he left the impression of his individuality. Alike in religion, in politics, in literature, and in philanthropy, his labours will be found among the earliest and most effective in the history of native Indian reform.

In chronicling a life of such manifold and simultaneous activities in various fields, the best way to avoid needless repetition will be to keep as closely as possible to the chronological order of events. I shall, therefore, divide the sixteen years of Rammohun's Calcutta life into four periods, which mark the successive stages in his treatment of the main problems of his day. These periods are (1) from 1814 to 1820; (2) from 1820 to 1824; 3) from 1824 to 1828; (4) from 1828 to September, 1830. The three years which followed, mostly spent in England, where he died in September, 1833, form a separate period altogether, and may be regarded as a general epilogue to the whole.*

Commencing with the first of these periods, we soon see that to Rammohun's mind the root evil of the whole wretched state of Hindu society was idolatry, and to destroy this was his first object. His multifarious researches in the various sacred books of India had shown him how comparatively modern was the popular Hinduism then current, and with what gross corruptions it had superseded the earlier forms of Hindu faith and practice. Single-handed as he was, he naturally sought the path of least resistance, and by appealing to the venerated authorities of the more ancient and spiritual scriptures, he endeavoured to purify and elevate the minds of his countrymen. For this purpose he selected some of the chief productions of the Vedantic system, "which (writes Pandit Siva Nath Sastri) were of unquestionable authority in matters of Hindu theology. With the general decline of learning, these writings had fallen into disuse in the province of Bengal, and there were very few men even amongst those who were reputed to be learned at that time who were familiar with their contents." In 1815 he published his translation of the Vedanta Sutra itself from the original Sanskrit into Bengali; and in 1816 he published a brief summary of this in Bengali, Hindustani and English. It had been his wish to "render a translation of the complete Vedanta into the current languages of this country," but this was never fully carried out. He recounts, however, how "during the interval between my controversial engagements with idolators as well as with advocates of idolatry, I translated several of the ten Upanishads of which the Vedanta or principal part of the Vedas consist." Of these the Kena and Isha upanishads appeared in 1816, and the Katha, Mundaka and Mandukya upanishads in 1817; and all of these except the last he translated into English also. These works he published with introductions and comments, and distributed them widely among his countrymen, free of charge.

The following extracts, written in 1816, will show the earnest feelings with which he started his propaganda.

My constant reflections on the inconvenient, or rather injurious rites, introduced by the peculiar practice of Hindu idolatry, which more than any other Pagan worship, destroys the texture of society, together with compassion for my countrymen, have compelled me to use every possible effort to awaken them from their dream of error: and by making them acquainted with their Scriptures, enable them to contemplate with true devotion the unity and omnipresence of Nature's God.

By taking the path which conscience and sincerity direct, I, born a Brahmin, have exposed myself to the complainings and reproaches, even of some of my relations, whose prejudices are strong, and whose temporal advantage depends upon the present system. But these, however accumulated, I can tranquilly bear; trusting that a day will arrive when my humble endeavours will be viewed with justice, perhaps acknowledged with gratitude. At any rate, whatever men may say, I cannot be deprived of this consolation: my motives are acceptable to that Being who beholds in secret and compensates openly! *

*(Final paragraphs to the Preface of his first English work, whose title was in itself a manifesto of the new crusade which he was initiating:- "Translation of an Abridgment of the Vedanta, or Resolution of all the Vedas; the most celebrated and revered work of Brahminical Theology: establishing the Unity of the Supreme Being: and that He Alone is the object of propitiation and worship. Calcutta, 1816.)

Some Europeans, endued with high principles of liberality, but not acquainted with the ritual part of Hindu idolatry are disposed to palliate it by an interpretation which, though plausible, is by no means well founded. They are willing to imagine that the idols which the Hindus worship are not viewed by them in the light of Gods or as real personi- fications of the divine attributes? but merely as instruments for raising their minds to the contemplation of those attributes, which are respectively represented by different figures. I have frequently had occasion to remark, that many Hindus also who are conversant with the English language, finding this interpretation a more plausible apology for idolatry than any with which they are furnished by their own guides, do not fail to avail themselves of it, though in repugnance both to their faith and to their practice. The declarations of this description of Hindus naturally tend to confirm the original idea of such Europeans, who from the extreme absurdity of pure unqualified idolatry, deduce an argument against its existence. It appears to them impossible for men, even in the very last degree of intellectual darkness, to be so far misled as to consider a mere image of wood or of stone as a human being, much less as divine existence. With a view, therefore, to do away with any misconception of this nature which may have prevailed, I beg leave to submit the following considerations.

Hindus of the present age, with a very few exceptions, have not the least idea that it is to the attributes of the Supreme Being as figuratively represented by shapes corresponding to the nature of those attributes, they offer adoration and worship under the denomination of gods and goddesses. On the contrary, the slightest investigation will clearly satisfy every inquirer that it makes a material part of their system to hold as articles of faith all those particular circumstances which are essential to the belief in the independent existence of the object of their idolatry, as deities clothed with divine power.

Locality of habitation and a mode of existence analogous to their own views of earthly things are uniformly ascribed to each particular god. Thus the devotees of Siva, misconceiving the real spirit of the Scriptures, not only place an implicit credence in the separate existence of Siva, but even regard him as an omnipotent being, the greatest of all the divinities, who, as they say, inhabit the northern mountain of Kailash; and that he is accompanied by two wives and several children, and surrounded with numerous attendants. In like manner the followers of Vishnu, mistaking the allegorical representations of the Shastras for relations of real facts, believe him to be chief over all other gods, and that he resides with his wife and attendants on the summit of heaven.

Similar opinions are also held by the worshippers of Kali, in respect to that goddess. And in fact, the same observations are equally applicable to every class of Hindu devotees in regard to their respective gods and goddesses. And so tenacious are those devotees in respect to the honour due to their chosen divinities that when they meet in such holy places as Haridwar, Prayag, Siva-Kanchi, or Vishnu-Kanchi in the Dekhan, the adjustment of the point of precedence not only occasions the warmest verbal altercations, but sometimes even blows and violence. Neither do they regard the images of these gods merely in the light of instruments for elevating the mind to the conception of those supposed being; they are simply in themselves made objects of worship. For whenever a Hindu purchases an idol in the market, or constructs one with his own hands, or has one made under his own superintendence, it is his invariable practice to perform certain ceremonies, called 'Pran Pratishtha,' or the endowment of animation, by which he believes that its nature is changed from that of the mere materials of which it is formed, and that it acquires not only life but supernatural powers. Shortly afterwards, if the idol be of the masculine gender, he marries it to a feminine one, with no less pomp and magnificence than he celebrates the nuptials of his own children. The mysterious process is now complete, and the god and goddess are esteemed arbiters of his destiny, and continually receive his most ardent adoration.

At the same time, the worshipper of images ascribes to them at once the opposite natures of human and of super-human beings. In attention to their supposed wants as living beings, he is seen feeding, or pretending to feed them every morning and evening; and as in the hot season he is careful to fan them so in cold he is equally regardful of their comfort, covering them by day with warm clothing, and placing them at night in a snug bed. But superstition does not find 1 minute here: the acts and speeches of the idols, and their assumptions of various shapes and colours, are gravely rel.ted by the Brahmins, and with all the marks of veneration are firmly believed by their deluded followers.

My reflections upon these solemn truths have been most painful for many years. I have never ceased to contemplate with the strongest feelings of regret, the obstinate adherence of my countrymen to their fatal system of idolatry, inducing, for the sake of propitiating their supposed Deities, the violation of every humane and social feeling. And this in various instances, but more especially in the dreadful acts of self-destruction and the immolation of the nearest relations, under the delusion of conforming to sacred religious rites. I have never ceased, I repeat, to contemplate these practices with feelings of regret, and to view in them the moral debasement of a race who, I cannot help thinking, are capable of better things, whose susceptibility, patience, and mildness of character, render them worthy of a better destiny. Under these impressions, therefore, I have been impelled to lay before them genuine translations of parts of their Scripture, which inculcates not only the enlightened worship of one God, but the purest principles of morality, accompanied with such notices as I deemed requisite to oppose the arguments employed by the Brahmins in defence of their beloved system. Most earnestly do I pray that the whole may, sooner or later, prove efficient in producing on the minds of Hindus in general, conviction of the rationality of believing in and adoring the Supreme Being only; together with a complete perception and practice of that grand and comprehens- ive moral principle - Do unto others as ye would be done by.

Such was the standing-ground from which Rammohun Roy opened his first regular campaign. The fame of his provincial discussions and writings had preceded his settle- ment in Calcutta, and when these were followed up by such increased and systematic opposition to the popular creed, great excitement was produced in Hindu society, and the orthodox feeling against Rammohun soon became very hostile.†

† (At the same time these publications created a very favourable impression among thoughtful Europeans, and spread the fame of Raja Rammohun Roy as a great religious reformer in Europe and America. The first English notice we find of Rammohun Roy occurs in the Periodical Accounts of the Baptist Missionary Society Vol. VI. pp. 106-109 of the date of 1816: "Ramamohuna Raya, a very rich Rarhee Brahmun of Calcutta is a respectable Sungskrita scholar and so well-versed in Persian, that he is called Mouluvee Ramamohuna Raya: He also writes English with correctness and reads with ease English mathematical and metaphysical works. He has published in Bengalee one or two philosophical works, from the Sungskrita, which he hopes may be useful in leading his countrymen to renounce idolatry." The narrative gives an account of Rammohun Roy's interview with the Serampore Missionaries and some particulars about his mode of life at this period. A fuller account is found in the Church of England "Missionary Register" for Sept. 1816 p. 370 in the course of a review of the Translation of the Vedanta Sutra: "We have been favoured with a sight of a tract printed at Calcutta in the present year (1816) with the following tittle:- "Translation of an Abridgement of the Vedant, etc."......by Rammohun Roy. Before we give an account of this curious tract, it may be advan- tageous to our readers to know something of the author." Then follows a brief account of the life and views of Rammohun Roy, with speculations as to the possibility of his becoming a Christian. The review of the Abridgement of the Vedant is very fair. The account closes with the following thoughtful remarks on the propaganda of Rammohun Roy: "The rise of this new sect, the zeal and subtlety displayed by its founder, with its obvious tendency to undermine the fabric of Hindu superstition, are objects of serious attention to the Christian mind. 'Who knows,' asks one

of the friends from whom we have received these communications, but this man may be one of the many instruments by which God, in his mysterious providence, may accomplish the overthrow of idolatry? "What may be the effect of this man's labours', says another correspondent, 'time will show. Probably they may bring the craft of Brahmanism and caste into danger."

A notice of the Abridgement of the Vedant is also found in the Monthly Repositary of Theology and General Literature for 1816 p. 512, which is interesting as affording from another quarter a view of the first English work of the Raja:-

"Two literary phenomena of a singular nature have very recently been exhibited in India. The first is a Hindu Deist. Rammohun Roy, a Brahmin, has published a small work, in the present year, at Calcutta, entitled 'An Abridgement of the Vedant'. It contains a collection of very remarkable texts from the Vedas, in which the principles of natural religion are delivered, not without dignity; and which treat all worship to inferior beings, together with the observance of rites and seasons, and the distinctions of food, as the aids of an imperfect religion, which may be altogether disregarded by those who have attained to the knowledge and love of God."

The records of the next year mark a striking progress of Rammohun Roy's fame, as evidenced by the following passage, extracted by the late Miss Mary Carpenter in her Last Days of Rammohun Roy from a letter of Rev. T. Belsham, Minister of Essex Street Chapel, London, as an introduction to a letter he had just received from a native convert to Christianity, William Roberts of Madras:-

"It is very remarkable that while the great doctrine of the unity and unrivalled supremacy of God is thus gradually working its way among the poorer classes of natives in the vicinity of Madras, it is at the same time making a triumphant progress among the higher castes of Hindus in the great and populous city of Calcutta. Rammohun Roy, a learned, eloquent and opulent Brahman, having by the proper exercise of his own understanding, discovered the folly and absurdity of the Hindu mythology and of idol worship, was led by conscientious sense of duty to proclaim this important discovery to his countrymen, and has publicly taught the doctrine of the divine unity and perfection to the native Hindus and has entered his protest against their impious, barbarous and idolatrous rites. Such a doctrine from a person of such exalted rank, at first excited great astonishment and gave infinite offence. But by degrees the courage, eloquence and perseverance of this extraordinary man prevailed over all opposition; and it is said that many hundreds of the native Hindoos, and especially of the young people, have embraced his doctrine."

The European reputation of Rammohan Roy, says Miss Mary Carpenter, as a remarkable man, and a reformer, was not confined to Great Britain. A French pamphlet respecting him was forwarded to the Editor of the "Monthly Repository," by the Abbe Gregoire, formerly Bishop of Blois, and which was afterwards inserted in the "Chronique Religieuse." The biographical part of this pamphlet was derived from communications from the learned M. D'Acosta, then the Editor of, The Times at Calcutta. The following extract presents several interesting features of the life of Rammohun Roy, as viewed by a foreigner: "There is probably, throughout India no Brahmin, who is less a Hindoo than he; and thousands of dupes who have suffered the loss of their caste have been less offenders against the peculiarities of their religion than he......Every six months he publishes a little tract in Bengalee and in English developing his system of theism; and he is always ready to answer the pamphlets published at Calcutta or Madras in opposition to him. He takes pleasure in this controversy; but although far from deficient in philosophy, or in knowledge, he distinguishes himself more by his logical mode of reasoning than by his general views. He appears to feel the advantage which it gives him with the Methodists, some of whom are endeavouring to convert him. He seems to have prepared himself for his polemical career from the logic of the Arabians, which he regards as superior to every other; he asserts, likewise, that he has found nothing in European books equal to the scholastic philosophy of the Hindoos. * Influenced, like those around him, with the spirit * of order, economy and knowledge of the value of money, acquired by their mercantile education, Rammohan Roy does not view the augmentation of property as the most important object: his fortune consists of the wealth he received from his ancestors: he does not give his mind to any kind of commercial speculation. He would consider that mode of life beneath his station and the dignities of a Brahmin. He derives no pecuniary advantage from his works; and in all probability desirous as he may be of power and distinction, he would not accept of the Government any place that should be merely lucrative; to solicit one of any description he would not condescend. ** Rammohun Roy, as has already been shown, is not yet forty years old; he is tall and robust; his regular features and habitually grave countenance assu:ne a must pleasing appearance when he is animated. He appears to have a slight disposition to melancholy. The whole of his conversation and manners show, at first sight, that he is above mediocrity. ** It is known that every member of his family verifies the proverb, by opposing with the greatest vehemence all his projects of reform. None of them, not even his wife, would accompany him to Calcutta, in consequence of which he rarely visits them in Burdwan, where they reside. They have disputed with him even the superintendence of the education of his nephews, and his fanatical mother shows as much ardor in her incessant opposition to him, as he displays in his attempts to destroy the idolatry of the Hindoos."

One more extract giving an impression which Rammohun Roy made on a European contemporary at this period, we shall record. It is taken from a "Journal of a Route across India, through Egypt to England, in the years 1817 and 1818 by Lieut - Col. FitzClarence " (afterwards Earl of Munster). He writes: "I became well acquainted with him, and admire his talents and achievements. His eloquence in our language is very great, and I am told he is still more admirable in Arabic and Persian. It is remarkable that he has studied and thoroughly understands the politics of Europe, but more particularly those of England; and the last time I was in his company he argued forcibly against standing armies in a free country, and quoted all the arguments brought forward by the Members of the Opposition. I think that he is in many respects a most extraordinary person. In the first place, he is a religious reformer, who has, amongst a people more bigoted than those of Europe in the middle ages, dared to think for himself. His learning is most extensive, as he is not only conversant with the best books in English, Arabic, Sanskrit, Bengali and Hindustani, but has even studied rhetoric in Arabic and English and quotes Locke and Bacon on all occasions. From the view he thus takes of the religion, manners and customs of so many nations, and from his having observed the number of different modes of addressing and worshipping the Supreme Being, he naturally turned to his own faith with an unprejudiced mind, found it perverted from the religion of the Vedas to a gross idolatry, and was not afraid, though aware of the consequences, to publish to the world in Bengali and English his feelings and opinions on the subject; of course he was fully prepared to meet the host of interested enemies, who, from sordid motives, wished to keep the lower classes in a state of the darkest ignorance. I have understood that his family have quitted him - that he has been declared to have lost caste - and is for the present, as all religious reformers must be for a time, a mark to be scoffed at. To a man of his sentiments and rank this loss of caste must be particularly painful, but at Calcutta he associates with the English; he is, however, cut off from all familiar and domestic intercourse; indeed from all communication of any kind with his relations and former friends.

His name is Rammohun Roy. He is particularly handsome, not of a very dark complexion, of a fine person, and most courtly manners. He professes to have no objection to eating and living as we do, but refrains from it, in order not to expose himself to the imputation of having changed his religion for the good things of this world. He will sit at table with us while the meat is on it, which no other Brahmin will do.')

Meanwhile he gathered around him a small circle of intelligent friends who sympathized more or less actively in his desire to enlighten his countrymen; and in 1815 he started a little society which he entitled the 'Atmiya Sabha', or Friendly Association, for the purpose of spiritual improvement. It met once a week, and its proceedings consisted in the recitation of texts from the Hindu Scriptures, and the chanting of theistic hymns composed by Rammohun and his friends. Rammohun's pandit, Siva Prasad Misra, was the first reciter, and a paid singer, Govinda Mala, was the first chanter. "The meetings were not quite public and were attended chiefly by Rammohun's personal friends. Among these may be mentioned Dwarkanath Tagore, Brajamohun Mazumdar, Holodhur Bose, Nanda Kisore Bose and Rajnarain Sen." ++ There was a remarkable man who also assisted Rammohun at this time, named Hariharananda Tirthaswami. This man, "during his peregrinations as a Hindu mendicant had come to Rungpur, and there met Rammohun, who had received him with great honour in recognition of his learning and liberality of spirit: and Tirthaswami, bound to Rammohun by love, followed him like a shadow. He practised the rules of Tantric Vamachara, and was a worshipper of One True God according to the Mahanirvana Tantra. Ram Chandra Vidyabagish, the first minister of the Brahmo Samaj was the younger brother of this man."

* (Among the associates of Rammohun Roy the following names also should be mentioned: Gopeemohun Tagore and his son Prasanna Kumar Tagore, Vaidyanath Mukerjee, father of late Justice Anukul Mukherjee, he was one of the organizers of the Hindu College and its first Secretary; Jaikrishna Sinha, Kasinath Mullik, Brindaban Mitra, grandfather of the late Dr. Rajendralal Mitra, Gopinath Munshee, Badan Chandra Roy; Chandra Sekhar Dev, Tarachand Chakravarti, Bhairab Chandra Datta, who afterwards became the Asst. Secretary of the Bethune School, Kalinath Roy, Zaminder of Taki, Boikuntha Nath Roy, one of the first trustees of the Brahmo Samaj, Annada Prasad Bandopadhyaya, Zaminder of Telinipara, Raja Kali Sankar Ghoshal.)

+(Father of Raj Narain Bose, who afterwards became a well-known figure in the Brahmo Samaj.)

++ (This sentence is taken from the Indian Mirror of July 1, 1865, from a brief sketch by Keshub Chandra Sen, entitled "Brahmo Samaj, or Theism in India.)

If Hariharananda Tirthaswami represented the extreme Eastern side of Rammohun's society, the extreme Western side was represented by David Hare, the active and bene- volent rationalist who did so much for native Bengal education. In his life by Pyarichand Mitra we read as follows:-

"Hare found an intimate friend in Rammohun Roy. He had begun to spread theism, denounce idolatry, was moving heaven and earth for the abolition of the suttee rite, and advocating the dissemination of English education as the means for enlightening his countrymen, The first move he (Hare) made, was in attending, uninvited, a meeting called by Rammohun Roy and his friends for the purpose of establishing a society calculated to subvert idolatry. Hare submitted that the establishment of an English school would materially help their cause. They all acquiesced in the strength of Hare's position, but did not carry out his suggestion." Hare, therefore, consulted Chief Justice Sir E. Hyde East, who inclined favourably to his ideas. The subject was mooted among leading Hindus, meetings were held at Sir E. H. East's house, and it was resolved that "an establishment be formed for the education of native youth." Rammohun Roy, fearing that his presence at the preliminary meeting might embarass its deliberations, had generously abstained from attending it, but his name had been mentioned as one of the promoters. Soon afterwards some of the native gentlemen concerned, told Sir Hyde East that they would

gladly accord their support to the proposed College if Rammohun Roy were not connected with it, but they would have nothing to do with that apostate. Hare communicated this to Rammohun Roy, who willingly allowed himself to be laid aside lest his active co-operation should mar the accomplishment of the project. This was early in 1816. So soon had Hindu orthodoxy taken alarm and so early had Rammohun been called upon to exercise that self-effacingness with which, many a time in his life, did he withhold his name from benevolent schemes for which he nevertheless worked, in order to smooth their reception by the general public, to whom his name was an offence.

About the end of Rammohun's third year in Calcutta, he wrote (fortunately for us) a brief summary of his proceedings to his old friend Mr. Digby, to whom he also sent his first two English publications, the Abridgement of the Vedant and the Kena Upanishad. These translations Mr. Digby reprinted in London in 1817, with a preface which beginning with the description of Rammohun quoted in the last chapter, goes on to give the following extract ("made without alteration") from "a letter I have lately received from him, inti- mately connected with the subject before me."

Rammohun Roy, India to Mr. John Digby, England, "I take this opportunity of giving you a summary account of my proceedings since the period of your departure froin India.

"The consequence of my long and uninterrupted researches in religious truth has been that I have found the doctrines of Christ more conducive to moral principles, and better adapted for the use of rational beings, than any others which have come to my knowledge; and have also found Hindus in general more superstitious and miserable, both in performance of their religious rites, and in their domestic concerns, than the rest of the known nations on the earth: I therefore, with a view of making them happy and comfortable* both here and hereafter, not only employed verbal arguments against the absurdities of the idolatry practised by them, but also translated their more revered theological work, namely Vedanta, into Bengali and Hindustani, and also several chapters of the Vedas, in order to convince them that the unity of God, and absurdity of idolatry, are evidently pointed out by their own Scriptures. I, however, in the beginning of my pursuits, met with the greatest opposition from their self-interested leaders, the Brahmins, and was deserted by my nearest relations; I consequently felt extremely melancholy; in that critical situation, the only comfort that I had was the consoling and rational conversation of my European friends, especially those of Scotland and England.

"I now with the greatest pleasure inform you that several of my countrymen have risen superior to their prejudices; many are inclined to seek for the truth: and a great number of those who dissented from me have now coincided with me in opinion. This engagement has prevented me from proceeding to Europe as soon as I could wish. But you may depend upon my setting off for England within a short period of time; and if you do not return to India before October next, you will most probably receive a letter from me, informing you of the exact time of my departure for England, and of the name of the vessel on which I shall embark."

* (To make men "comfortable" may at first sound rather a low aim for a religious reformer; but the preface to the Kena Upanishad explains

Rammohun's meaning, which was simply to break the superstitious fetters that made utterly needless discomfort an essential feature of orthodox Hindu life. In this preface he expresses his desire "to correct these exceptionable practices which not only deprive Hindus in general of the common comforts of society, but also lead them frequently to self-destruction. ... A Hindu of caste can only eat once between sunrise and sunset - cannot eat dressed victuals in a boat or ship - nor clothed - nor in a tavern, nor any food that has been touched by a person of a different caste - nor if interrupted while eating, can he resume his meal.)

Mr. Digby returned to India in November, 1819, and was again employed in the Bengal Civil Service. During 1821 and 1822 he was stationed at Burdwan, where he would doubtless have many opportunities of meeting his old friend. Rammohun's much longed for visit to England did not take place until the end of 1830. It is interesting to know how early he had formed that desire.

The year 1817 saw further progress of the movement. Rammohun's publications now began to call forth learned and animated replies from the defenders of Hinduism. The Madras Courier, in December, 1816, contained a long letter from the head English master in the Madras Government College, Sankara Sastri, controverting Rammohun's views as shown in his writings, and pleading for the worship of Divine attributes as virtual deities. Rammohun reprinted this letter with a masterly reply entitled 'A Defence of Hindu Theism,' in which he not only defended his own position very clearly, but carried the war into the enemy's camp by exposing the degrading character of the legends attached to so many of the Hindu incarnations, and pointing out how mischievous must be the effect of regarding such narratives as sacred records. Another defender of Hinduism appeared some months later in the head Pandit of the Government College at Calcutta, Mrityunjaya Vidyalankar, who published a tract entitled 'Vedanta Chandrika.' To this Rammohun replied in 'A Second Defence of the Monotheistical System of the Vedas.' In this tract, substantially the same arguments as before were put forth, but with still greater fullness and force. These writings were, however, largely supplemented and strengthened by Rammohun's numerous oral discussions and conversations with his friends, disciples and opponents, of which we can only now get occasional glimpses. Pandit S. N. Sastri states in his 'History of the Brahmo Samaj' that:

"At times the Atmiya Sabha got intereststing discussion meetings which would attract all classes of people. The most remarkable of these meetings was the one held in December, 1819, where Rammohun Roy had a face-to-face fight with his idolatrous adversaries. A learned Madrasi Pandit, called Subrahmanya Sastri, renowned at that time for his erudition, publicly challenged him to a polemical combat. Rammohun Roy accepted it with pleasure, and in the presence of a large gathering of people, headed by Radha Kanta Dev, the acknowledged leader of the orthodox Hindu community, silenced his adversary by the great cogency of his reasoning, as well as by the long array of scriptural authorities that he quoted in favour of his views." *

* (This discussion was held at the house of Behari Lal Chaubay in Barabazar where the Atmiya Sabha used to meet at this period.)

[Defeated in theological debate, his opponents renewed their attack upon him in the law courts. "Shortly after" this debate Rammohun's nephew (his brother's son) "brought an action against him in the Supreme Court in order to disinherit him from any participation in the ancestral property, on the score of his being an apostate from the Hindu religion."† The endeavour was made to prove that he had broken caste and so forfeited his civil rights. The proceedings lasted some two years, and involved him in great expense, but ended in a complete victory for Rammohun. But during these two years he considered it advisable to discontinue holding the meetings of the Atmiya Sabha, which earlier litigation had compelled him to have convened in the houses of friends instead of his own, as previously.] ++

† So Nagendranath Chattopadhyaya in his 'Biography of the Raja' (p. 62) and G. S. Leonard in his "History of the Brahma Samaj" (Newman & Co., Calcutta, 1879) p. 35.

++K. S. Macdonald in his lecture on the Raja (Herald Office, Calcutta, 1876) thinks that this giving up of these meetings "does not look well," "seemingly because he was afraid their very existence would prejudice his worldly interests." Mr. Macdonald apparently forgets that during the latter part of these two years Rammohun was in regular attendance on Mr. W. Adam's unitarian services and was openly identified with the Unitarian Committee. For the sentences enclosed in brackets and notes, the continuator is responsible.

An interesting sign of the progress of Rammohun's views is recorded at the beginning of 1820. A native called as a witness in a court of law refused to take the waters of Ganga. He declared himself a follower of Rammohun

Roy, and consequently not a believer in the imagined sanctity of the river. He was allowed to affirm as quakers do. Our reformer may thus be regarded as a pioneer in the abolition of oaths in the courts of law.

We must now take up the other main branch of Rammohun's propaganda, agitation against suttee. His first tract on this subject appeared in November, 1818, in the form of a dialogue between an opponent and an advocate of the custom; and in February, 1820, this was followed by a second tract giving a later dialogue between the same inter- locutors. But before speaking of these in detail, some brief account must be given of the state at which the controversy had arrived at that time.

A Sati, long since anglicised as suttee - means literally a faithful woman, from 'sat' - truth; but the term has long been practically narrowed to designate a widow who is burned on the funeral pile of her husband. This "rite" (as it is euphemistically called) was never universal in India, but it has been practised more or less extensively in various localities and amongst various classes in that country. M. Barth, in his admirable work on 'The Religions of India,' says (p. 59):-

"A custom which. could beyond a doubt reckon its victims by myriads, the immolation, viz., more or less voluntary * of the widow on the funeral pile of of her husband, is not sanctioned by the Vedic ritual, although certain hints in the symbolism connected with funerals (particularly in the Atharvaveda) come very near it, and in a measure fore- shadow it. In the Atharvaveda we see the widow could marry again under certain conditions, which in the course of time orthodox usage strictly debarred her from doing. The custom of the suicide of the Sati is nevertheless very ancient since as early as the days of Alexander the Great found it was observed among one of the tribes at least of the Punjab. The first Brahmanical testimony we find it is that of the Brihaddevata, which is perhaps of quite as remote antiquity; in the epic poetry there are numerous instances of it. At first it seems to have been peculiar to the military aristocracy, and it is under the influence of the sectarian religions that it has especially flourished. Justice requires us to add that it was only at a period comparatively modern that it ceased to meet with opposition."

Sir John Malcolm in one of his 'Reports on Central India,' says that "the Mohameddan rulers endeavoured, as much as they could without offending their Hindu subjects, to prevent it." The zeal of the Emperor Akbar in the matter is well known, and the Asiatic Journal of January, 1824, states that the practice "was discouraged and even forbidden by the Moghul Government, and the Peshwa was in the habit of personally exerting himself to dissuade widows from becoming suttees, making suitable provision for those who yielded to his arguments."

When the European powers came to obtain footing in India, they also usually seemed to have endeavoured to stop the suttee rite. The French, the Dutch, and the Portuguese colonies all exerted themselves in this direction, and with fair success. The English were no less humanely shocked by the practice, and frequently made efforts to stop it, but the official class were considerably hampered by the dread of offending native prejudices and thus imperiling the British power in India. At last, however, serious efforts were made by philanthropists in England, both in the House of Commons and in the East India House, and in 1821 the first Blue Book on the subject was issued.

* (It has been established on the testimony of European eye-witnesses that at the beginning of the nineteenth century, at any rate, force was used to prevent the victims from escaping from the burning pyre. Mr. J. Peggs published a booklet under the name of "The Suttee's cry to Britain" in which he wrote:- "The use of force by means of bamboos is, we believe, universal through Bengal. In the burning of widows as practised at present in some parts of Hindustan, however voluntary the widow may have been in her determination, force is employed in the act of immolation. After she has circumambulated and ascended the pile, several natives leap on it, and pressing her down on the wood, bind her with two or three ropes to the corpse of her husband, and instantly throw over the two bodies, thus bound to each other, several large bamboos, which being firmly fixed to the ground on both sides of the pile, prevent the possibility of her extricating herself when the flames reach her. Logs of wood are also thrown on the pile, which is then inflamed in an instant.")

From this valuable storehouse of evidence we find that the first recorded British action in this matter took place in the very year of Rammohun's birth, 1772; when a Captain Tomyn, of Tripetty in Southern India, hearing that a widow was about to be sacrificed, went straightway to the spot, and led her away to a place of safety. This truly British course drew down upon him a formidable riot from a large and indignant crowd. But the first deliberate official step taken on this subject was the refusal, in January 1789, of a British magistrate to permit the performance of a suttee at Shahabad. His letter to the Governor-General in Council, Lord Cornwallis, is so terse and sensible, that it is worth preserving :-

*My Lord. cases sometimes occur in which a Collector having no specific orders for the guidance of his conduct, is necessitated to act from his own sense of what is right. This assertion has this day been verified in an application from the relatives and friends of a Hindu woman, for my sanction to the horrid ceremony of burning with her deceased husband. Being impressed with a belief that this savage custom has been prohibited in and about Calcutta, and considering the same reasons for its discontinuance would probably be held valid throughout the whole extent of the Company's authority, I positively refused my consent. The rites and superstitions of the Hindu religion should be allowed with the most unqualified tolerance, but a practice at which human nature shudders I cannot permit within the limits of my jurisdicion, without particular instructions. I beg, therefore, my Lord, to be informed whether my conduct in this instance meets your approbation.

Lord Cornwallis's reply informed Mr. Brooke that the Government approved of his refusal to grant the application for permission of the suttee: but they did "not deem it advisable to authorize him to prevent the observance of it by coercive measures, or by any exertion of his official powers; as the public prohibition of a ceremony, authorized by the tenets of the religion of the Hindus, and from the observance of which they have never been restricted by the ruling power, would in all probability tend rather to increase than diminish their veneration for it, and consequently prove the means of rendering it more prevalent than it is at present."

Sixteen years later, in January 1805, Mr. J. R. Elphinstone, a magistrate of Zillah Behar, acted in a similar way, forbidding the sacrifice of a young widow of only twelve-years-old (who was "extremely grateful for my interposition") but as he was "not aware of the existence of any order or regulation to prevent such a barbarous proceeding," and as native prejudices might cause trouble, he wrote to headquarters, requesting definite instructions on the subject. Hereupon, Lord Wellesley sent a letter (Feb. 5th, 1805) to the Nizamat Adawlat, the chief judicial authority in India at that time, requesting that court to ascertain the precise amount of sanction given by the Hindu Shastras to the practice of suttee. The Nizamat sent in its reply in four months (June 5th, 1805), enclosing the opinion of a pandit and suggesting certain rules for the guidance of Government officials which might slightly restrict the range of the practice. But no such rules were drawn up, and nothing whatever was done for seven years, a discreditable hiatus, but one which was probably owing, at least in part, to the frequent changes in the personnel of the Government during that period. In 1812, a magistrate of Bundelcund being perplexed as to his duty concerning suttees, wrote (Aug. 3rd) to the Nizamat Adawlat for instructions: the Nizamat sent his letter to the Governor-General (Lord Moira, afterwards Marquis of Hastings) and after eight months more delay the instructions were at last drawn up and issued, April 17th, 1813. Their principle was "to allow the practice in those cases in which it is countenanced by the Hindu religion and law, and to prevent it in others in which it is by the same authority prohibited" I.e. where the woman is unwilling or is under sixteen, or is pregnant, or drugged, or intoxicated. These instructions were afterwards extended (in January 1815) by the important item of prohibiting suttee when the widow had very young children, an extension which was brought in by the humane refusal of some magistrates to sanction such sacrifices, and in June 1817 a full and elaborate summary of the whole series of instructions was drawn up by the Government officials. It is quite clear from the various letters and despatches given in the Blue Book that from this time forth the British authorities did really care earnestly about the matter. Regular statistics on the subject were started in 1815, with which date commenced a series of lists of the suttees performed all over British India, with the details of name, age, caste, of each victim - truly awful records for any Christian Government.

One of these replies is so important as to deserve special notice. Mr. H. Oakely, a magistrate of Zilla Hughli, writes (Dec. 19, 1818) saying how earnestly he has sought to discover the reason of the great frequency of suttees in his district, which yielded the largest number of victims in the list, 376 in the four years ending with 1818. One cause he finds in the nearness to Calcutta. "It is notorious (he says) that the natives of Calcutta and its vicinity exceed all others in profligacy and immorality of conduct;" and while the depraved worship of Kali, "the idol of the drunkard and the thief," is "scarcely to be met with in the distant provinces." it abounds in the metropolis. Elsewhere, "none but the most abandoned will openly confess that he is a follower of Kali. In Calcutta we find few that are not. . . . By such men, a suttee is not regarded as a religious act, but as a choice enter tainment; and we may fairly conclude that the vicious propensities of the Hindus in the vicinity of Calcutta are a cause of the comparative prevalence of the custom." This view seems to be confirmed by the large number of suttees in the other districts near Calcutta, Burdwan (Rammohun's own district) ranking only second to Hughli. But besides this local cause, Mr.

Oakely attributes much to another cause of general application, viz. : to the attempts of Government to "regulate" the practice. He says:-. Previous to 1813, no interference on the part of the police was authorised, and widows were sacrificed, legally or illegally as it might happen; but the Hindus were then aware that the Government regarded the custom with natural horror, and would do anything short of direct prohibition to discourage and gradually to abolish it. The case is now al- tered. The police officers are ordered to interfere, for the purpose of ascertaining that the ceremony is performed in conformity with the rules of Shastras; and in that event, to allow its completion. This is granting the authority of Government for burning widows; and it can scarcely be a matter of astonishment that the number of sacrifices should be doubled, when the sanction of the ruling power is added to the recommendation of the Shastras.

He ends by saying, "I do not hesitate in offering my opinion that a law for its abolition would only be objected to by the heirs, who derive worldly profit from the custom, Brah- mins, who partly exist by it, and by those whose depraved nature leads them to look on so horrid a sacrifice as a highly agreeable and entertaining show; at any rate the sanction of Government should be withdrawn without delay."

Mr. Ewer, summarizing the replies to his circular of inquiry, expressed his agreement with the views of Mr. Oake ly and of other magistrates who wrote to the same effect; and finally, the Governor-General reluctantly acquiesced in the inference that the Government action in the matter had really tended to increase instead of to discourage the sacrifices, and therefore suspended any additional regulations for the time.

Meanwhile two native petitions were sent up to the Governor-General which appeared to tell on the opposite side. They are not mentioned in the Blue Book, and I have only seen the second of them. It is given in full in the Asiatic Journal of July 1819, which states that it seems to have been sent up in August, 1818 and that it "was signed by a great num- ber of the most respectable inhabitants of Calcutta." Its immediate occasion was to counteract a petition recently sent up to Government by certain other inhabitants of Cal- cutta, which had prayed for the repeal of the orders then in force against illegal proceedings in cases of suttee. The counterpetition challenges the title of the previous supplicants to represent "the principal inhabitants of Calcutta," and warmly endorses the humanity and justice of the aforementioned Government order. In forcible language, some of the chief horrors of the suttee practice are enumerated. For instance:-

"Your petitioners are fully aware from their own knowledge or from the authority of credible eye-witnesses that cases have frequently occurred when women have been induced by the persuasions of their next heirs, interested in their destruction, to burn themselves on the funeral pile of their husband; that others who have been induced by fear to retract a resolution rashly expressed in the first moments of grief, of burning with their deceased husbands have been forced upon the pile and there bound down with ropes, and pressed with green bamboos until consumed with the flames; that some, after flying from the flame, have been carried back by their relations and burnt to death. All these instances, your petitioners humbly submit are murders according to every Shastra, as well as to the common sense of all nations."

In conclusion, these petitioners declare that they "look with the most lively hope to such further measures relative to the custom of burning widows as may justly be expected from the known wisdom, decision, and humanity which have ever distinguished your Lordship's administration."

It is evident that the writer of the above took hold of the regulation system from the side of prohibition, regarding the police interference at "illegal" suttees as a step towards the final abolition of the practice altogether, and looking to Lord Hastings in the hope of further protection. And no doubt a small number of suttees was really prevented by the regulation system, as we find by occasional records of such instances in the Blue Books. But the balance on the whole was so enormously on the other side that it is not surprising to find, among the letters of the magistrates and other high class officials con- sulted, a very large proportion of opinions against the system altogether; and the conviction is often put forth that the practice of suttee might be abolished by law without any danger to the British rule. Lord Hastings left India on January I, 1829; but his successor Lord Amherst, wrote with equal humanity on the subject, and concurred in the same policy of standing still until he knew in which direction to move. Perhaps, as a new comer, he may have been additionally cautious in the matter. At any rate, the impasse remained for some years more.

And now we come to Rammohun Roy. It was in this eventful year 1818, that his influence in this matter began to be definitely felt.* He used to go down to the Calcutta burning-grounds and try to avert the Suttee sacrifices by earnest persuasion.† Two of such cases have been recorded, one very briefly;- the other is described in the Asiatic Journal for March 1818, which states that the priests were induced to light the pile first,

Rammohun having maintained that the Shastra required this, and left it open to the widow to ascend the pile and enter the flames afterwards if she chose, his expectation of course being that she would not so choose. But this case (if it be accurately reported) proved exceptional; the two widows both fulfilled the suttee's ideal, and "deliberately walked into" the flames, the younger widow having previously "with great animation, addressed herself to the bystanders in words to this effect:- 'You have just seen my husband's first wife perform the duty incumbent on her, and will now see me follow her example. Henceforward, I pray, do not attempt to prevent Hindu women from burning, otherwise our curse will be upon you."

* [The efforts of Rammohun Roy to suppress this great social evil commenced at a much earlier date. One of the main causes which drew upon him the anger and persecution of the orthodox Hindu community was his condemnation of suttee. The widow of his elder brother Jaganmohun became a suttee on 8th April, 1810. Raja Rammohun was then at Rungpur and could have heard of the event some time after its occurence. But when he heard of it he took his mother to task for it. His views on the question had been formed and freely expressed long before this. In his early youth he was present at the burning of a widow, and the cruel scene made such a deep impression on him that he resolved never to rest until this inhuman custom were abolished.)

+ [In these efforts he had often to incur the displeasure and insult of the relatives of the suttee.)

No record is given of the actual ordeal, which often proved fatal to the fortitude of many suttees who had dared it, as we have seen with Rammohun's own sister-in-law. But assuming the unbroken courage of the two widows here described, it needs not to be added that such heroism was quite exceptional, as may be seen from the details given in the Calcutta petition, quoted above, as well as from the habit prevalent in Bengal of tying down the victims to prevent their escape.

It was in August, 1818, that this petition was presented to Lord Hastings. How far Rammohun was concerned in it does not appear. It bears traces of his hand, and most likely he wrote a good deal of it, though there is one paragraph reflecting very harshly on the Mohammedans which is so unlike him that it must have come from another source. On the 30th of November following Rammohun issued an English translation of his first work on the subject; a Conference between an Advocate for, and an Opponent of, the Practice of Burning Widows Alive. The brief preface states that the tract is a literal translation of one in Bengali which "has been for several weeks past in extensive circulation in those parts of the country where the practice of widows burning themselves on the pile of their husbands is most prevalent."

A Second Conference followed, fourteen months later (Feb. 20, 1820) and was dedicated to Lady Hastings in the following words. "The following tract being a translation of a Bengali essay, published some time ago, as an appeal to reason in behalf of humanity, I take the liberty to dedicate to your Ladyship; for to whose protection can any attempt to promote a benevolent purpose be with so much propriety committed?"

As Rammohun was far too discreet to have published such a dedication without leave from its object, we may conclude that it virtually implied the Governor-General's good- will to his movement.

These tracts are very characteristic of their author. He threw his argument into a dramatic form, making the 'Opponent" (of suttee) quite as good a Hindu as the "Advocate," and ready to admit that "all those passages you have quoted are indeed sacred law, and it is clear from those authorities that if women perform con-cremation or post-cremation, they will enjoy heaven for a considerable time" (previously estimated at thirty-five millions of years). But he calmly points out that all this brings suttee under the category of acts "performed for the sake of gratifications in this world or the next"; which are declared by the highest Hindu authorities to be only of an inferior order of merit. The Katha Upanishad declares that "faith in God which leads to absorption is one thing; and rites which have future fruition for their object another. Each of these, producing different consequences, holds out to man inducements to follow it. The man who of these two chooses faith, is blessed; and he, who for the sake of reward practices rites, is dashed away from the enjoyment of eternal beatitude." And the author of the 'Mitakshara' decides that, "the widow who is not desirous of final beatitude, but who wishes only for a limited term of a small degree of future fruition, is authorized to accompany her husband."

Thus far the abstract argument is of a purely Hindu nature. The "Opponent" then shows that Manu, their great law-giver, expressly enjoyed that the widow should live on as an ascetic, and should "continue till death forgiving all injuries" (a significant hint!), "performing harsh duties, avoiding every sensual pleasure, and cheerfully practising the incomparable rules of virtue which have been followed by such women as were devoted to one only husband." Other high authorities are quoted in confirmation of this view.

By this process of argument the "Opponent" brings the discussion up to the critical point. The "Advocate" flatly denies that women are capable of true faith or permanent virtue, and avows that they are burned in order to prevent them from going astray after the husband's death. Arrived at this issue, Rammohun drops the dramatic dress and enters upon a thorough defence of women in general and Indian women in particular, which shows how closely he had observed, and how ardently he longed to see them delivered from the miseries of their lot. This defence is so characteristic of himself and of the situation that I give it entire, but must first call attention to one golden sentence concerning the relative trustworthiness of the two sexes which is, alas! not applicable to India alone.

Women are in general inferior to men in bodily strength and energy; consequently the male part of the community, taking advantage of their corporeal weakness, have denied to them those excellent merits that they are entitled to by nature, and afterwards they are apt to say that women are naturally incapable of acquiring those merits. But if we give the subject consideration, we may easily ascertain whether or not your accusation against them is consistent with justice. As to their inferiority in point of understanding, when did you ever afford them a fair opportunity of exhibiting, their natural capacity? How then can you accuse them of want of understanding? If, after instruction in knowledge and wisdom, a person cannot comprehend or retain what has been taught him, we may consider him as deficient; but as you keep women generally void of edu- cation and acquirements, you cannot, therefore, in justice pronounce on their inferiority. On the contrary, Lilavati, Bhanumati, the wife of the prince of Karnat, and that of Kalidas, are celebrated for their thorough knowledge of all the Shastras: moreover in the Brihadaranyaka Upanishad of the Yajurveda it is clearly stated, that Yagnavalkya imparted divine knowledge of the most difficult nature to his wife Maitreyi, who was able to follow and completely attain it!

Secondly. You charge them with want of resolution, at which I feel exceedingly surprised: for we constantly perceive, in a country where the name of death makes the male shudder, that the female, from her firmness of mind, offers to burn with the corpse of her deceased husband; and yet you accuse those women of deficiency of resolution.

Thirdly. With regard to their trustworthiness, let us look minutely into the conduct of both sexes, and we may be enabled to ascertain which of them is the most frequently guilty of betraying friends. If we enumerate such women in each village or town as have been deceived by men, and such men as have been betrayed by women, I presume that the numbers of the deceived women would be found ten times greater than that of the betrayed men. Men are, in general, able to read and write, and manage public affairs, by which means they easily promulgate such faults as women occasionally commit, but never consider as criminal the misconduct of men towards women. One fault they have, it must be acknowledged, which is, by considering others equally void of duplicity as themselves, to give their confidence too readily, from which they suffer much misery, even so far that some of them are misled to suffer themselves to be burnt to death.

In the fourth place, with respect to their subjection to the passions, this may be judged of by the custom of marriage as to the respective sexes; for one man may marry two or three, sometimes even ten wives and upwards; while a woman, who marries but one husband, desires at his death to follow him, forsaking all worldly enjoyments, or to remain leading the austere life of an ascetic.

Fifthly. The accusation of their want of virtuous knowledge is an injustice. Observe what pain, what slighting, what contempt, and what afflictions their virtue enables them to support! How many Kulin Brahmins are there who marry ten or fifteen wives for the sake of money, that never see the greater number of them after the day of marriage, and visit others only three or four times in the course of their life. Still amongst those women, most, even without seeing or receiving any support from their husbands, living dependent on their fathers or brothers, and suffering much distress, continue to preserve their virtue; and when Brahmins, or those of other tribes, bring their wives to live with them, what misery do the women not suffer? At marriage the wife is recog- nised as half of her husband, but in after conduct they are treated worse than inferior animals. For the woman is employed to do the work of a slave in the house, such as, in her turn, to clean the place very early in the morning, whether cold or wet, to scour the dishes, to wash the floor, to cook night and day, to prepare and serve food for her husband, father and mother-in-law, brothers-in-law, and friends and connections! (for amongst Hindus more than in other tribes relations long reside together, and on this account quarrels are more common amongst brothers respecting their worldly affairs). If in the preparation or serving up of the victuals they commit the smallest fault, what insult do they not receive from their husband, their mother-in-law, and the younger brothers of their husband! After all the male part of the family have satisfied themselves, the women content themselves with what may be left, whether sufficient in quantity or not. Where Brahmans or Kayasthas are not wealthy, the women are obliged to attend to their cows, and to prepare cow dung for firing. In the afternoon they fetch water from the river or tank; and at night perform the office of menial servants in making the beds. In case of any fault or omission in the performance of those labours, they receive injurious treatment. Should the husband acquire wealth, he indulges in criminal amours to her per- fect knowledge, and almost under her eyes, and does not see her, perhaps once a month. As long as the husband is poor she suffers every kind of trouble, and when he becomes rich she is altogether heart-broken. All this pain and affliction their virtue alone enables them to support. Where a husband takes two or three wives to live with him, they are subjected to mental miseries and constant quarrels. Even this distressed situation they virtuously endure. Sometimes it happens that the husband, from a preference for one of his wives, behaves cruelly to another. Amongst the lower classes, and those even of the better class who have not associated with good company, the wife, on the slightest fault, or even on bare suspicion of her misconduct, is chastised as a thief. Respect to virtue and their reputation generally makes them forgive even this treatment. If, unable to bear such cruel usage, a wife leaves her husband's house to live separately from him, then the influence of the husband with the magisterial authority is generally sufficient to place her again in his hands; when, in revenge for her quitting him, he seizes every pretext to torment her in various ways, and sometimes even puts her privately to death. These are facts occurring every day, and not to be denied. What I lament is, that seeing the women thus dependent and exposed to every misery, you feel for them no compassion that might exempt them from being tied down and burnt to death.

This noble defence may fitly close our record of Rammohun's first regular campaign. At this point we must leave his controversies on suttee and Idolatry, to take up other phases of his many-sided activity.

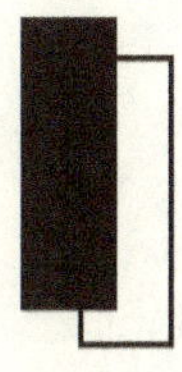

Regular and Irregular Campaigns against Trinitarian Orthodoxy (1820 -1824)

We now enter upon a wholly new scene of Rammohun's career, his relations to Christianity. It may be remembered that in his letter of 1817 to Mr. Digby, he said:-"The consequence of my long and uninterrupted researches into religious truth has been that I have found the doctrines of Christ more conducive to moral principles, and more adapted for the use of rational beings, than any other which have come to my knowledge." With his habitual thoroughness, he took the trouble to acquire the Greek and Hebrew languages (the latter he learned, it is said, from a Jew, in six months) that he might gain a full understanding of both the Old and the New Testaments; and the remarkable mastery of their contents which is shown in his later writings bears witness to the success of his study. The result was the publication, in 1820, of his celebrated work entitled 'The Precepts of Jesus, the Guide to Peace and Happiness'; extracted from the Books of the New Testament, ascribed to the Four Evangelists with translations into Sanskrit and Bengali. As the preface to this book has, I think, been but imperfectly understood, and as it throws important light on the then state of his mind, I give it nearly entire:-

"A conviction in the mind of its total ignorance of the nature and of the specific attributes of the Godhead, and a sense of doubt respecting the real essence of the soul, give rise to feelings of great dissatisfaction with our limited powers, as well as with all human acquirements which fail to inform us on these interesting points. On the other hand, a notion of the existence of a supreme superintending power, the Author and Preserver of this harmonious system, who has organized and who regulates such an infinity of celestial and terrestrial objects; and a due estimation of that law which teaches that man should do unto others as he would wish to be done by, reconcile us to human nature, and tend to render our existence agreeable to ourselves and profitable to the rest of mankind. The former of these sources of satisfaction, viz., a belief in God, prevails generally; being derived either from tradition and instruction, or from an attentive survey of the wonderful skill and contrivance displayed in the works of nature.

The latter, although it is partially thought also in every system of religion with which I am acquainted, is principally inculcated by Christianity. This essential characteristic of the Christian religion I was for a long time unable to distinguish as such amidst the various doctrines I found insisted upon in the writings of Christian authors, and in the conversations of those teachers of Christianity with whom I have had the honour of holding communication. Amongst those opinions, the most prevalent seems to be, that no one is entitled to the appellation of Christian who does not believe in the divinity of Christ and of the Holy Ghost, as well as in the divine nature of God, the Father of all created beings. Many allow a much greater latitude to the term Christian, and consider it as comprehending all who acknowledge the Bible to contain the revealed will of God, however they may differ from others in their interpretations of particular passages of scripture; whilst some require from him who claims the title of Christian only an adherence to the doctrines of Christ, as taught by himself, without insisting on implicit confidence in those of the Apostles, as being, except when speaking from inspiration, like other men, liable to mistake and error. That they were so is obvious from the several instances of differences of opinion amongst the Apostles recorded in the Acts and Epistles."

On the relative claims of those different conceptions of Christianity, which had been so extensively and confidently debated, he declines entering into discussion, and continues thus :-

"I confine my attention at present to the task of laying before my fellow creatures the words of Christ, with a translation from the English into Sanskrit and the language of l'engal. I feel persuaded that by separating from the other matters contained in the New Testament the moral precepts found in that book, these will be more likely to produce the desirable effect of improving the hearts and minds of men of different persuasions and degrees of understanding. For, historical and some other passages are liable to the doubts and disputes of freethinkers and anti-Christians, especially miraculous relations, which are much less wonderful than the fabricated tales handed down to the natives of Asia, and consequently could be apt at best to carry little weight with them. On the contrary, moral doctrines, tending evidently to the maintenance of peace and harmony of mankind at large, are beyond the reach of metaphysical perversion, and intelligible alike to the learned and to the unlearned. This simple code of religion and morality is so admirably calculated to elevate men's ideas to high and liberal notions of one God, who has equally subjected all living creatures, without distinction of caste, rank, or wealth, to change, disappointment, pain and death, and has equally admitted all to be partakers of the bountiful mercies which he has lavished over nature, and is also so well fitted to regulate the conduct of the human race in the discharge of their various duties to God, to themselves, and to society, that I cannot but hope the best effects from its promulgation in the present form."

From this we may see that the very last thing Rammohun desired or anticipated for his book was theological controversy. It was that from which he was trying to escape. To him, the "essential chracteristic of the Christian religion" was its ideal humanity, its tendency to promote "the peace and harmony of mankind at large," and to raise them to "high and liberal notions of one God who has equally admitted all to be partakers of (his) bountiful mercies." It was this which he thought would improve the hearts and minds of "men of different persuasions," and in his sanguine soul he could not but "hope the best effects form its promulgation in the present form." What effect his work might have pro- duced on his countrymen if he and they had been able to discuss it together without interruption, can never now be known. For before he had had time to make the transla- tions into Sanskrit and Bengali which he had somewhat prematurely announced on his title page, the book was attacked by the chief missionaries of the day in their periodical 'The Friend of India,' and Rammohun was at once immersed in a sea of controversy which lasted for years. A unique opportunity was thus worse than wasted, and made the occasion of increased strife. No doubt all this was providentially overruled for eventual good; but it is impossible not to regret that the Christians of that day and hour had not been wiser.

Here we must digress a little. At this time (1820) Christianity was very imperfectly represented in Bengal. Henry Martyn was dead, and Reginald Heber had not yet arrived. The bishopric of Calcutta, established in 1814, was occupied by Dr. Middleton, a man of scholarly attainments and plodding industry but of somewhat rigid and unsympathetic temperament. The Church of Scotland was represented by the Rev. Dr. Bryce, a clever and rather liberal-minded man, whose ministry Rammohun attended for some time, but who was so eccentric and indiscreet that he gradually alienated most of his friends, and Rammohun among them. The chief missionary activity of that time was in the hands of the English Dissenters, especially the celebrated Baptist Mission of Serampore, near Calcutta, under the presidency of Dr. Carey and Marshman. Carey was originally a poor shoemaker, with very little general education, but with a great taste for languages, and an ardent desire to convert the heathen. Marshman was a successful and earnest school- master and a most valuable colleague to the enthusiastic but unpractical Carey. Their joint mission was started in 1799, and they had been working zealously ever since. How soon Rammohun made their acquaintance does not appear, but their "Periodical Account" for the year 1816 contains the following notices of him and his doings:-

"Rama-Mohuna-Raya, a very rich Rarhee Brahmun of Calcutta, is a respectable Sanskrit scholar, and so well versed in Persian, that he is called Mouluvee-Rama-Mohuna-Raya: he also writes English with correctness, and reads with ease English, Mathematical and metaphysical works. He has published, in Bengalee, one or two philosophical works from the Sanskrit which he hopes may be useful in leading his countrymen to renounce idolatry. Europeans breakfast at his house, at a separate table, in the English fashion; he has paid us a visit at Serampore, and at a late interview, after relating an anecdote of Krishna, relative to a petty theft of this God, he added, "The sweeper of my house would not do such an act, and can I worship a god sunk lower than the man who washes my floors?' He is at present a simple theist, admires Jesus Christ, but knows not his need of the atonement, He has not renounced his caste, and this enables him to visit the richest families of Hindoos. He is said to be very moral; but is pronounced to be a most wicked man by the strict Hindoos."

Of this man Mr. Yates writes thus, in a letter dated August, 1816:-

'I was introduced to him about a year ago: before this, he was not acquainted with any one who cared for his soul. Some time after I introduced Eustace Carey to him, and we have had repeated conversations with him. When I first knew him he would talk only on metaphysical subjects such as the eternity of matter, the nature and qualities of evidence etc. but he has lately become much more humble, and disposed to

converse about the Gospel. He has many relations, Brahmuns, and has established religious worship among them. He maintains the unity of God, and hates all heathen idolatries. He visited Eustace lately and stayed to family prayer, with which he was quite delighted. Eustace gave him Dr. Watt's Hymns; he said he would treasure them up in his heart.* He has been to Serampore once, and has engaged to come and see me in the course of a few weeks. He has offered Eustace a piece of ground for a school."

* (That was what Rammohun Roy actually did. He carried the volume with him throughout his life. Shortly after his death Dr. Carpenter stated that "it was a common practice with the Raja, as he went o public worship, to read some of Dr. Watt's Hymns for children.")

One might have thought that these worthy men, who expressed such care for Rammohun's soul, would have given some sort of fraternal welcome to his spontaneous recommendation of the teachings of Christ to his countrymen. But unfortunately they belonged to the narrowest school of Calvinistic orthodoxy, and not only held the doctrine of the Atonement in its harshest form, but were so engrossed by it as to regard that alone as "the Gospel." A review of Rammohun's book soon appeared in the Friend of India, by a "Christian Missionary," Rev. Deocar Schmidt, who feared that the "Precepts" might "greatly injure the cause of truth." Dr. Marshman added some editorial comments, in which he spoke of Rammohun as "an intelligent Heathen, whose mind is as yet completely opposed to the grand design of the Saviour's becoming incarnate."

All this hurt Rammohun's feelings very much, and he quickly replied with "An Appeal to the Christian Public in defence of the 'Precepts of Jesus,' by a Friend to Truth, In this he defended himself with much spirit from the charge of being a "heathen" (which term he regarded as virtually synonymous with an idotator), and claimed to be a believer in one true and living God," and not only that, but also in the truths revealed in the Christian system." He proceeds:- "I should hope neither the Reviewer nor the Editor can be justified in inferring the heathenism of the Compiler, from the facts of his extracting and publishing the moral doctrines of the New Testament, under the title of a "Guide to Peace and Happiness"his styling the "Precepts of Jesus" a code of Religion and morality, his believing God to be the Author and Preserver of the Universe, or his considering those sayings as adapted to regulate the conduct of the whole human race in the discharge of all the duties required of them... Although he was born a Brahman he not only renounced idolatry at a very early period of his life, but published at that time a treatise in Arabic and Persian against that system; and no sooner acquired a tolerable knowledge of English, then he made his desertion of idol worship known to the Christian world by his English publication - a renunciation that, I am sorry to say, brought severe difficulties upon him, by exciting the displeasure of his parents, and subjecting him to the dislike of his near as well as distant relations, and to the hatred of nearly all his countrymen for several years. I therefore presume that among his declared enemies, who are aware of those facts, no one who has the least pretension to truth, would venture to apply the designation of heathen to him"

He then vigourously defends the principle on which his selection of Precepts was made, and illustrates it by copious and cogent passages from the words of Christ himself. He recalls the emphasis laid by Christ on the two-fold law of love as that on which hung all the Law and the Prophets; His charge to the rich young man to keep the command- ments, "This do and thou shalt live"; and the description of the last Judgment in Matt. xxv., which declares eternal destiny decided by the discharge or neglect of the duties of human beneficence.

"These precepts (he proceeds) separated from the mysterious dogmas and historical records, appear to the Compiler to contain not only the essence of all that is necessary to instruct mankind in their civil duties, but also the best and only means of obtaining the forgiveness of our sins, the favour of God, and strength to overcome our passions and to keep His commandments."

After this he goes on to point out how unsatisfactory have been the results of the missionary methods of propagating Christianity.

The Compiler, residing in the same spot where European missionary gentlemen and others for a period of upwards of twenty years have been, with a view to promote Christianity, distributing in vain amongst the natives numberless copies of the complete Bible, written in different languages, could not be altogether ignorant of the cause of their disappointment. He, however, never doubted their zeal for the promulgation of Christianity, nor the accuracy of their statement with regard to immense sums of money being annually expended in preparing vast numbers of copies of the Scriptures; but he had seen with regret that they have completely counteracted their own benevolent efforts, by introducing all the dogmas and mysteries taught in Christian Churches to people by no means prepared to receive them; and that they have been so incautious and inconsiderate in their attempts to enlighten the natives of India, as to address their instructions to them in the same way as if they were reasoning with persons brought up in a Christian country, with those dogmatical notions imbibed from their infancy. The consequence has been, that the natives in general, instead of benefiting by the perusal of the Bible, copies of which they always receive gratuitously, exchange them very often for blank paper; and generally use several of the dogmatical terms in their native language as a mark of slight in an irreverent manner; the mention of which is repugnant to my feelings. It has been owing to their beginning with the introduction of mysterious dogmas and of relations that at first sight appear incredible, that, notwithstanding every exertion on the part of our divines, I am not aware that we can find a single respectable Moosulman or Hindoo, who was not in want of the common comforts of life, once glorified with the truth of Christianity, constantly adhering to it.

From what I have already stated, I hope no one will infer that I feel ill-disposed towards the Missionary establishments in this country. This is far from being the case. I pray for their augmentation, and that their members may remain in the happy enjoyment of life in a climate so generally inimical to European constitutions; for in proportion to the increase of their number, sobriety, moderations, temperance, and good behaviour, have been diffused among their neighbours as the necessary consequence of their company, conversation, and good example.

A letter written at this time to a friend, Colonel B gives Rammohun's own account of the controversy which had been commenced.

As to the opinion intimated by Sir Samuel J, respecting the medium course in Christian dogmas, I never have attempted to oppose it. I regret only that the followers of Jesus, in general, should have paid much greater attention to enquiries after his nature than to the observance of his commandments, when we are well aware that no human acquirements can ever discover the nature even of the most common and visible things and moreover, that such inquiries are not enjoined by the divine revelation. On this consideration I have compiled several passages of the New Testament which I thought essential to Christianity, and published them under the designation of 'Precepts of Jesus,' at which the Missionaries of Srirampoor [Serampore] have expressed great displeasure, and called me, in their review of the tracts, an injurer of the cause of truth. I was, therefore, under the necessity of defending myself in an "Appeal to the Christian Public," a few copies of which tract I have the pleasure to send you, under the care of Captain Sand entreat your acceptance of them.

I return with my sincere acknowledgments, the work which Sir S. J. was so kind as to lend me. May I request the favour of you to forward it to Sir S. J., as well as a copy of each of the pamphlets, with my best compliments, and to favour me with your and Sir S. J's opinion respecting my idea of Christianity, as expressed in those tracts, when an opportunity may occur; as I am always open to conviction and correction?

This appeal elicited certain "Remarks" from Dr. Marshman in the Friend of India of May 1820. Dr. Marshman disavows any uncharitable purpose in the use of the word Heathen which, he thinks, "cannot be candidly construed into a term of reproach," but refuses to call Christian anyone who does not accept "the Divinity and Atonement of Jesus Christ, and the Divine Authority of the whole of the Holy Scriptures." Quite conformably to this narrow limitation of the term Christian, he passes on to a singularly negative version of Christianity.

The leading doctrines of the New Testament... may be summed up in the two following positions: That God views all sin as so abominable that the death of Jesus Christ alone can expiate its guilt; and that the human heart is so corrupt that it must be renewed by the Divine Spirit before a man can enter heaven.

In the first number of the quarterly series of the 'Friend of India' published in September 1820, the worthy Baptist sets himself to prove this version of his faith from the sayings of Jesus.

To this essay Rammohun replied in a "Second Appeal" published in 1821, nearly six times the length of the first. He repudiates any desire to challenge the credibility of the miracles recorded in the New Testament, or to put them on a level with the marvels of Hindu mythology. He had only recognized the fact that the Hindu mind was as it were sodden with stories of miracles, and he had hoped to direct his countrymen to those precepts of the moral sublimity of which had first moved him to admiration of Christianity. He describes himself by implication as "labouring in the promulgation of Christianity." He then opposes the main positions advanced by Dr. Marshman. He disputes the consonance with justice of Dr. Marshman's theory of the atonement, but he declares that he has "repeatedly acknowledged Christ as the Redeemer, Mediator, and Intercessor with God on behalf of his followers." He confesses himself moved by his reverence for Christianity and its author to vindicate it from the charge of Polytheism, for he regards Trinitarianism as essentially polytheism. He has little difficulty in disposing of Dr.Marshman's endeavours to prove the doctrine of Trinity from the Old Testament. On the new Testament he resorts to exegetical methods familiar to Unitarians, in order to establish the impersonality of the Holy Spirit. On the baptismal formula he avers that "it is proper that those who receive" the Christian religion, "should be baptized in the name of the Father, who is the object of worship; of the Son, who is the Mediator; and of that influence by which spiritual blessings are conveyed to mankind, designated in the Scriptures as the Comforter, Spirit of Truth, or Holy Spirit." He makes an excursion into pre-Nicene history and recalls how "in the first and purest ages of Christianity, the followers of Christ entertained" very "different opinions on the subject of the distinction between Father, Son and Holy Spirit" without being excommunicated. The precepts of Jesus, which no other religion can equal much less surpass, do not, he insists, depend on the metaphysical arguments and mysteries with which they have been associated.*

By this time the controversy had, it will be seen, concentrated itself on two main points, which he thus defines in an "Advertisement" to the "Second Appeal."

"First, that the 'Precepts of Jesus' which teach that love to God is manifested in beneficence towards our fellow-creatures, are a sufficient Guide to Peace and Happiness; and secondly, that omnipresent God, who is the only proper object of religious veneration, is one and undivided in person."

Naturally the last-named point soon became the main question at issue; and as the Unity of God was the main passion of Rammohun's life, he soon threw himself with his whole heart into the contest which was thus so strangely brought home to him from a quite unexpected quarter. At this point, the beginning of the year 1821, we must stop to record a singular event which accentuated the controversy in no small degree.

* The passage enclosed in brackets was inserted by the Continuator with Miss Collet's approval.

[Rammohun's studies in the Scriptures and interest in the Christian religion had led him into frequent intercourse with English missionaries. He appears in close cooperation with two members of the Baptist Mission at Serampore, Rev. William Yates and Rev. William Adam, both according to Rammohun's testimony "well reputed for their Oriental and classic acquirements." How this came about is related by Mr. Adam in a letter to the committee of the Baptist Missionary society dated June 11, 1821:-

I have for some time past been engaged with Rammohun Roy and Mr. Yates in translating the four Gospels into Bengali. The two translations of Dr. Carey and Mr. Ellerton are declared by Rammohun Roy to abound in the most flagrant violations of native idiom, and he accordingly applied to Mr. Yates and myself for our assistance in translating them anew from the original. This we readily have given. Our Lord's 'Sermon on the Mount' is printed separately at the expense of the B__A__S

On September 30, 1822, Mr. Adam writes to Mr. Edward Poole:-

I am at present just finishing a careful revisal of a new translation of the Gospel of St. Matthew in Bengali, originally executed by Rammohun Roy, the Rev. Mr. Yates, and myself. Mr. Yates has since declined his assistance so that it now entirely rests with Rammohun Roy and myself.

The difficulty with Mr. Yates arose when the Revisers began with the fourth Gospel. They got as far as the third verse in safety, but there they struck on the Greek preposition, 'dia' and the Revision was wrecked. At first Mr. Yates agreed to translate. "All things were made through him," but by the next session of the Committee he had discovered in the substitution of through for by a suggestion of Arianism and on the following day withdrew from the enterprise altogether on account of the tendency towards heresy which had transpired. During these discussions, Mr. Adam tells us, Rammohun "sat, pen in hand, in dignified reticence, looking on listening, observing all, but saying nothing." This project and the manner of its termination naturally drew "heretic" and "heathen" into an intimacy more frequent and confidential, with the result that Mr. Adam finally renounced his belief in the doctrine of Trinity and avowed himself a Unitarian.

The arguments advanced in Rammohun's Second Appeal published about this time may be taken to indicate the kind of consideration which decided Mr. Adam. This singular event was made public in the latter half of 1821.] *

*The passage between brackets was inserted by the Continuator with Miss Collet's approval.

The story of Mr. Adam's conversion has been told so often and with such frequent inaccuracies that I am glad to be able to produce the following letter in which he communicates the fact to an English friend.

It is now several months since I began to entertain some doubts respecting the Supreme Deity of Jesus Christ, suggested by frequent discussions with Rammohun Roy, whom I was endeavouring to bring over to the belief of that Doctrine, and in which I was joined by Mr. Yates, who also professed to experience difficulties on the subject. Since then I have been diligently engaged in studying afresh the Scriptures with a view to this subject, humbly seeking divine guidance and illumination, and I do not hesitate to confess that I am unable to remove the weighty objections which present themselves against this doctrine. I do not mean to say that there are no difficulties in rejecting it, but the objections against it compared with the arguments for it, appear to me like a mountain compared with a molehill. +

† At this point Miss Collet ceased writing. The rest of the work is from the hands of the Continuator. The point at which her revision of his manuscript ended is indicated later.

We cannot wonder at the profound impression which this Occurrence produced. At anytime the fact of a Christian missionary being converted by "an intelligent heathen" would be sure to excite widespread remark. But in the days when Evangelical orthodoxy enjoyed an almost undisputed ascendancy, and in quarters like those of the Baptist Mission where the tradition of Calvinism stamped the dominant Evangelicalism with its own rigidity, the shock must have been startling in the extreme. The convert was half-humorously, half-savagely, called "The second fallen Adam." The animosity usually harboured by the orthodox against a renegade was rendered doubly bitter by the fact that the converstion was apparently due to the dispassionate examination of the Scriptures by an open-minded Hindu, missionary ardour and Protestant devotion to the Bible being both wounded in their tenderest place. The Unitarians in England and America naturally accepted the intelligence as of a veritable Daniel come to judgment and were shaken, as we shall see by and by, into new missionary enthusiasm.

But the news was not made public property until the latter part of 1821, and before then Rammohun's literary and polemical activity had assumed certain fresh phases. Some explanation of the turn it took is suggested by an incident which occurred about this time.*

* Bp. Middleton died July 8, 1822. His overtures to Rammohun Roy would most probably take place after 'The Precepts of Jesus' came out, which was in the beginning of 1820. The incident occurred, Mr. Adam informs us, during "the hot season." Mr. Adam's statement that "he never afterwards visited the Bishop" implies that a considerable interval elapsed before the Bishop's death. Hence, we are safe in concluding that the time of the incident fell in hot season of 1820 or 1821.

Of this Mr. Adam is our informant. According to his narrative,-

"One day in the hot season, about midday, I was engaged in my usual studies, when 1 was informed that a native gentleman was at the gate of my compound and desired to see me. This was an unusual hour for a call. I went to the gate and found that it was Rammohun Roy, whom I instantly requested to alight from his carriage and enter the house. The unusualness of the hour was fully justified by the explanation he gave me. On invitation he had been to see Dr. Middleton, the Bishop of Calcutta. Rammohun Roy's house was probably about two miles from the Bishop's palace and my dwelling was intermediate between the two. He called on me both for refreshment to his body and sympathy in his mental trouble. His first request was that he should be permitted to remove his turban, which was of course granted, and the second that he should have some refreshment, but that before it was brought and he partook of it, my servants should be sent away, since if they had seen him eat under my roof they would have bruited abroad that he had lost caste. This was promptly and quietly attended to, and when he felt cool and refreshed, he proceeded to state what had disturbed his mind.

With much indignation he informed Mr. Adam that the Bishop had sent for him, had entered into a long argument to persuade him to accept of Christianity, and, not content with this singular stretch of the laws of hospitality, had wound up by expatiating on "the grand career which would open to him by a change of faith." "He would be honoured in life and lamented in death, honoured in England as well as in India; his name would descend to posterity as that of the modern Apostle of India." The Bishop's meaning was doubtless innocent enough, but the keen truth-loving Hindu seemed to feel it as a modern version of the Tempter's "All these things will I give thee, if thou wilt fall down and worship me." "The sting of the offence was this," reports Mr. Adam: "he was asked to profess the Christian religion, not on the force of evidence, or for the love of truth, or for the satisfaction of his conscience, or for the benefit of his fellowmen, but for the sake of the honour and glory and fame it might bring him. This was utterly abhorrent to Rammohun's mind. It alienated, repelled, and disgusted him." He never met the Bishop again.

As may readily be imagined, and as the foregoing incident shows, a very warm friendship was springing up between Rammohun and Mr. Adam. The latter, fortunately for us, left on record a great many of their mutual communications in letter and manuscript, which have been placed at the disposal of the writer of this work. His testimony to the impression made upon him by Rammohun's character may be here most properly cited :-

I was never more thoroughly, deeply, and constantly impressed than when in the presence of Rammohun Roy and in friendly and confidential converse with him, that I was in the presence of a man of natural and inherent genius, of powerful understanding, and of determined will, a will determined with singular energy and uncontrollable self-direction, to lofty and generous purposes. He seemed to feel, to think, to speak, to act, as if he could not but do all this, and that he must and do it only in and from and through himself, and that the application of any external influence, distinct from his own strong will, would be the annihilation of his being and identity. He would be free or not be at all. Love of freedom was perhaps the strongest passion of his soul, freedom not of action merely, but of thought. . . . This tenacity of personal independence, this sensitive jealousy of the slightest approach to an encroachment on his mental freedom was accompanied with a very nice perception of the equal rights of others, even of those who differed most widely from him.

The effect on such a nature of the attitude assumed to him by organized Christianity in India can be readily conceived. A Brahman by birth, he had commended to his own countrymen the 'Precepts of Jesus' as surpassing those of any other religion as a guide to peace and happiness, and he had undertaken to help in translating the whole of the four Gospels into Bengali. As a result he had been assailed by the Baptist editor, he had been forsaken by one of his Baptist co-translators whose orthodoxy deterred him from making a correct version; and by the Anglican Bishop, he had been, as he understood, offered the bribe of worldwide fame, to induce him to accept Christianity. Such an experience of English Christianity in its established and nonconforming phases was not likely to conciliate Rammohun Roy. We can scarcely wonder that the latter half of 1821 witnessed a vigorous polemic on his part against the tactics of Christian missionaries.

The 'Sumachar Dúrpun,' a periodical issued from the Mission Press at Serampore, came out on the 14th of July with an onslaught on the pantheism of the Vedanta Shastra, arguing that while inconsistent with polytheism it logically destroyed the reality of the universe and the responsibility of the human soul, as well as the perfectness of God. It also invited replies. But on Rammohun taking the missionaries at their word and sending a reply, they, with a lack of fairness and indeed with a stupidity which was simply fatuous, refused to insert it. Rammohun accordingly brought out under the name of his pandit, Shivaprusad Surma, The Brahmunical Magazine, as "a vindication of the Hindu religion against the attacks of Christian missionaries." The first two numbers contain the provocative article reprinted from the 'Sumachar Durpun' and the suppressed reply. Rammohun is at great pains to represent the Vedantic system as more of a monotheism than a pantheism. He firmly avers that God is the creator of the world, but grants that matter is eternal. "We find the phrases 'God is all and in all,' in the Christian books; and I do not suppose they mean by such words that pots, mats, etc. are gods. I am inclined to believe that by these terms they mean the omnipresence of God." Similar language in the Vedant could be similarly explained. Polytheism he represents as only an accommodation to the ignorance of the unenlightened, and he cites by way of retort the anthropomorphisms of the Old Testament and the human experiences of the Eternal Son. Does not the New Testament tell us, he asks in effect, of One God begetting another, and of the former taking the shape of a Dove, the latter appearing as Man? Similar stories in their own religion Hindu philosophers regard as fictions meant only "to engage the minds of persons of weak understanding." But the missionaries insist that the incarnations in Dove and Man are real. A reply in the Friend of India, No. 38, led to a vigorous rejoinder in the third number of the Brahmunicàl Magazine. Rammohun here directs his attack on the doctrine of Trinity. He discards Trinity in Unity as an inconceivable idea, and charging Trinitarians with Tritheism he pronounces them polytheists. In answer to aspersions on Hindu morals, he suggests that the domestic life of Europeans might not compare favourably with that of Hindus. He concludes with a pious dignity which admirably contrasts with the tone of his opponent. The Editor had had the impious effrontery to declare that Hinduism evidently owed its origin to the Father of Lies alone. "Shivaprusad Surma" makes answer, "we must recollect that we have engaged in solemn religious controversy and not in retorting abuse against each other."

In these pseudonymous articles, Rammohun writes, it will be observed, as a devout and aggrieved adherent of Hinduism, His preface to the first number of the Magazine makes complaint of Christian missions in India as constituting a departure from the promise of the British authorities not to interfere with the religion of their subjects, and as taking an undue advantage of the fact that Christianity is the religion of the conqueror. He suggests, in effect, that "the superiority of the Christian religion" should not be advocated "by means of abuse and insult, or by affording the hope of worldly gain," but "by force of argument alone." His protest against the religious insolence which proclaimed the whole of the wonderful development of Indian faith, from the Rig Veda down to Rammohun Roy himself, as solely of Satanic origin, was timely and well- deserved; and his hostility to Christianity as then instituted in India was quite compatible with his previously expressed reverence for its Founder and for his real religion.

It is refreshing to turn for a moment from these theological wranglings to get a glimpse of Rammohun's cosmopolitan sympathies in the political sphere. When the intelligence reached India that the people of Naples after extorting a Constitution from their despotic King were crushed back into servitude by the Austrian troops, in obedience to the joint mandate of the crowned heads of Russia, Prussia, Austria, Sardinia, and Naples, Rammohun felt it keenly. In a letter to Mr. Buckingham, of date August 11, 1821, he declares himself much "depressed by the late news from Europe." "From the late unhappy news" he goes on,

I am obliged to conclude that I shall not live to see liberty universally restored to the nations of Europe, and Asiatic nations, especially those that are European Colonies, possessed of a greater degree of the same blessing than what they now enjoy. Under these circumstances I consider the cause of the Neapolitans as my own, and their enemies as ours. Enemies to liberty and friends of despotism have never been, and never will be ultimately successful

These noble words reveal how profoundly Rammohun felt with the late Russell Lowell that, "In the gain or loss of one race all the rest have equal claim"; and that

'Wherever wrong is done to the humblest and the weakest', neath the all-beholding Sun that wrong is also done to us.

In September, 1821, the Calcutta Unitarian Committee was originated. *

* "The Committee was formed in September, 1821," says Mr. William Adam in a letter under date of June 26, 1827, to Mr. R. Dutton, "and its present members are Theodore Dickens, a barrister of the Supreme Court, George James Gordon, a merchant of the firm of Mackintosh & Co., William Tate, an attorney, B. W. Macleod, a surgeon in the Company's service, Norman Kerr, an uncovenanted servant of the Company, Rammohun Roy, Dwarkanath Thakoor, Prusunnu Coomar Thakoor, Radhaprusad Roy, and myself. It will be observed that nearly all the European names are Scottish.

It was composed of a few native gentlemen among whom Rammohun was leader, and several Europeans, civilians and others, including Mr. Adam, whose conversion had just been announced. "Proselytism," Mr. Adam explains, "is not our immediate object. We aim to remove ignorance and superstition, and to furnish information respecting the evidences, the duties, and the doctrines of the religion of Christ." The methods chosen were "education, rational discussion, and the publication of books both in

English and in the native languages." In January, 1822, Mr. Adam writes that he has with the assistance of a few friends rented a house in which Christian worship is regularly conducted. "Rammohun Roy is one of the warmest of our supporters." As we shall see presently, the Anglo-Hindu school, commenced under the auspices of this Committee, was almost exclusively supported by Rammohun. The "Unitarian press" was entirely his property. Mr. Adam, in his new role of Unitarian minister, seems to have depended for his financial support chiefly on Rammohun's bounty. So that the whole organization was principally in Rammohun's hands. We may regard the formation of this Unitarian Committee as a distinct and an important stage in his career as founder.

This avowed and organized connection with Unitarian Christianity led Rammohun into correspondence with several of its votaries in England and America. On October 27, 1822, we find him writing to "a gentleman of Baltimore,"

I have now every reason to hope that the truths of Christianity will not be much longer kept hidden under the veil of heathen doctrines and practices, gradually introduced among the followers of Christ, since many lovers of truth are zealously engaged in rendering the religion of Jesus free from corruptions. .

It is a great satisfaction to my conscience to find that the doctrines inculcated by Jesus and his Apostles are quite different from those human inventions which the missionaries are persuaded to profess, and entirely consistent with reason and the revelation delivered by Moses and the prophets. I am, therefore, anxious to support them, even at the risk of my own life. I rely much on the force of truth, which will, I am sure, ultimately prevail. Our number is comparatively small, but I am glad to inform you that none of them can be justly charged with the want of zeal and prudence.

I wish to add, in order that you may set me right, if you find me mistaken, my view of Christianity is that in representing all mankind as the children of one eternal Father, it enjoins them to love one another, without making any distinction of country, caste, colour, or creed; notwithstanding they may be justified in the sight of the Creator in manifesting their respect towards each other, according to the propriety of their actions and the reasonableness of their religious opinions and differences.

Writing to the same gentleman a few months later, on December 9, 1822, he declares,

Although our adversaries are both numerous and zealous, as the adversaries of truth always have been, yet our prospects are by no means discouraging, if we only have the means of following up what has already been done.

We confidently hope that, through these various means, the period will be accelerated, when the belief in the Divine Unity and in the mission of Christ will universally prevail.

These avowals, of readiness to support the doctrines of Christ even at the risk of his life, and of hope in the ultimate universality of faith in the mission of Christ, naturally led to the impression that Rammohun was to all intents and purposes a Unitarian Christian.

Despite his hopefulness of its eventual success, the Unitarian movement seems to have very speedily received a decided rebuff. For, six months later, July 2, 1823, Rammohun writes to Mr. Samuel Smith, "From the disappointment which we have met in our endeavour to promote the cause of Unitarianism, I scarcely entertain any hope of success." On the 4th of August following, Mr. Buckingham writes of Rammohun's exertions, "He has done all this to the great detriment of his private interests, being rewarded by the coldness and jealousy of all the great functionaries of Church and State in India, and supporting the Unitarian Chapel, the Unitarian Press, and the expense of his own publications. out of a private fortune of which he devotes more than one-third to acts of the purest philanthropy and benevolence."

His controversy with the missionaries was kindled afresh in the quarterly 'Friend of India' which appeared in December, IS21. The editor, Rev. Dr. Marshman, devoted 128 closely printed pages to an attempted refutation of Rammohun's Second Appeal to the Christian Public. His arguments are directed to the defence of the old Evangelical doctrines of Atonement and of the Deity of Christ with the consequent doctrine of Trinity. He lays the whole of the Scriptures, Old as well as New Testament, under contribution for proof texts of those dogmas, with a disregard of the laws of historical exegesis which even to the orthodoxy of today is bewildering. Dogmas which did not actually emerge until, at the earliest, in the beginning of the Christian era, are proved by passages in the Pentateuch, in the Psalms and in the Prophets. One example may suffice : "In Psalm xlv.," avers the learned Editor, "we have the Eternal Deity of the Son fully revealed." Evangelical religion has its answer to Rammohun's objections, but its exponents in India were not then aware how much must be conceded to the modern critical spirit before that answer can be effectively made. But Dr. Marshman sinned against higher than merely critical canons. Because the reverent Hindu impugns the Baptist's conception of the Supreme Being who they both adore, Dr. Marshman accuses him of "arraigning his maker of gross injustice" and of "charging Him with having founded all the religion of the patriarchs and prophets, of the apostles and primitive saints, of the blessed in Heaven throughout eternity, on an act of palpable iniquity." And of this Hindu Theist he dares to ejaculate, "May his eyes be opened ere it be for ever too late !"

On the 30th of January, 1823, Rammohun issued his rejoinder, The Final Appeal to the Christian Public in Defence of the Precepts of Jesus is a voluminous document. His four pages of mild and inoffensive preface to 'The Precepts of Jesus' had evoked such extensive criticism as to draw from him a first "Appeal in Defence" of 20 pages, a "Second Appeal" of 150 pages, and now a "Third and Final Appeal" of 256 octavo pages

The last work bears evidence of the unfortunate change of attitude into which the missionaries suffered themselves to be betrayed by the progress of this polemic. It announces that while all the previous works of the author on the subject of Christianity had been printed at the Baptist Mission Press, Calcutta, the acting proprietor had, after the Second Appeal appeared, declined, "although in the politest manner possible" to print any other production of Rammohun on the same subject. Rammohun was therefore obliged to purchase his own type and to rely on native superintendence. The title page declares the work "Printed at the Unitarian Press, Dhurmtollah, Calcutta."+ "I am well aware,' says Rammohun in his preface, "that this difference of sentiment has already occasioned much coolness towards me in the demeanour of some whose friendship I hold very dear." But his devotion to the truth of Monotheism which he held to be not less imperilled by Christian Trinitarianism than by Hindu polytheism, left him no option but to pursue the controversy.

† "There is a Unitarian press, also the property of Rammohun Roy, at which several pamphlets and tracts have been and continue to be printed, almost all bearing on the Unitarian controversy or tending to promote philanthropic objects." Letter of Mr. Wm. Adam, July 27 1816.

The "Final Appeal" controverts Dr. Marshman's arguments and Scriptural "proofs" step by step; first as dealing with the Atonement, and next with the Trinity. Into the windings of this devious disputation we need not wander. Suffice it to say that, while the methods of exposition of the Hindu are more modern than those of his Christian opponent, many of his exegetical expedients are more apt to amuse than to convince a theologian of the present day. Yet the acquaintance which he shows with Hebrew and Greek and with expository literature is, considering his antecedents, little less than marvellous. It is interesting to observe that he rebuts Dr. Marshman's appeal to the authority of inter- pretative tradition by a reminder of the position of the first Protestants in face of the unbroken Catholic tradition; and the charge of imputing iniquity to his maker he courteously and even with a sense of pain retorts upon his critic. It is also interesting to place beside his anonymous or pseudonymous defence of Hinduism, this question which appears in the preface above his own proper signature:-

Could Hinduism continue after the present generation, or bear the studious examination of a single year, if the belief of their idols being endued with animation were not carefully impressed on the young before they come to years of understanding?

His objection to Dr. Marshman "condemning those whose sentiments as to the person of Jesus Christ are precisely the same" as Newton's and Locke's, is significant, for he goes

on to describe these "sentiments" which we may perhaps infer that he himself holds -thus,-" that He is the anointed Lord and King promised and sent from God" and "is worthy of worship for his mediation and meritorious death, but by no means perfect God and perfect Man."

Not content with this bulky "Final Appeal," Rammohun proposed in the preface to start in the following April a monthly magazine "to be devoted to Biblical criticism and to subject Unitarian as well as Trinitarian doctrines to the test of fair argument." "If any one of the missionary gentlemen, for himself and in behalf of his fellow-labourers, would send an essay in defence of their distinctive tents, Rammohun would publish the same at his own expense. This proffer led to a curious controversy. A certain fiery doctor of medicine, R. Tytler by name, considered it "a general challenge to all Christians who profess a belief in the divinity of Christ," and accordingly he offered to meet Rammohun in either public or private disputation. Rammohun replied pointing out that what he had asked for was literary discussion, and declaring his willingness to examine any arguments which Dr. Tytler might commit to writing on behalf of the doctrine of Trinity, provided they were sent "by a missionary gentlemen under his signature." The sagacious Hindu was not going to be drawn from his quest after sober and temperate theological controversy by the truculent polemic of an irresponsible layman. The layman thereupon writes to the Bengal Hurkaru, April 40, 1823, in a towering passion, charging this Unitarian Goliath with shrinking from the conflict to which he had challenged the hosts of Israel, so soon as the first layman appeared against him. He is especially indignant at the idea of his being required to secure the warrant of a missionary's signature to his lucubrations, as if he were going to turn Anabaptist! Whence it appears that the irate doctor did not love the Baptist persuasion. Rammohun Roy replied under date May 1st, quoting the precise words of his challenge and indicating the doctor's non-compliance with the specified terms. To a more courteous proffer of literary battle from an anonymous correspondent, Rammohun, on May 3rd, answered, reasonably enough, that he did not engage to encounter all professors of the Trinity "of whatever rank or situation, character or peculiar state of mind," but with accredited theologians only.

But for dealing with amateur theologians of the minatory order, he had methods of his own. He would answer a fool according to his folly. In the Hurkaru of May 3rd, Dr. Tytler explodes with indignation at Rammohun's informing him of his entire indifference whether a man professed belief as a Christian in the divinity of Christ or of "any other mortal man," or as a Hindu in the divinity of Thakur Trata Ram or Munu. The idea of putting Christian theology on a level with Hindu mythology drove the doctor into a frenzy of italics, capitals, large capitals and notes of exclamation. Rammohun adopted in reply an artifice as innocent in its transparency as it was pungent in its satire. He wrote under the assumed name of Ram Doss and under the assured profession of Hindu orthodoxy, to propose to Dr. Tytler a joint crusade against "the abominable notion of a single God" advocated by Rammohun Roy and others. He argues that Christian and Hindu orthodoxy rested on the common basis, the manifestation of God in the flesh, and drew a parallel between the incarnations of Ram and of Christ. Trinity in Unity on the one side and on the other the 330, 000,000 of persons in the Hindu Godhead were equally matters of faith, inscrutable to reason. This covert satire stung the pugnacious doctor into styling Ram Doss "the wretched tool" of "the damnable heresy of Unitarianism" which was the same as Hindu idolatry and like it proceeded from the Devil. He signed this effusion characteristically, "Your inveterate and determined foe in the Lord." Dr. Tytler's qualifications for controversy may be further seen in his assertion that "there is no book at present in possession of Hindus of higher antiquity than the entrance of the Mussulmans into India," and that "the histories of Buddha, Shalivahana and Krishna comprise nothing more than perverted copies of Christianity."

The correspondence which went on for the most of the month of May was published in pamphlet form under the title: 'A Vindication of the Incarnation of Deity' as the common basis of Hinduism and Christianity against the schismatic attacks of R. Tytler, Esq., M.D., by Ram Doss."

Possibly to the same time belongs 'A Dialogue between a Missionary and Three Chinese Converts,' which is published in the English works of the Rajah. This little tract is written with the desire of making out that the impression produced on Chinese minds by the teaching of three Gods who are one God and one of whom died, is bewildering and ridiculous.

On November 15 in the same year appeared the fourth and last number of the Brahmunical Magazine. The cover of the pseudonym Shivaprusad Surma is further kept up by an opening explanation that in default of reply from Rammohun Roy to the missionary attacks upon the Vedanta system this magazine had been published. This artifice of self-multiplication and self-concealment by aid of pseudonyms certainly savours more of the journalist than of the national religious reformer; but, however we may explain it, Rammohun seems to have had quite a liking for such tactics. The Magazine is occupied first with a defence of the Vedantic system and then with an onslaught on the doctrines of the Trinity and Atonement. The writer greatly enjoys himself in putting together ten different versions of the Trinity presented by English divines, from the Sabellian view of Dr. Wallis to the explanation of the newly-arrived Bishop Heber of Calcutta that the second and third persons in the Trinity are simply the Angels - Michael and Gabriel! He suggests that so various and contradictory a creed is scarcely likely to make many converts. He concludes by laying down" for the information of the missionary gentlemen," 'our religious creed," which we may probably regard as the faith of the real author:-

"In conformity with the precepts of our ancient religion, contained in the Holy Vedanta, though disregarded by the generality of the moderns, we look up to ONE BEING as the animating and regulating principle of the whole collective body of the universe, and as the origin of all individual souls, which in a manner somewhat similar vivify and govern their particular bodies; and we reject idolatry in every form and under whatsoever veil of shophistry it may be practised, either in adoration of an artificial, a natural, or an imaginary object. The divine homage which we offer consists solely in the practice of Daya, or benevolence towards each other, and not in a fanciful faith, or in certain motions of the feet, arms, head, tongue, or other bodily organs, in a pulpit or before a temple."

In 1823, and possibly as a sort of practical conclusion to the course of controversy, Rammohun issued a short tract entitled 'Humble Suggestions' to his countrymen who believe in the One True God. It is stated to be " by Prusunnu Koomar Thakoor." As his editor, Jogendra Chunder Ghose, remarks at this point, "The Raja was fond of writing anonymously and of giving the names of others to his own works." This "advertisement" is prefixed.

My object in publishing this tract is to recommend those to whom it is addressed to avoid using harsh or abusive language in their intercourse with European missionaries, either respecting them or their objects of worship,however much this may be countenanced by the example of some of these gentlemen. This is the tract :-

Those who firmly believe on the authority of the Vedas that "God is One only, without an equal," and that "He cannot be known either through the medium of language, thought or vision: how can he be known except as existing, the origin and support of the Universe?" and who endeavour to regulate their conduct by the following precept, "He who is desirous of eternal happiness should regard another as he regards himself, and the happiness and misery of another as his own," ought to manifest the warmest affection towards such of their own countrymen as maintain the same faith and practice, even although they have not all studied the Vedas for themselves, but have professed a belief in God only through an acquaintance with their general design. Many along the ten classes of sunnyasees, and all the followers of Gooroo Nanuk, of Dadoo, and of Kubeer, as well as of Suntu, etc., profess the religious sentiments above mentioned. It is our unquestionable duty invariably to treat them as brethren. No doubt should be entertained of their future salvation, merely because they receive instructions, and practise their sacred music in the vernacular dialect. For Yajnavalkya, with a reference to those who cannot sing the hymns of the Vedas, has said "The divine hymns, Rik, Gatha, Panika, and Dukshubihita should be sung; because by their constant use man attains supreme beatitude". "He who is skilled in playing on the lute (veena), who is intimately acquainted with the various tones and harmonies and who is able to beat time in music, will enter without difficulty upon the road of salvation." Again the Shivu Dhurmu as quoted by Rughoonundun, says, "He is reputed a Gooroo who according to the capacity of his disciple instructs him in Sanskrit whether pure or corrupt, in the current language of the country, or by any other means."

Amongst foreigners, those Europeans who believe God to be in every sense ONE, and worship Him alone in Spirit, and who extend their benevolence to man as the highest service to God, should be regarded by us with affection, on the ground of the object of their worship being the same as ours. We should feel no reluctance to co-operate with them in religious matters, merely because they consider Jesus Christ as the Messenger of God and their spiritual teacher; for oneness in the object of worship and sameness of religious practice should produce attachment between the worshippers.

Amongst Europeans, those who believe Jesus Christ to be God himself, and conceive him to be possessed of a particular form, and maintain Father, Son, and Holy Ghost to be one God, should not be treated in an unfriendly manner. On the contrary, we should act towards them in the same manner as we act towards those of our countrymen who without forming any external image meditate upon Ram and other supposed incarnations and believe in their unity.

Again, those amongst Europeans who believing Jesus Christ to be the Supreme Being, moreover construct various images of him, should not be hated. On the contrary, it becomes us to act towards those Europeans in the same manner as we act towards such as believe Ram, etc., to be incarnations of God and form external images of them. For, the two last mentioned sects of foreigners are one and the same with those of the two similar sects among Hindoos although they are clothed in a different garb.

When any belonging to the second and third classes of Europeans endeavour to make converts of us, the believers in the only living and true God, even then we should feel no resentment towards them, but rather compassion, on account of their blindness to the errors into which they themselves have fallen. Since it is almost impossible, as every day's experience teaches us, for men when possessed of wealth and power, to perceive their own defects.

So terminated Rammohun's polemic against the Trinitarian missionaries. But, even while that was in full course, he was involved in repelling attacks from an entirely opposite quarter. A defender of the conventional Hindu faith, who styled himself an "Establisher of Religion," brought out a brochure in Bengali, entitled "Four Questions," which was manifestly levelled at the reformer and his associates. From Rammohun's reply in the same language, which appeared in 1822 (20th of Magh, 1229, Bengali era), and which was entitled "Answers to Four Questions," we gather the chief points at issue between him and his orthodox fellow countrymen. The style of both combatants is indirect, allusive, sinuous; with many covert personal references which are now scarcely intelligible, but all wrapped round the main point, which was -had the reformers put themselves outside the pale of Hinduism? The first question ran thus-

Do these professors of knowledge and their childish followers, having examined the mysteries of the Shastras, wish to give up their own religion and adopt that of foreigners? Is it proper, according to the Shastras, for gentlemen to associate with such good-intentioned people?

In other words, ought not Rammohun and his accomplices to be boycotted as renegades? Rammohun retorts with a 'tu quoque.' The "practiser of religion," as he calls his pragmatic rite-observing opponent, failed just as much as "the inquirer into religion" to practise a millionth part of what the minute rules of Hinduism required. "The practiser," with his father and grandfather, had served men of an alien faith, had used Mahometan tooth-powder and perfumes, had studied Mahometan lore with Mahometans, had instructed men of an alien faith in his own Shastras. These things were as much violations of strict Hindu law as any ritual offence charged to "the inquirer."

The second question inquires whether the religion of those who oppose native manners and customs, who ignorantly claim to know God, and who wear the Sacred Thread without affection, is not as the religion of the tiger and the cat ? Reply is made by enquiring whether "the establisher" observes the native customs of the Vaisnavs, who eat no fish. Does he follow all the usages of his own sect? If not, does he perform the requisite penance? An effective contrast is drawn between the man who outwardly appears to fulfil the strictest prescriptions of his religion, but at home eats fish and abuses everyone; and the man who makes no pretences but holds to the saying of Maha Nirban, "the eternal religion consists in the knowledge of God and the performance of those practices most beneficial to man."

The third question asks what religion sanctions the taking of life by a Brahman, and scornfully enquires as to the fate in this and in the next world of "merciful searchers into knowledge," who daily cause kids to be killed for their table. The answer affirms that according to the Shastras "it is not a sin to eat flesh that has been offered to Gods and to ancestors." But if the eating of animal food incur the punishment of hell, does not the Establisher himself eat fish?

The fourth question asks what must be done with "certain well-known persons" who "throw off fear of religion and of public opinion, cut their hair, drink wine and consort with infidels." It is answered that the Shastras forbid only "vain cutting of the hair," and enjoin the drinking of consecrated wine. Critics are significantly reminded that Brahmans who consort with the Mohammedan wives of their own servants and with Chandal courtesans ought properly to forfeit then brahmanhood.

These pungent replies called forth a rejoinder of more than two hundred pages from "the Establisher of religion." This brought Rammohun again into the field. In 1823 (12th of Pous, 1230, Bengali era) he published his Pathya Pradana ("Medicine for the Sick"). Its preface describes the last work of his opponent - whom he calls henceforth not the establisher but "the destroyer of religion"- as merely one long tirade of abuse. Rammohun declines to retaliate, remarking that in giving medicine to boys that are sick the physician does not lose his temper over their kicks and screams. The "Medicine" he administers is compounded from the Shastras. In giving it, he rebuts false interpretations put upon his former answers.

The controversy was thus, it appears, analogous to that between the "tithing of mint and anise and cumin," and "the weightier matters of the law." Against the Rabbinism of the Hindu religion, Rammohun appealed to its Prophetism.

On the 16th of June in this year (1823), Rammohun, who had emerged successfully from the proceedings instituted against him by his nephew some three years previously, was drawn once more into the law courts. The Rajah of Burdwan sued him for Rs. 15,002, being principal and interest on a bond for Rs. 7,501, which was given by Rammohun's father for arrears of land revenue, and which fell due so far back as 1797. Rammohun's defence was (1) that having been disinherited by his father he could not be held to have inherited his father's debts; (2) that no demand for payment had been made during his father's life-time or since until now, and (3) that a debt not claimed for twelve years ceased to be legally binding. He argued that the action was brought out of malice, with a desire to ruin him, because Rammohun's son-in-law, Dewan to the plaintiff's son lately deceased, had acted as vakeel for the widowed Ranees and extorted from the Rajah what was legally, though not customarily, their due. For this exacting vindication of widows' rights, the Rajah naturally blamed Rammohun, and relying on his immense wealth was bent on breaking him. The proceedings now begun lasted over more than eight years. Defeated in the Provincial

Court of Calcutta, the Rajah appealed to the higher tribunal - the Sudder Dewanee Adaulut and the judicial decision which finally worsted him was not pronounced until Nov. 10, 1831.

It is a remarkable commentary on the many-sidedness and elastic sympathy of Rammohun's character that just at the time when he was anonymously satirizing or loftily compassionating the propaganda of Trinitarian Christians, we find him avowing attendance on a Presbyterian Church and giving his name and countenance to a petition for the despatch of Presbyterian missionaries to India. To Rammohun we may trace some share in the origination of Alexander Duff's great missionary work. Dr. Bryce, Church of Scotland Chaplain in Calcutta, declared himself disabused by Rammohun Roy of Abbe Dubois' opinion that no Hindu could be made a true Christian; and, to quote Dr. Bryce's own words,

"Encouraged by the approbation of Rammohun I presented to the General Assembly of 1824 the petition and memorial which first directed the attention of the Church of Scotland to British India as a field for missionary exertions, on the plan that is now so successfully following out, and to which this eminently gifted scholar, himself a Brahmin of high caste, had specially annexed his sanction."

On the 8th December, 1823 - within less than a month of the appearance of the Brahmanical Magazine, No. iv- Rammohun added this written testimony to the minute of St. Andrew's Kirk Session on the proposal mentioned by Dr. Bryce:-

As I have the honour of being a member of the Congregation meeting in St. Andrew's Church (although not fully concurring in every article of the Westminster Confession of Faith), I feel happy to have an opportunity of expressing my opinion that, if the prayer of the memorial is complied with there is a fair and reasonable prospect of this measure proving conducive to the diffusion of religious and moral knowledge in India."

The parenthesis disclaiming complete concurrence with the Presbyterian creed, coming as it does from "Ram Doss," seems to carry with it a flavour of fine irony; but its mildness of statement was probably due only to the Rajah's exceeding urbanity. Rammohun's active assistance of Duff's earliest efforts will be noticed later. Scotsmen will doubtless regard it as a compliment to their national type of religion that while this cultured theist was horrified by the overtures of the Anglican bishop and was antagonized by the Baptist editors, he was induced to beg for the presence in his country of Scottish Presbyterian missionaries.

But his sympathies most naturally lay with the suggestion which had been elicited, on his work becoming known in England and America, of starting a Unitarian propaganda in India. In 1823 Rev. Henry Ware, Unitarian Minister of Harvard College, Cambridge, United States, addressed a number of questions to Rammohun on "The Prospects of Christianity and the means of Promoting its Reception in India." Rammohun, in a letter dated February 2, 1824, explains that his delay in replying was due to his engrossing "controversies with polytheists both of the West and East." Before proceeding to answer seriatim the questions presented, he remarks:-

There is one question ("whether it be desirable that the inhabitants of India should be converted to Christianity" which I pause to answer, as I am led to believe, from reason, what is set forth in Scripture, that "In every nation he that feareth God and worketh righteousness is accepted with him," in whatever form of worship he may have been taught to glorify God. Nevertheless I presume to think that Christianity, if properly inculcated, has a greater tendency to improve the moral, social, and political state of mankind than any other known religious system.

He expresses his delight that so great a body of the American people "have engaged in purifying the religion of Christ from those absurd idolatrous doctrines and practices, with which the Greek, Roman, and Barbarian converts to Christianity have mingled it from time to time." Able friends of truth, he adds, have made similar efforts in England, but there they have against them the power and revenues of the established Church. In America they had to fight "only prejudice unarmed with wealth or power." He concludes with a reference to the political future of the United States which reveals the wide outlook and sympathy of the man. He was writing shortly after the Missouri compromise (1821) had relaxed the first great tension between the "free" North and the slave-holding South; and these are his words:-

I presume to say that no native of these States can be more fervent than myself in praying for the uninterrupted happiness of your country and for what I cannot but deem essential to its prosperity - the perpetual union of all the States under one general government.

He goes on to amplify his desire for the maintenance of Federal unity. He then deals with the string of questions propounded. On the number and quality of converts he speaks guardedly, but leaves the impression that there are no converts save a very few of low caste or none, ignorant, and influenced by mercenary motives. He quotes Abbe Dubois as a greater authority than himself, who said that it was impossible to convert a Hindu to Christianity. The chief causes assigned by him for the slow advance of Christianity in India are the reliance of the natives on their sacred books, their early prejudices, their dread of losing caste, and the fact that "the doctrines which the missionaries maintain and preach are less conformable with reason than those professed by Moosulmans and in several points are equally absurd with the popular Hindu creed." From this last drawback alone was the promulgation of Unitarian Christianity exempt. The sincere conversion of the few enlightened Hindus to Trinitarian Christianity is "morally impossible," but "they would not scruple to embrace or at least to encourage, the Unitarian system of Christianity, were it inculcated on them in an intelligible manner." To the question whether and if so how Unitarians could aid the cause of Christianity in India, Rammohun returns the reply:-

Everyone who interests himself in behalf of his fellow creatures, would confidently anticipate the approaching triumph of true religion should induce you and your friends to send to Bengal as many serious and able teachers of European learning and science and Christian morality unmingled with religious doctrines, as your circumstances may admit, to spread knowledge gratuitously among the native community, in connection with the Rev. Mr. Adam. . . .

Unitarian missionary schools giving instruction in the rudiments of a European education in the English language and in Christian morality, mingling with it very little instruction relative to the doctrines of Christianity, would, he held, be of great use,"the only way," in fact, "of improving their understanding and ultimately meliorating their hearts." "I may be fully justified in saying that two-thirds of the native population of Bengal would be exceedingly glad to see their children educated in English learning." "To the best of my knowledge, no benefit has hitherto arisen from the translation of the Scriptures into the languages of the East, nor can any advantage be expected from the translations in circulation." To the question whether any important impression will ever be made "except by the conversion and through the influence of persons of education," Rammohun answers characteristically, "Christianity, when represented in its genuine sense in any language whatever, must make a strong impression on every intelligent mind, especially when introduced by persons of education and respectability." As the place most likely for successful propaganda he recommends Calcutta.

As a result of prospects thus advanced and of anticipated support from English-speaking lands, Mr. Adam, aided by Rammohun and the Unitarian Committee, proceeded to organize a Unitarian Mission in Calcutta. To its growing fund we find that Rammohun subscribed Rs. 5,000, Dwarkanath Thakoor Rs. 2,500, and Prusunnu Coomar Thakoor Rs. 2,500. Writing on June 4th, 1824, to Dr. T. Rees, of the Unitarian Committee in London, Rammohun reports:-

As to the state of the Unitarian Society in Calcutta, our Committee have not yet been able to purchase a suitable piece of ground for a chapel and school. They will, I hope, soon succeed in their endeavours. We have collected, partly by purchase and partly by gift, a great number of works and established a pretty respectable library in Calcutta.

From this letter we learn that Mr. Adam is now styled "the Unitarian Missionary in Bengal." Rammohun prefaces the report with expressions of lively delight that the London Unitarians had reprinted his 'Precepts of Jesus' and the two Appeals in its defence. He goes on naively to declare his grief and disappointment that George IV ., -whom he generously describes as "the most accomplished person of his time, of most enlightened acquirements and most liberal sentiments"should not have used his royal influence to relieve the members of the established Church from "the fetter" of the Thirty-nine Articles and from the repetition of the damnatory clauses of the "Athanasian Creed."

It is interesting to note that six days after Bishop Heber arrived in Calcutta (he came October 10th, 1823, and wrote the letter on the 16th) he informs the Dean of St. Asaph, "Our chief hindrances are some Deistical Brahmins who have left their old religion and desire to found a sect of their own, and some of those who are professedly engaged in the same work with ourselves, the Dissenters."

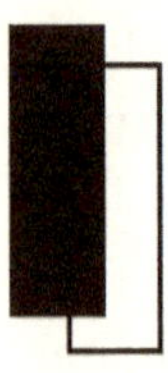

Journalistic and Educational
Pioneer-work (1821 -1826)

It is characteristic of Rammohun's many-sided activity that during the period of his energetic and voluminous theological controversy, he was busily engaged in promoting native journalism and native education. His role was essentially that of the enlightener; his one aim in publishing treatises on Unitarian divinity, in founding schools and colleges, and in conducting two newspapers was to enlighten the minds of his fellow-countrymen. He was certainly not the man to overlook the enormous value of the newspaper as an instrument for diffusing intellectual light. The relaxation in 1819 of the previously very stringent rules of press censorship enforced by the British Government was accepted by him as an invitation to the development of native journalism.

The regulation requiring every newspaper before it was issued to be submitted to a Government official was dispensed with Lord Hastings, the then Governor-General contented himself with prohibiting animadversions on the actions of Government, discussions likely to create religious alarm among the natives, or otherwise to stir up dissension, relying for the rest on "the prudence and discretion of the editors."

In a copy of Mr. Buckingham's Calcutta Journal in the latter part of 1821 appeared the "prospectus of a Bengalee weekly newspaper to be conducted by natives, printed and circulated in Bengalee and English." It was to be called Sambad Kaumudi or "The Moon of Intelligence." It was to deal with "religious, moral and political matters; domestic occurrences; foreign as well as local intelligence." The intimation of the price at which the new weekly was to be had is couched in terms of superabundant Oriental courtesy:-

To enable us to defray the expenses which will necessarily be attendant on an undertaking of this nature, we humbly solicit the support and patronage of all who feel themselves interested in the intellectual and moral improvement of our countrymen, and confidently hope that they will with their usual liberality and munificence, condescend to gratify our most anxious wishes, by contributing to our paper a monthly subscription of two rupees, in acknowledgment of which act of their benignity and encouragement, we pledge ourselves to make use of our utmost efforts and exertions to render our paper as useful, instructive and entertaining as it can possibly be.

The first number appeared December 4. 1821.* Its "address to the Bengal public" announced "the public good."

* [There is a considerable doubt as to the date of the first publication of the Sambad Kaumudi, most probably it appeared first in July 1819. In the list of Bengali publications compiled by Rev. Long in 1852 the Sambad Kaumudi is mentioned as a newspaper printed at the Sanskrit Press from 1819. The Christian Observer of Calcutta in 1840 in the list to be its "guiding star." It gratefully acknowledges Lord Hastings' action in removing the shackles from the Press. It promises to reprint in Persian, Hindustani and English such of its articles as seem to merit translation. It invokes the assistance of the Literati, and not the least significant promise of all - it offers to publish "respectful expression" of native grievances.

"A newspaper conducted exclusively by natives in the native language," it describes itself as "a novelty at least if not a desideratum." We may regard it therefore as the parent, and Rammohun Roy as the founder, of native journalism in India.+ Its consequent significance for the future of the Empire justifies the statement here of the contents of a few of its earlier numbers.

No. I.-The Editor's address to the Bengali community.

An Appeal to the Government for the establishment of a School for the gratuitous instruction of the children of poor but respectable Hindus.

An account of a miser prince of newspapers extinct before that date mentions the Sambad Kaumudi as first published in 1819. The India Gazette of July 1819 had a note about the pamphlet of Rammohun Roy on the suttee, mentioning that it was reprinted in a Bengali newspaper and expected much good from it. The Bengali newspaper was evidently the Sambad Kaumudi. One of the colleagues of Rammohun Roy in editing Sambad Kaumudi was Bhawani Charan Banerjee, who contributed considerably to its columns. But when Rammohun Roy began to write against suttee in the Sambad Kaumudi with great vehemence Bhawani Charan Banerjee withdrew his assistance and started another paper under the name of Samachar Chandrika which appeared in 1823. All these facts

lead to the conclusion that the Sambad Kaumudt first appeared in 1819.
Edi.]

+ Two other native papers were started about the same time, one in
Persian called the 'Jami Jehan Numa' and run in opposition to the liberal
views of the Mirat, the other in Bengali, and known as the 'Sumachar
Chandrica.'

No. II.- An Address to the natives, enumerating the advantages of reading newspapers.

Letter proposing to raise a fund to water the Chitpore Road. Account of
implicit faith in a Guru and an extraordinary gift.

Letter suggesting 22 instead of 15 as the legal age for succeeding to
hereditary property. Satirical account of the lavish generosity at the funerals
of certain rich natives, who when alive were notorious for niggardliness.

Humble address to the Government soliciting the extension of trial by
jury to the Mofussil, Zila and Provincial Courts of Judicature.

No. III.- An Appeal to the Government to relieve the Hindu community from the inconvenience consequent upon there being only one Ghat for the burning of dead bodies; whereas an immense space of ground has been granted for the burial of Christians.

Appeal to Government for the prevention of exportation of the
greatest part of the produce of rice from Bengal to foreign ports. Appeal
to Government to enable the middle class of native subjects to avail
themselves of the treatment of European physicians.

Appeal to the Calcutta magistrates to resort to rigorous measures for
relieving the Hindu inhabitants of Calcutta from the serious grievance
of Christian gentlemen driving their buggies amongst them and cutting
and lashing them with whips, without distinction of sex or age, while
they quietly assembled in immense numbers to see the images of their
deities pass in the Chitpore Road, when many of them, through terror and
consternation caused by the lashing inflicted on the spectators, fell down
into drains, while others were trampled under foot by the crowd.

This last heading gives a vivid glimpse of the way in which "Christian
gentlemen" from Britain failed to make either their rule or their religion
beloved by the natives. It also shows us how readily Anglo-Indians. writing
in the Indian Free Press would call "public attention at home" to the new
venture "ere it is too late," and cry "Obsta principiis." No. VI., it may be

noted, contains "an appeal to the rich Hindus of Calcutta to constitute a society for the relief of destitute widows, upon the principles of the Civil and Military Widows' Fund, established by order of Government." No. VII. urges on Hindu parents to get their children instructed in the native grammar before imposing on them the study of foreign languages. No. VIII. prints the plea of a philanthropist, who observing the misery caused by prejudices of caste, urges the Hindus not to debar themselves thereby from mechanical pursuits, but to cultivate "such arts as would tend to their comfort, happiness and independence."

The Sambad Kaumudi was for the common people. But Rammohun desired to supply information and guidance to the educated classes also, and in a form more peculiarly suited to their needs. In the following year (1822) he started a weekly newspaper in Persian, called the Mirat-al-Akhbar or 'Mirror of Intelligence.' This came out on Fridays, as the Bengali organ on Tuesdays. The style of the new weekly may be gathered from an article which appeared in its issue of Oct. 11, 1822, on "Ireland; the Causes of its Distress and Discontents." The article opens with a short statement of the geographical position and political history of the island. "The Kings of England having shut their eyes against justice, gifted away to their own parasites the estates of the Irish noblemen." The account of the causes of Irish discontent is given with grave naivete:-

Although all the inhabitants of this island call themselves the followers of the religion of Jesus Christ (upon whom and the rest of the prophets of God be peace and blessing!), yet a great number of them on account of their differing in some particular point of faith from the religion adopted by the King of England, follow their own clergymen and Pope in the performance of religious duties, and refuse adherence to the royal divines of the established Church of England; and in consequence the stipends of their own divines are not defrayed from the revenue of the land but depend on the contributions of private individuals. Besides this, on account of the stipends of the royal clergymen who are appointed to officiate in Ireland, the Government of Ireland exact taxes every year from those who positively refuse to be led by these clergymen in religious matters. How admirable is the observation of Saadi (on whom be mercy!)-

Do not say that these rapacious Ministers are the well-wishers of his Majesty:

For in proportion as they augment the revenue of the State, they diminish his popularity;

O statesman, apply the revenue of the King towards the comfort of the people; then during their lives they will be loyal to him.

This Persian poetry Mr. Gladstone only succeeded in translating into Parliamentary enactment in 1869. The second cause adduced is still (1897) an unsolved problem:-

The nobles and other landed proprietors of Ireland pass their time in England, either with a view to raise themselves at Court, or to have all the luxuries of life at their command. And they spend in England an immense sum of the revenue of their lands, which they collect by means of stewards or farmers; and consequently the tradespeople in England benefit by the liberal manner in which they spend their money, instead of the people of Ireland. And their rapacious stewards or farmers, for their own advantage and in order to show their zeal for the interest of their masters unmercifully increase the rent of the land and extort those rents from the peasantry. So that many from their improper behaviour are now deprived of the means of subsistence.

The natives are noted for their good natural abilities and open disposition, as well as for their generosity and hospitality. Foreigners are of the opinion that from the climate of Ireland the people are of quick apprehension and easily provoked (God knows best!)

The practical upshot of these explanations of the situation is to announce the ravages of famine in Ireland and to give the names of "a number of respectable European gentlemen of liberal principles and a body of liberal natives of this country," who have, "for the love of God," subscribed for the relief of the starving Irish. Irishmen who are proud of their nationality will not readily forget this tribute of appreciation and succour from one of the earliest pioneers of the National movement in India.

The National aspirations of Greece were not, however, favourably regarded by the Mirat. In an article published in November, 1822, quoted by a Calcutta paper as "expressing

the feeling of the thinking part of the natives generally," the writer rejoices in the receipt of the news of Turkish victory over the rebellious Greeks. He is manifestly jubilant that the Tsar with his grand army and his resolve "to conquer Turkey and destroy Islamism" was held back by Austria and England. Of the Greeks it is said, "Having returned from the deserts of rebellion, they have now taken up their abode in the city of comfort and obedience." Editorial information or prescience was this time at fault, since the Greek rebellion which broke out in 1821 only ended in the achievement of Independence in 1832. For this attitude to Greece, Mohammedan sympathy with Turkey was of course responsible.

Such free criticism of English policy in Europe as well as satiric reference to British insolence in treatment of natives on the public roads, naturally aroused European susceptibilities. John Bull, a Calcutta print, is ridiculed by the Hurkaru (of September 2, 1822) for translating the Persian amiss and in its jealous apprehension rendering tursa "Christians" as "Infidels." The Mirat was not lacking in loyalty. It was most eulogistic in its remarks on Lord Hastings, the then Governor-General.

But the end of 1822 saw the close of Lord Hastings' Governor-Generalship with its liberal and enlightened policy. Between his departure and the arrival of Lord Amherst, his successor, the Hon. John Adams officiated as Acting Governor-General. This temporary elevation of an inferior official was marked by characteristically official measures for the restriction of liberty. A single paragraph from the Mirat in February attests the arbitrary measures being adopted:-

The eminently learned Dr. Bryce, the head minister of the new Scotch Church, having accepted the situation of Clerk of the Stationery belonging to the Honourable Company, Mr. Buckingham the editor of the [Calcutta] Journal observed directly as well as indirectly that it was unbecoming of the character of the minister to accept a situation like this; upon which the Governor-General, in consideration of his disrespectful expression, passed an order that Mr. Buckingham should leave India for England within the period of two months from the date of the receipt of this order, and that after the expiration of that period he is not allowed to remain a single day in India.

The Journal was suppressed, and at the close of 1823 Mr. Arnot, Mr. Buckingham's assistant editor, was arrested and put on board a home-going ship.

The notice expelling Mr. Buckingham was followed up, suddenly and without notice, on March 14th, by a rigorous Press Ordinance from the acting Governor-General in Council. The preamble stated that "matters tending to bring the Government..... into hatred and contempt, and to disturb the peace..... of society have of late been frequently published and circulated in newspapers." The Ordinance prescribed that henceforth no one should publish a newspaper or other periodical without having obtained a license from the Governor-General in Council, signed by the Chief Secretary.

Before this regulation could come into force, the law required it to be fixed up in the Supreme Court for twenty days, and then if not disallowed, registered. It was accordingly entered on March 15th. On the 17th, Council moved the Court to allow parties feeling themselves aggrieved by the new regulation to be heard. Sir Francis Macnaghten, the sole Acting Judge, fixed the 31st for the hearing of objections, but suggested that in the meanwhile the objectors would do well to state their plea in a memorial to Government. Foremost among those objectors was Rammohun Roy. He and his friends set about promoting the suggested petition, but, as he afterwards stated, "in preparing this memorial in both the English and the Bengalee languages, and discussing the alterations suggested by the different individuals who wished to give it their support and signature so much time was necessarily consumed, that it was not ready to be sent into circulation for signature until the 30th of March." Consequently only fifteen natives had time to read and sign it; and the Government had no time, even if they wished, to act. Another memorial of the same tenor was hastily drawn up next day, signed by Rammohun and five other distinguished native gentlemen, and by counsel submitted to the Supreme Court. This memorial was attributed by its opponents to an English author, but was really, as was generally acknowledged later, the work of Rammohun. It may be regarded as the Areopagitica of Indian history. Alike in diction and in argument, it forms a noble landmark in the progress of English culture in the East.

The memorial first sets out the loyalty and attachment of the natives to British rule. They had trusted the Government with millions of their money. Relying on the Government, landlords had improved, instead of impoverishing as formerly, their estates. They had prayed for British victory during the Napoleonic wars. They rejoiced in the literary and political improvements due to British influence. They were most loyal in Calcutta, where British sway was best known. Possessing the same civil and religious liberty along with a lighter taxation, they were not inferior in loyalty to British-born subjects. Among the institutions which tended to improve the minds and ameliorate the condition of the natives was the native Press, and chiefly the newspaper Press, with its four native newspapers-two in Persian, two in Bengali. These journals had done nothing to disparage the Government or to promote dissension. "Native authors and editors have always restrained themselves" from publishing matter obnoxious to the Government. Yet the Ordinance had been issued, requiring a license revocable at pleasure for all newspapers. The first positive objection advanced against this new measure will probably strike all Westerns who are not Quakers or Tolstoyans with some surprise. In order to secure the license, the applicant was apparently required to make an affidavit or statement on oath. But, the Memorial proceeds:-

Those natives who are in more favourable circumstances and of respectable character, have such an invincible prejudice against making a voluntary affidavit, or undergoing the solemnities of an oath that they will never think of establishing a publication which can only be supported by a series of oaths and affidavits, abhorrent to their feelings and derogatory to their reputation amongst their countrymen.

Light is thrown on this intense antipathy by a letter in the India Gazette, dated Dec. 9, 1824, from which the following sentences may be quoted:-

I have frequently inquired of Hindus the reason of their objecting to swear; and the answers I have received have been, "If I put my hand into the Gunga Jul [Ganges Water], I put my hand into the fire of hell"; or "Should I happen to say one word which is not true, I shall be tormented during a hundred transmigrations"; or "I shall sink my ancestors into places of torment." They can make no distinction between voluntary and involuntary misstatements. *

*The Grand Jury at the Calcutta Sessions in October, 1825, proposed the substitution of a solemn declaration for an oath in the case of natives, declaring "it is notorious that by forcing a Hindu of any of the superior classes to swear, we inflict on him a disgrace in his own eyes and in the eyes of his fellow-citizens."

The Memorial goes on to show that "a complete stop" in the diffusion of knowledge of a certain kind will result from the new Ordinance. The better informed natives will be prevented instructing the people in the admirable system of British Government. Natives will be precluded from acquainting the Government with the errors and injustice which its executive officers may commit in various parts of the country. After this deprivation of a right which they had not abused, the natives could no longer feel justified in boasting of the privilege of British protection. But surely the British Government will not follow the precedent of Asiatic despotism in hoping to preserve power by keeping the people in darkness. Experience proves that a good Government grows stronger as its subjects become more enlightened. Every good ruler, aware of human imperfection and amenable to reverence for the eternal Governor, must be conscious of the liability to error involved in managing a great Empire and of the need of ready means of ascertaining consequent grievances. But the only effectual means is "Unrestrained liberty of publication", subject to the regular law of the land.

On this memorial being read, its prayer was supported by the speeches of Counsel, Mr. Fergusson and Mr. Turton. But Sir Francis Macnaghten gave his decision in favour of the Press Ordinance. In doing so, he absolutely ignored the native memorial, "not alluding to it in the most distant manner, nor to the arguments it contained." He further scandalized the memorialists by announcing that, before the Ordinance was entered or its merits argued in court, he had pledged himself to Government to give it his sanction.

There was but one resource left to the defenders of a free Press, and of that resource Rammohun did not hesitate to avail himself. He and his coadjutors appealed to the King in Council. The Appeal is one of the noblest pieces of English to which Rammohun put his hand. Its stately periods and not less stately thought recall the eloquence of the great orators of a century ago. In a language and style forever associated with the glorious vindication of liberty, it invokes against the arbitrary exercise of British power the principles and traditions which are distinctive of British history.

An eloquent recognition of the benefits of British rule, benefits which had led Hindus to regard the English rather as deliverers than conquerors, sets in effective contrast a statement of the grievance complained of. The native press had aided in diffusing these blessings and in inculcating an appropriate gratitude. The Friend of India, an organ of European missionaries, had acknowledged the valuable service rendered by the native newspapers and expressly declared that the liberty they possessed had not been abused by them "in the least degree." The sudden withdrawal of this unabused liberty could only have as its motive the desire to afford Government and all its functionaries complete immunity from censure or exposure or public remark. The law of the land being competent to deal with any offences committed by newspapers against public order, the new and arbitrary restrictions, if meant seriously, seemed to suggest that Government intended to interrupt the regular course of justice and take the law into its own hands. A free Press had never yet caused a revolution; but revolutions had been innumerable where no free Press existed to ventilate grievances. If this avenue of redress should be closed to the natives, they would consider "the most peculiar excellence of the British Government of India" done away, and themselves condemned to perpetual oppression and degradation. It placed their civil and religious rights "entirely at the mercy of such individuals as may be sent from England to assume the executive authority, or" and here comes a politely covered thrust at Acting Governor John Adams "rise into power through the routine of office, and who from long officiating in an inferior station, may have contracted prejudices against individuals or classes of men, which ought not to find shelter in the breast of the legislator." Subordinate officials being fallible, Government ought to welcome the check imposed on them by the fact or dread of publicity. Even on the lowest ground, regarding India merely as a valuable property, the British nation would act wisely in seeing that so important an asset should have good care taken of it. Under Mohammedan rulers, Hindus had enjoyed every political privilege in common with Moslems, but under British sway they were not allowed) similar equality with their conquerors; and the slight compensation offered them in the liberty of their Press was a right they were the less prepared to forego. The Appeal concludes with the alternative; either let His Majesty restore the freedom of the Press or let him appoint an independent Commission to investigate from time to time the condition of his Hindu subjects, restraint of some kind being absolutely necessary to preserve them from the abuses of uncontrolled power.

Argument and eloquence, however, proved of no avail against the Anglo-Indian dread of native criticism. The Privy Council in November, 1825, after six months' consideration, declined to comply with the petition, presented by Mr. Buckingham, late of the Calcutta Journal, against the Press Ordinance of 1823.

Not many months after that Ordinance came into force, the Mirat ceased to appear. It lived in all only some sixteen months. The editor declared his inability to go on publishing under what he considered degrading conditions, and lamented that he, "one of the most humble of men," should be no longer able to contribute towards the intellectual improvement of his countrymen. The Asiatic Journal of January, 1824, in recording the announcement, objects to it as having a "direct tendency to reflect on the act of Government." So sensitive were Anglo-Indian susceptibilities that even the negative protest of a journalist ceasing to publish his paper was resented. Rammohun did not carry his protest so far as to stop the Sambad also. It was continued, and in fact survived its founder for several years.

The question arises, why, if both must not be sacrificed, was the Mirat selected for sacrifice ? Two reasons probably weighed with Rammohun: the greater cost and the greater risk of Government interference. The Mirat was addressed to a cultured constituency. The outlay involved in its production would therefore be larger, and its circulation smaller; while its more critical attitude would naturally excite the keener suspicion in the breast of thin-skinned officials.*

* At this point Miss Collet's revision of the continuator's manuscript ceases altogether. Of his work up to this point she sent (dictated) expressions of generous approval. The "few points" in this chapter which, she said, required "touching up," she regretted she was not then strong enough to specify. She reserved them for the next interview,-which, alas! never took place.

The educational purpose which inspired Rammohun's journalism led him into several more distinctively academic enterprises. His share in founding, along with Sir E. H. East and Mr. David Hare, the old Hindu College, has already been noticed. In 1822, he opened on his own account an Anglo-Indian School for imparting a free education in English to Hindu boys. With the exception of a few subscriptions from other friends, the whole of the funds required were supplied by Rammohun. Mr. William Adam, who was one of the visitors, thus speaks of the School in 1827:- -

Two teachers are employed, one at a salary of 150/- Rs. per month, and the other at a salary of 70/- Rs. per month; and from 60 to 80 Hindu boys are instructed in the English language. The doctrines of Christianity are not inculcated, but the duties of morality are carefully enjoined, and the facts belonging to the history of Christianity are taught to those pupils who are capable of understanding general history.

From reports of examinations, the school seems to have proved a fair success. The founder's control over it was not less real and continuous than his support of it. Mr. William Adam strongly desired to make it a public institution, to solicit for it public subscriptions, and to put it under the control of the Unitarian Committee. But Rammohun firmly refused his consent to the scheme. Mr. Adam was much distressed and felt it his duty accordingly to restrict his activity as a visitor. Even in that narrowed sphere he came into collision with Rammohun's strong will. He complained that his fellow visitor, whom he considered quite unsuited for the post, upset the plans and practices which Mr. Adam had painfully introduced into the school. But Rammohun would not part with the obnoxious visitor, whose popularity with the natives was great; and Mr. Adam resigned in high dudgeon. This occurred in 1828.

Shortly after the opening of this school, in 1823,-the year most crowded with his theological polemic, we find Rammohun in the thick of a great educational controversy. The British Government was known to be appropriating funds for the promotion of Indian education; and the kind of promotion most desirable was the subject of eager dis- cussion. Should the Government seek simply to develop and deepen the education already in vogue in India? Or should it boldly endeavour to introduce the innovations of European science and European culture? The "Orientalists" clamoured for the exclusive pursuit of Oriental studies. They were hotly opposed by the "Anglicists," chief among whom was Rammohun Roy. The Government seemed inclined to yield to the Orientalist view and announced the intention of establishing a Sanskrit College in Calcutta. The step drove Rammohun, undaunted by the scant courtesy which his former appeals to the British authorities had received, to address a Letter on English Education to Lord Amherst, the new Governor-General. In this letter he expresses profound regret that the Government was proposing to found a Sanskrit College-"to impart such knowledge as is already current in India." Such a seminary would, he argues, resemble those existing in Europe before Lord Bacon's day, and would only "load the minds of youth with grammatical niceties and metaphysical distinctions of little or no practical use." The Sanskrit language by reason of its great difficulty had been for ages a lamentable check to the diffusion of knowledge; but if it must be studied for the sake of the information it contains, its study might be promoted by grants to existing institutions where it was already taught. Rammohun sees no advantage in requiring young men to spend the best years of their life in the study of philological niceties. A more remarkable feature of his contention is its criticism of the Vedanta. He had, it will be remembered, translated large portions of the Vedanta into modern tongues. He had warmly defended its teachings against the attacks of the missionaries. Nay, in the fourth number of the Brahmanical Magazine which was published almost in the very month in which this Letter was written, he was still engaged in defending Vedantic doctrine. Yet he now writes:-

Neither can much improvement arise from such speculations as the following, which are the themes suggested by the Vedanta, in what manner is the soul absorbed in the Deity? What relation does it bear to the Divine

Essence? Nor will youths be fitted to be better members of society by the Vedantic doctrines which teach them to believe that all visible things have no real existence, that as father, brother have no actual entity they consequently deserve no real affection, and therefore the sooner we escape from them and leave the world the better.

This last objection to the Vedantic doctrines is precisely that advanced by the missionaries in the 'Sumachar Darpan' and assailed by Rammohun in the Brahmuanical Magazine. The apparent breach of consistency involved in its endorsement here, will be considered subsequently.

After further objections to the "imaginary learning" of Hindu schools, he summarily assures Lord Amherst that "the Sanskrit system of education would be the best calculat- ed to keep this country in darkness." What he wants to see established is "a more liberal and enlightened system of instruction, embracing mathematics, natural philosophy, chemistry, anatomy, with other useful sciences." This, he urges "may be accomplished with the sums proposed, by employing a few gentlemen of talent and learning educated in Europe and providing a College furnished with necessary books, instruments, and other apparatus."

Of this letter Bishop Heber wrote in March, 1824 *:- Rammohun Roy, a learned native, who has sometimes been called, though I fear without reason, a Christian, remonstrated with this [Orientalist] system last year, in a paper which he sent me to be put into Lord Amherst's hands and which for its good English, good sense, and forcible arguments, is a real curiosity, as coming from an Asiatic."

The patronizing tone of these remarks reveals only too plainly the unfortunate attitude which Christian missionaries, even the most devout, assumed towards natives of India, who were, to say the very least, certainly not their inferiors.

"It was owing, perhaps, to this agitation," remarks Jogendra Chunder Ghose on this letter to Lord Amherst, "that the foundation stone of the building intended for the Sanskrit College was laid in the name of the Hindu College (February, 1824), and the Hindu College was located there together with the Sanskrit College."

Within about a year of the completion of this Sanskrit and Hindu College, we find Rammohun taking a new and important step in his career as educational reformer. We learn from Mr. William Adam, writing under date July 27, 1826, that:- Rammohun Roy has lately built a small but very neat and handsome college, which he calls the Vedanta College, in which a few youths are at present instructed by a very eminent Pandit, in Sanskrit literature, with a view to the propagation and defence of Hindu Unitarianism. With this institution he is also willing to connect instructions in European science and learning, and in Christian Unitarianism, provided the instructions are conveyed in the Bengali or Sanskrit language. The Western reader may perhaps be surprised to find Rammohun scarcely two years after his opposing the Government scheme of a Sanskrit College because of its promoting instruction in the Vedantic philosophy,himself founding Sanskrit and Vedanta College. It may at first appear as much of a paradox as his advancing in the Letter to Lord Amherst the same arguments against the Vedanta which he had denounced in the Brahmanical Magazine. But to understand these seeming inconsistencies we must bear in mind the complex nature of the Vedantic system and the different practical issues bound up in the several controversies. The teachings of the Vedanta lend themselves to a remarkable diversity of theological interpretation. They are appealed to equally by dualistic and non-dualistic schools of thought. They contain passages which breathe a lofty and ethical theism; in other places they seem to countenance a pantheism that is simply acosmism, the denial of all finite existence; and they also include much that, judged by the standards of Western culture, is puerile and fantastic where it is not demonstrably false. According as the Vedanta is taught with or without a proper selective adjustment of its widely various contents, its value as a subject of instruction may be set high or low. In the ordinary Hindu schools it was taught in false perspective, with a discrimination exercised if at all, in favour of what was trivial, incorrect, polytheistic. Rammohun therefore opposed with all his might the suggestion that the British Government should perpetuate or encourage this kind of Vedantic instruction. At the same time he saw in the Vedanta rightly handled and "rightly divided" a means for leading his countrymen out of their prevailing superstition and idolatry into a pure and elevated Ttheism. Their devotion to the Vedantic scriptures was the lever by which Rammohun hoped to lift them into a simpler and nobler faith. Therefore, he founded the Vedanta College and therefore also he controverted the missionaries' wholesale disparagement of the Vedanta. If the missionaries had succeeded in discrediting the Vedanta, they would in Rammohun's eyes have broken down the bridge which enabled men to pass from Hindu polytheism to Hindu theism. He thus combated both the conservative Christian who advocated indiscriminate rejection and the conservative Hindu who advocated the indiscriminate retention of Vedantic teaching; and he provided for a discriminating instruction in the ancient system which should have the approval of liberal Hindus and liberal Christians.

This method is illustrated by a tract on Different Modes of Worship which appeared in January 18, 1825. It was written in Sanskrit by Rammohun Roy under the name of Shivaprusad Surma, and it was translated into English, with English annotations, by Rammohun Roy under the name of "A Friend of the Author." It propounded the difficulty: Some shastras enjoin worship by means of idols, others dissuade from it: how to reconcile the contrary advice? It finds answer in certain sayings of Vyas in the Bhagavat and of Shreedhur his commentator, to the effect that idol worship, along with ritual observances, is only of value so long as a man has not yet become conscious that the Lord of the Universe dwells in all beings. When he attains that consciousness, his worship becomes the discharge of the four duties of "charity to the needy," "Honour to others," "Friendship," and "An equal regard to all creatures," under the observant conviction that "the all-powerful Lord is in the heart watching over the soul." The writer remarks in a note that "worship through matter" was sanctioned in Judaism though forbidden in Christianity. This reference suggests that Rammohun conceived of his Hindu Unitarianism standing to historic Hinduism as the New Covenant stood to the Old: a development of the spiritual core at the expense of the ritual and material kernel.

His Vedanta College and his translations from the Vedanta served alike as witness to his continuity with the historic past of India and as the implement enabling him to connect her with a progressive future. But of his equal readiness to avail himself of the powerful solvents of English influences we are reminded by his publication in 1826 of a Bengali Grammar in English. His Anglo-Hindu school and his "Anglicist" remonstrances had shown how eager he was to introduce the better-educated classes of India into the new world of European literature; the Bengali Grammar reveals his anxiety to facilitate the inroad of the aggressive European in the dialect and understanding of the common people. In his 'Introduction to the Grammar' (June 12) he refers to "the persevering exertions of many European philanthropists in the noble attempt to ameliorate the moral condition of [the] inhabitants"; who "with a view to facilitate intercourse between themselves and the natives" and without expectation of finding any literary treasures in the language, labour to acquire the vernacular. This circumlocution in describing the missionaries and the careful avoidance of any reference to their distinctively religious work are significant; and are still more so when taken along with the express declaration which follows that he intended the Grammar "as a humble present for these worthy persons," to aid them "in their own studies or in directing those of others." Of this contribution to missionary philology Mr. W. Adam wrote at the time. "The work throws much new light upon the idioms of the language, but the arrangement is defective in consequence of the desultory mode of composition he indulges in." A Bengali version of it was brought out by the author in 1833. Bengali owes much to Rammohun. It was his writings chiefly which raised it into a literary language. As by Wiclif in England and Luther in Germany, so also by Rammohun in Bengal, the despised dialect of the common

people was made the vehicle of the highest ideas and became thereby permanently elevated. Reformation in religion has often proved ennoblement in language. During the whole of this period of theological controversy and journalistic and educational activity Rammohun never left out of sight the more directly philanthropic projects to which he had early given himself. The campaign against suttee was not allowed to flag. He used the Sambad Kaumudi as a regular weapon in this agitation. It was an agitation slowly but steadily affecting the attitude of the British authorities to the whole question. Of this the proceedings of the Nizamut Adaulut on the 25th of May, 1821, supply striking proof. The Chief Judge Leycester, while of opinion that suttee could not be put down generally, advised its suppression "by proclamation" in divisions where it was little in practice, viz., Dacca, Moorshedabad and Bareilly and in Allahabad, Futtehpore, Bundelcund, and Calpee. The second judge, Mr. Courtney Smith, to his lasting honour be it recorded, demanded the "entire and immediate abolition" of suttee. The two other judges, of those who drew up "Minutes" on the subject, pronounced against abolition as likely to imperil public order, but one of them, Mr. Dorin, suggested that the barbarous rite should be sup pressed in a single district, say the Hooghly district, by way of experiment and example. He emphasized the extremely significant fact that, in answer to a circular sent out the pre vious year to the magistrates of the Lower Provinces, "about one half of the magistrates" declared in favour of total abolition at once. The reply of Lord Hastings, made on the 17th of the following July, stated that he could not approve any of the three suggestions, not feeling that the time had arrived for either experimental, gradual, or entire prohibition. He expressed the hope that the more educated natives would "gradually become disposed to abandon the practice." He had doubtless in mind the propaganda of Rammohun Roy and his followers.

As though to lend confirmation to this hope, the indefatigable reformer in the course of the same year (1822) published a valuable tract on "Modern Encroachments on the Ancient Rights of Females according to the Hindu Law of Inheritance." In this he applied to social reform the method he had found fruitful in theological discussions. He appealed from the present to the past and against the prescription of custom set the authority of antiquity. By numerous citations he proves that "all the ancient law-givers unanimously award to a mother an equal share with her son in the property left by her deceased husband, in order that she may spend her remaining days independently of her children." But unfortunately later jurists made void, by their expositions, this salutary law. As a consequence "both stepmothers and mothers have, in reality, been left destitute in the division of their husband's property and the right of a widow exists in theory only among the learned but unknown to the populace." Hence, "a woman who is looked upto as the sole mistress by the rest of a family one day, on the next becomes dependent on her sons and subject to the slights of her daughters-in-law." On the death of their husbands women had only three courses before them:-

Firstly. To live a miserable life as entire slaves to others without indulging any hope of support from another husband.

Secondly. To walk in the paths of unrighteousness for their maintenance and independence.

Thirdly. To die on the funeral pile of their husbands, loaded with the applause and honour of their neighbours.

Having shown that Hindu antiquity, far from demanding suttee, had made honourable provision for the maintenance of the widow, Rammohun passes on to attack the institution of polygamy, which had made difficult the fulfilment of the ancient law of female inheritance. Where plurality of wives was most frequent, as in Bengal, the number of female suicides was proportionately great. "This horrible polygamy among the Brahmans is directly contrary to the law given by ancient authors." A second marriage while the first wife was alive was allowed only on the ground of specified physical or moral defects.

It is interesting to learn from Mr. William Adam's letters of 1826, Rammohun's personal antipathy to polygamy. He was, as we have previously related, married by his father at nine years of age to two child-wives. To both he felt himself bound to remain faithful, but on the death of one (in 1824), who was the mother of the children, he became in practice as in theory a monogamist. It is sad to find that even so his married life was not too happy. The Asiatic Journal for November, 1833, states in its obituary notice that "Rammohun Roy has left in India a wife from whom he has been separated on what account we know not) for some years."Babu N.N. Chatterjee states that Rammohun "lived apart from his wives simply because they were Hindus, and he was considered an outcast by them. His wives did not like to live with him." All the more commendable, therefore, is his uniform and chivalrous championship of womanhood. So strongly was he opposed to polygamy that (Mr. Adam tells us) he inserted clauses in his will disinheriting any son or more remote descendant who had more than one wife at the same time. But he was, we are informed, a monogamist not on religious grounds but on grounds of expediency.

In his tract on the subject, Rammohun further recalls ancient authorities to show that a daughter was entitled to receive a fourth part of the portion which a son could inherit. This had been so far set aside by modern practice that the daughter was deprived of any portion if there were a son surviving and was even-in express violation of ancient law-sold in marriage. He concludes the tract with a guarded hope that not merely Hindu Pandits but European judges might be called in to pronounce on cases of disputed inheritance.

Lord Hastings' despatch of August 15, 1822, which was written a few months before his departure from India, and which may therefore be taken to sum up the views formed during his Governor-Generalship, shows the very high importance which the British Government attached to Rammohun's campaign against suttee. After deploring the increase in the number of victims during the previous year, which he attributed to the fanatic spirit roused by the divided state of feeling among the Hindus, "his lordship in council does not despair of the best effects resulting from the free discussion of the matter by the people themselves, independently of European influence and interposition; and it only remains for him to watch carefully the indications of a change of sentiment amongst the people and to encourage to the utmost every favourable disposition." He thus went out of office with the hope that the practice would be extirpated not by the peremptory authority of the Government but by persuasive arguments of Rammohun and his following. He had reason highly to appraise the effect of their humane propaganda. It is interestingly attested in Bishop Heber's Journal. From a conversation with Dr. Marshman, January 15, 1824, he learns in the first place that suttee had increased in recent years, an increase which the Baptist imputed to "the increasing luxury of the higher and middling classes, and to their expensive imitation of European habits," which made them eager to avoid the expense of maintaining widows. "But," Dr. Marshman is reported to have said, "the Brahmans have no longer the power and popularity which they had when he first remembers India, and among the laity many powerful and wealthy persons agree, and publicly express their agreement, with Rammohun Roy in reprobating the custom, which is now well known to be not commanded by any of the Hindu sacred books, though some of them speak of it as a meritorious sacrifice." But opinion among the Government officials was, Bishop Heber remarks, still divided as to the practicabilty of prohibition. The Nizamat Adaulut was indeed, slowly moving towards the desired end. Mr. Haringay, one of the judges, proposed in a minute of June 28, 1823, to issue further regulations enabling the police to prevent suttees taking place until full inquiry had been made. At the same time he personally approved suppression. His brother judges however held that to impose fresh regulations and safeguards was to deepen in the native mind the impression of the rite being legalized and countenanced by Government. Rather than add new ragulations, the majority of the Court were (July 23, 1824) of opinion that it would be preferable to pass an enactment for the future prohibition of suttees throughout the country. The pressure of public opinion in Great Britain and in their own Court, led the Directors to express themselves very vigorously on the subject to the new Governor-General, in a despatch of June 17, 1823. On Dec. 3rd 1824, Lord Amherst in the course of his reply, declared:-

We entirely participate with your honourable Court in the feelings of detestation with which you view the rite and in your earnest desire to have it suppressed, and we beg to assure you that nothing but the apprehension of evils infinitely greater than those arising from the existence of the practice could induce us to tolerate it for a single day.

The famine in the southern provinces of the Deccan in 1824 called forth from fourteen native signatories a singularly Catholic appeal, which if not composed (as it was not signed) by Rammohun Roy, shows how his inter-religion views were spreading. The appeal was for funds to establish in the famine-stricken districts chatrams, or charitable inns, for Hindus, Moslems, Christians, as the case might require, each providing the food needed by the respective religionaries. Christians were adjured to contribute in the name of Christ, and the duty was enforced by reference to His teachings. Moslems were similarly reminded of the precept and example of their Holy Prophet and Ali; and Hindus were referred to humane sayings of Krishna and Bhisma. The Appeal proceeds:

We conjure those of the three faiths of Christians, Mussulmans, and Hindus, in the name of our common Creator and God, to show the affection that man, as a commoner of nature, should bear to his fellowman, by relieving so many individuals of those three religions who are dying daily for want of their usual sustenance.

The same wide sympathy with men of different faiths which breathes through this Appeal is illustrated by a project which Rammohun cherished a year later. Writing in 1826, Mr. William Adam announces that Rammohun "is about commencing a life of Mohammed who has, he thinks, been much misrepresented both by his friends and his enemies." The line he took over the 'Precepts of Jesus,' against non-Christians and orthodox alike, suggests the line which this biography of the prophet of Arabia would have followed. It is a matter of profound regret that the idea was never carried out. A study of the founder of Islam by the founder of the Brahmo Samaj would doubtless have formed a valuable contribution to the religious development of modern India.

The close of this period was temporarily clouded for Rammohun by grave domestic anxiety. His son was "the confidential native servant of the Burdwan Collector of Revenue" and was prosecuted on a charge of embezzlement of the public money. He seems, writes Mr. Adam, "to be the victim, partly of the negligence of his employer and the envy of his fellow servants." It was only a part of the campaign of persecution carried on in the law courts against the hated reformer. Suspense of the issue weighed heavily on Rammohun's mind. We find him under the pressure of neglecting his correspondence with English and American friends, as Mr. Adam feels bound to explain to them. The youth was acquitted in the Circuit Court in February, 1826, but the case was carried thence before the Nizamut Adaulut. Happily, Mr. Adam was able to write in August of the same year that "Rammohun Roy is very well, having lately brought the prosecution against his son to a successful issue." But the end of this vexatious forensic attack was not yet.

The intensity of fatherly affection which Rammohun here displayed sets in a more remarkable light the method of education he had adopted with his growing boys. Mr. William Adam, in his lecture on Rammohun, declares:-

He employed no direct means, no argument or authority, no expostulation or entreaty to turn his sons from the idolatrous practices and belief, in which they had been educated by the female members of his family and by the Brahman priests whom they consulted and followed. He gave them a good education; by his personal demeanour secured a place in their esteem and affection; set them an example in his life and writings; and then left them to the influence of idolatrous associations on the one hand, and to the unfettered exercise of their reason on the other. His eldest son, the hope of his heart, for some time after attaining mature age, continued an idolator; but before his father's death, with his. younger brother, abandoned the superstition of the country, and zealously co- operated with his father.*

* From Rakhal Das Haldar, in his notes to the lecture, we learn concerning these youths, that the elder died without leaving male issue, and that the younger, Rama Prasad Ray, "lived to attain eminence at the bar of the highest Judicial Tribunal of Bengal, and was the first native Justice elect of the High Court at Fort William, though he was prevented by death from sitting on the Bench."

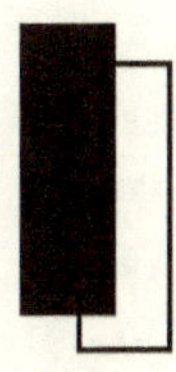

Founding the Brahmo Samaj (1826 -1828)

We now enter on the most distinctive period of Rammohun's crowded career. What has already transpired has made it abundantly evident that he was above all and beneath all a religious personality. The many and far-reaching ramifications of his prolific energy were forthputtings of one purpose. The root of his life was religion. He would never have been able to go so far or to move his countrymen so mightily as he did but for the driving power of an intense theistic passion. The years in which he stands out as the founder of a distinct religious community must therefore be regarded as the most characteristic epoch in his history.

It is fortunate for us that just at the opening of this period we have an authoritative statement of Rammohun's attitude to the two great historic faiths between which he stood. In a letter to Dr. Tuckerman, dated Feb. 18-20, 1826, Mr. William Adam thus explains the Reformer's relation to Hinduism and Christianity, an explanation which, it will be seen, Rammohun himself endorsed:-

Mr. Tuppin in one of his letters asks - Does Rammohun Roy profess to be a Christian ?......I find it difficult to give a definite answer to this question, but the nearest approach to the truth, although I hope and believe that it is not the truth itself, would perhaps be to say that he is both a Christian and a Hindu, Christian with Christians and a Hindu with Hindus. And before you say either that I am contradicting myself, or that he is insincere in his religion, you must candidly weigh all the circumstances in which he is placed. In the first place then, his relinquishment of idolatry is absolute, total, public, uncompromising; and when you reflect who he is and what he is, this is of itself an invincible test of integrity of religious principle and conduct. But his relinquishment of idolatry is not inconsistent with the retention of his Brahmanical rights, and observance of the rules of caste, the latter of which is necessary to the former and both are necessary to enable him to be useful to his countrymen, the thing which he has most at heart. On the other hand, although he may safely relinquish idolatry, he cannot safely profess Christianity. The profession would involve loss of caste, loss of property, loss of influence, loss of everything but a name; and while be employs caste, property, influence everything to promote, not the nominal profession merely, but the enlightened belief and salutary influences of Christianity, his claim to be a practical although not a nominal Christian would seem to be undoubted. In this point of view, Hinduism furnishes the antidote to its own inherent intolerance. There is another reason for the course he has pursued. The profession of Christianity would identify him in the opinion of Hindus not with the respectable and liberal portion of the Christian population, but with the low, ignorant and depraved converts recently made by the English, or long since made by the Portuguese, missionaries, and in the opinion of Mussulmans who hold him in high esteem, with Trinitarians generally; for such Mussulmans suppose all Christians to be. In other words, the profession of Christianity would inevitably, in the present circumstances of this country, identify him with persons from whom he differs as widely as from those with whom he is now identified. He has, therefore, only a choice of evils, and he has hitherto chosen that which, although he groans under its bondage, leaves him greater liberty and usefulness than he could otherwise possess. I have thus given you the view of his circumstances and conduct which I have reason to suppose he would himself give you if he were now writing to you; and I have only further to add that... I do not feel these reasons to be quite so convincing as they appear to him.... I have no doubt

that in his opinion they possess all the force necessary fully to justify him in the sight of God and his own conscience in the course which he has pursued.

Since writing the preceding paragraph, I have had an opportunity of showing it to Rammohun Roy, who considers it a correct representation of his feelings and sentiments.

In a later letter to Dr. Tuckerman, of date Oct. 14, 1826, Mr. Adam remarks:-

You inquire whether Rammohun Roy is a Unitarian Christian, . . or only a Theist, and on this point I beg to refer you to my No. VI., which contains all the information I can give you respecting it... In addition to the particulars then given, he permits me now to say that failing the male heirs of his own body, of whom there are two, he has bequeathed the whole of his property to our Mission; and while he regrets the appearance of ostentation which this statement may bear, he leaves it to yourself to judge whether he would have been likely to do so if he did not sincerely embrace the Christian religion and ardently desire to extend its blessings to his countrymen.

To Dr. Tuckerman's inquiry concerning the rites of caste which Rammohun as a Brahman observed, Mr. Adam (June 24, 1827) answered:-

All the rules in the present state of Hindu society he finds it necessary to observe relate to eating and drinking. He must not eat of the food forbidden to Brahmins nor with persons of a different religion from the Hindu or of a different caste or tribe from his own. This is the only remnant of the rules of caste to which he still adheres, and even this remnant I have reason to know he frequently but secretly disregards... Both in the marriages and deaths that happen within his domestic circle he rigidly abstains in his own person from every approach to the idolatrous rites usually practised on such occasions, although he does not prohibit the other members of his family from engaging in them if they think proper.

This compliance with the rules of caste must, one would think, have been extremely distasteful to Rammohun, inasmuch as he considered caste to be one of the gravest of the many ills under which his country laboured. In a private letter written about this time (January 18, 1828) he thus expresses himself:-

I agree with you that in point of vices the Hindus are not worse than the generality of Christians in Europe and America; but I regret to say that the present system of religion adhered to by the Hindus is not well calculated to promote their political interest. The distinction of castes, introducing innumerable divisions and sub-divisions among them has entirely deprived them of patriotic feeling, and the multitude of religious rites and ceremonies and the laws of purification have totally disqualified them from undertaking any difficult enterprise.... It is, I think, necessary that some change should take place in their religion, at least for the sake of their political advantage and social comfort. I fully agree with you that there is nothing so sublime as the precepts taught by Christ and there is nothing equal to the simple doctrines he inculcated.

He goes on to deplore the way in which they were disregarded and distorted by Christians, but hopes for a change to be effected by the growing spirit of inquiry and humanity. It is said that Rammohun "translated into Bengali a work called 'Bastra Suchit' written by a Buddhist named Buddha Ghosh, opposing caste. This is an interesting link of connection between the ancient and most famous movement for reforming Hinduism, and its modern successor. It illustrates anew Rammohun's readiness to borrow books or arguments from any religion, Mohammedan, Buddhist, or Christian, if only thereby he might purify Hinduism.

In a letter of introduction to Jeremy Bentham, of Nov. 14, 1830, Mr. J. Young, whom some one called "his dearest friend in India," says of Rammohun:-

He has externally maintained so much, and no more, of Hindoo custom as his profound knowledge of their sacred books enabled him to justify relaxing, however, little by little, yet never enough to justify his being 'out of the pale.' I need not say that in private it is otherwise, and that prejudices of all sorts are duly contemned by our philosopher.

His impartial attitude towards other faiths was not yet understood by his Unitarian allies. From many other passages in their letters partly cited above, it is pretty evident that both Mr. Adam and Dr. Tuckerman had convinced themselves that Rammohun accepted what they called "the Divine authority of our Lord." He certainly was very closely identified with the Unitarian Mission. The Unitarian services had, for the time, been given up; as a consequence, we find Mr. Adam writing of Rammohun, in February, 1826, "at present he does not attend anywhere," but expressing the confidence that as soon as Unitarian worship was resumed he would as before be among the most regular worshippers. From the letter of October 14, 1826, cited above, we learn that Rammohun had made provision in his will for Mr. Adam's family, a tribute to the cause as well as to the friendship of the Unitarian missionary. Earlier in the same year he had been "so much gratified by the perusal of the 'One Hundred Arguments for the Unitarian Faith,' " sent him by the American Unitarian Association" that he ..."caused an edition to be printed at his own Press for distribution in Calcutta."

Along with Dwarkanath Thakur, Prusunnu Coomar and Radha Prasad Roy, and six Englishmen he served on the Unitarian Committee. In the renewal of that Committee's activity in 1827 he had a prominent share. On Mr. Adam (whose journalistic venture, the Calcutta Chronicle, was ruthlessly suppressed by the Government a few months later) resuming operations as missionary, Rammohun's son, Radha Prasad, offered a site adjoining the Anglo-Hindu school for a native chapel and school. The cost of the proposed building was put at three or four thousand rupees which, Mr. Adam wrote (to Rev. W. J. Fox, Aug. 1. 1827), "Rammohun Roy thinks he will be able to collect among his native friends." Unitarians in Britain had despatched, some months previously, about 15,000 rupees.* * Pending the anticipated erection, the Committee rented the Harkaru public rooms which were attached to the Harkaru newspaper and library; and there morning service was commenced by Mr. Adam on Sunday, August 3, 1827.

Thus began Rammohun's second attempt to find his Church - his fellowship of worship and propaganda - under the auspices of Unitarian Christianity.

His literary activity revived about this time and in directions characteristic of it. "For a period of more than two years," he wrote to Mr. J. B. Estlin, February 7, 1827, "owing to the most afflicting circumstances arising from the hostile feelings of some individuals towards my family. I found myself totally unable to pursue any undertaking or carry on correspondence, even with those whom I sincerely loved and revered." But, his son's trial having ended satisfactorily in 1826, he managed to publish in the following year "A translation into English of a Sanskrit Tract inculcating the Divine worship; esteemed by those who believe in the revelation of the Vedas as most appropriate to the nature of the Supreme Being." This is really a commentary, partly composed of sayings of the sages, on "the Gayatree, the most sacred text of the Vedas." The version given of that mystic formula reads, "We meditate on the cause of all, pervading all, and internally ruling all material objects, from the sun down to us and others." As though by way of offset to this excursion into the Vedic Scriptures, we find+ Rammohun engaged with Mr. Adam in translating the 'Sermon on the Mount' into Sanskrit, the idea being eventually to turn the whole of the 'Precepts of Jesus' into that language. Towards the close of the year, he published a little tract entitled "Answer of an Hindu to the Question. " Why do you frequent a Unitarian place of worship instead of the numerously attended Established Churches?" It bears the signature of Chandra Shekar Deb, a disciple of Rammohun; but, as Mr. Adam informed Dr. Tuckerman in a letter dated Jan. 18, 1828, it was entirely Ram- mohun's own composition. Mr. Adam adds, "I regret that he continues to publish these things in the name of another, but I cannot succeed in dissuading him from it." This persistent assumption of other people's names is indeed a puzzle. There seems to have been a secretive strain in Rammohun's blood, which made him favour this pseudonymous authorship. The answer simply amounted to saying that in a Unitarian place of worship he heard nothing of Incarnation, Union of Two Natures, or Trinity, doctrines which he regarded as only a variant of the anthropomorphic and polytheistic mythology of popular Hinduism.

But the Unitarian exotic did not thrive. Its roots would not strike. The English morning service begun in August was very indifferently attended. "* From the first it "received little support from avowed Unitarians." "Even a majority of the Committee regularly absented themselves. An evening service was tried in November. It was attended at first by 60 to 80, but gradually "dwindled almost to nothing."+ Mr. Adam was surprised to find the native members of his Committee stoutly opposed to the erection of a native chapel for lectures in the native language. Their plea was that "anything said or written in the vernacular tongue will be degraded and despised in consequence of the medium through which it is conveyed." English, Persian, and Sanskrit were the only languages which would secure respect. Mr. Adam endeavoured to console him. self by a course of "familiar lectures on the First Principles of Religion" which he began in October "for the exclusive benefit of the natives... in the native part of the city" in Rammohun's Anglo-Hindu school, in fact. His audiences at first ranged from 12 to 25. But even Rammohun did not attend, and in the end poor Mr. Adam was left "with scarcely a single individual to address. " Before things had reached this pass, he made gallant efforts to turn the tide. On the 30th of December, 1827, he got the Unitarian Committee to adopt a proposal which he had drafted so long ago as May of the previous year, to constitute themselves into "a more complete organization" to be known as "the British Indian Unitarian Association. "This step was intended to deepen the local esprit de corps and bring members into closer touch with Unitarians in Great Britain and America. But the Sunday congregations went on declining. Then Mr. Adam, thinking it wise to give up the services before the attendance had become ridiculously small, proposed that he should be sent on a missionary journey to Madras. But the Committee refused consent, on Rammohun's representations chiefly, that the funds could not stand the cost and that Mr. Adam was indispensable to Calcutta. There was no way out but to face failure and confess it. Mr. Adam had been baffled in all his plans. As we saw in our last chapter, he had tried to run the Anglo-Hindu school as a Mission agency, but had been so frequently baulked by Rammohun's autocratic will as in the end to be compelled to resign all share in its management. His congregations both British and native had run down almost to zero. He accordingly requested the Committee to point out some other form of missionary service which would justify him in receiving the stipend which came to him from abroad for that purpose. The Committee saw no "fit mode in which Mr. Adam can employ himself as a Unitarian missionary," and could therefore no longer disburse the stipend referred to. Poor Mr. Adam retired heartbroken." This decisive act seems to have taken place in the first half of 1828.

We are now brought to the verge of the foundation of the Brahmo Samaj. We have described Mr. Adam's futile endeavours somewhat fully, because it was upon the ruins of the Unitarian Mission that the new theistic Church was reared. Between the two movements there was the most direct connection. Religious beginnings are often lost in obscurity, but not so in this case. There are two accounts of the origin of the Brahmo Samaj: distinct and independent, but quite harmonious.

The popular and best known may be given first."+ In those days a newspaper was published, named the 'Harkara.' In the office of the Harkara the Rev. Mr. Adam had established an association under the name of the Unitarian Society. . . One day at the close of worship, Rammohun Roy with his disciples was returning from the Harkara office. On the road Tara Chand Chakravarti and Chandra Shekar Deb said, 'What need is there for us to go to the prayer house of strangers to perform our worship? We ought to erect a house of our own in which to worship one God.' This proposal was the first germ of the Brahmo Soamaj. The proposer, Chandra Shekar Deb, is now living.

+ The following is taken from "Little Stories about Rammohun W Roy," 2nd part, from Tattwabodhini No. 445, month Bhadra. 1828 (Bengal era). The recounter, Babu Rajnarain, whose father was a disciple and coadjutor of Rammohun Roy, states that he gave Kisori Chand Mitra for his Life of Rammohun, which appeared 36 years previously in the Calcutta Review, "these' anecdotes and others taken from the lips of my father.

When this event happened we have no precise indication. It could scarcely have occurred before or during the time when Rammohun was actively organizing the British Indian Unitarian Association (Dec. 30, 1827). It probably took place in the early part of 1828, when the Unitarian congregations were fast dwindling away. Whenever it was made, the suggestion at once impressed Rammohun. He consulted his comrades, Dwarkanath Thakur and Roy Kalinath Munshi. On their approving the idea, he called a meeting at his house, when these and other friends, including Prasanna Kumar Thakur and Mothuranath Mullick agreed to carry it out. A site at Shimla in Calcutta was first thought of, but subsequently abandoned; and until a suitable place could be found and building erected, it was decided to hire a house belonging to Kamal Lochan Bose, at Jorasanko, in the Chitpore Road, and there commence public worship.*

The other account makes Mr. Adam the proximate initiator of the Samaj. It is given in his letters, written while the new movement was in its earliest stages. In a letter to Mr. John Bowring, London, under date, Feb. 5, 1828, he writes:-

I must add before I conclude, that I am endeavouring to get the Hindu Unitarians in Calcutta to unite in forming an Association auxiliary to the British India Association, and for the establishment of the public worship of the One God among themselves, for the printing of tracts and for the diffusion of religious knowledge generally among their countrymen. To prevent prejudice from being excited, it will be necessary to keep Christianity out of view at present in connection with this auxiliary, but it will really be (what it perhaps may not be nominally) an auxiliary to our views, and a highly valuable one, too, if I can succeed in creating the necessary degree of interest to begin and carry it on.

On April 2, of the same year, he writes to Dr. Tucker-man, announcing the discontinuance of the native service, and remarking,-

Since then I have been using every endeavour in my power to induce Hindu Unitarians to unite among themselves for the promotion of our common objects, and I am not without hopes of succeeding, although I have a great deal of apathy to struggle against.

On January 22, 1829, writing to Dr. Tuckerman, he recalls the fact that "one of the resolutions"-presumably passed in connection with the formation of the British Indian Unitarian Association had invited all Unitarians, whether Christian or Hindu, to form themselves into Associations, etc., and proceeds,

There has accordingly been formed a Hindu Unitarian Association, the object of which is, however, strictly Hindu and not Christian, i.e., to teach and practise the worship of One Only God on the basis of the divine authority of the Ved, and not of the Christian Scriptures. This is a basis of which I have distinctly informed Rammohun and my other native friends that I cannot approve.

But he has, he says, encouraged them to go forward, as he considers it "a step towards Christianity" and thinks that "the friendly feeling which happily exists between Christian and Hindu Unitarians should be preserved." He has, therefore, recommended his Committee to make a grant of 500 rupees to the Hindu Association, and has himself occasionally attended their services. This "Hindu Association" is, of course, the Brahmo Samaj.

There is no discrepancy between the two narratives. The idea may have arisen quite spontaneously without as well as within the circle of Hindu reformers. From the "great deal of apathy," indeed, which Mr. Adam complains of on April 2, it would seem that Chandra Sekhar Dev had not then made the suggestion on which Rammohun acted so eagerly. And from this it would follow that Mr. Adam really originated the idea, Rammohun having had it pressed on his notice since the beginning of February. The Hindu may have hung back until the project was broached by his own followers and their readiness to take action thereby attested. But, even if Mr. Adam can claim the credit of first suggesting the distinct organization for worship, we must remember that he was only a secondary agency. He and all his associations were spiritually begotten by Rammohun Roy. And the Brahmo Samaj was but the last development of a series of tentative social efforts which reached back to the very beginning of Rammohun's reforming career. Even when at Rungpur (1809-1814) he held meetings for religious discussion. In 1815 he founded the Atmiya Sabha and kept it going month by month until 1819. After that he still continued lecturing to a private circle of friends and followers. In 1821 he converted Adam from Trinitarianism and organized with him the Unitarian Committee. He had assisted in its resuscitation and re-organization in 1827. And now the group of comrades and disciples which had hung around him these many years were at last ready to form an independent community, no longer for dialectical or educational purposes only, but for worship, for distinctly religious fellowship. The share which Unitarianism had in the birth of the Brahmo Samaj was distinctly maieutic not maternal.

The great commencement took place on Wednesday, the 20th of August, 1828. Then the native theistic Church of modern India was born. It was at first called simply Brahma Sabha, the Society of God. The inaugural preacher was Ramchandra Surma. His discourse was upon the spiritual worship of God. His text, which was taken from various parts of the Hindu Scriptures, read, "God is one only without an equal. In whom abide all worlds and their inhabitants. Thus he who mentally perceives the Supreme Spirit, in all creatures, acquires perfect equanimity, and shall be absorbed into the highest essence, even into the Almighty."

All worship, whether of natural objects, images, persons was indirectly worship of the Supreme; but direct worship was the most excellent. Its superior excellence was attest- ed by revelation (" the Vedas, the Institutes of Manu, and all Scriptures of acknowledged authority"), by reason, which discarded all outward ceremonies and found worship to consist in self-discipline, self-realization, and service of others, and by experience; for while indirect worshippers quarreled with each other's partial views of

God, the direct worshiper had quarrel with none, for he adored the One God whom they also under howsoever imperfect and differing forms actually adored.

This sermon was translated into English by Tarachand Chakravarti, and published. In sending copies to a friend named Captain A. Froyer (Nov. 19), Rammohun spoke of it as "exhibiting the simplicity, comprehensiveness and tolerance which distinguish the religious belief and worship formerly adopted by one of the most ancient nations on earth and still adhered to by the more enlightened portion of their posterity."

Mr. Adam thus describes (to Dr. Tuckerman, January 22, 1829) the order of their weekly meeting, which was usually held on a Saturday evening, between 7 and 9:-

The service begins with two or three of the Pandits singing, or rather chanting in the cathedral style, some of the spiritual portions of the Veda, which are next explained in the vernacular dialect to the people by another Pandit. This is followed by a discourse in Bengali... and the whole is concluded by hymns both in Sanskrit and Bengali, sung with the voice and accompanied by instrumental music, which is also occasionally interposed between other parts of the service. The audience consists generally of from 50 to 60 individuals, several Pandits, a good many Brahmins, and all decent and attentive in their demeanour.

The Calcutta John Bull, of August 23, 1828, in reporting the opening ceremony in somewhat similar terms observes that in delivering the sermon the officiating minister lectured "from a separate room, that the Vedas may not be desecrated by being in the same apartment with the profanum vulgus of hearers." Two Telugu Brahmans were permanently secured for the recital of the Vedas. Utsavananda Vidyavagisa read from the Upanisads, and Ram Chandra Vidyavagisa explained them in Bengali. Tarachand Chakravarti was appointed the first secretary.

The new departure caused no little disappointment among European residents. The John Bull laments that the liberal Hindus have "from Unitarianism very naturally slid into pure Deism," and bewails the lost hope of Rammohun Roy becoming the great agent in Christianizing India. Even Mr. Adam's eyes were considerably opened. In the letter last cited he declares-

Rammohun Roy, I am persuaded, supports this institution, not because he believes in the divine authority of the Veda, but solely as an instrument for overthrowing idolatry. To be candid, however, I must add that the conviction has lately gained ground in my mind that he employs Unitarian Christianity in the same way, as an instrument for spreading pure and just notions of God, without believing in the divine authority of the Gospel.

But, however unpopular with Europeans, the new departure made its way among the educated Hindus of Calcutta. The numbers in which they attended, and the rapid increase in the funds of the Society showed a marked contrast to the fate of the earlier efforts put forth by the Unitarian Committee. The Samaj had evidently come to stay. It was no exotic imported from abroad. However suggested, it was an indigenous product of the Hindu mind; and it took root and grew.

As Rammohun and his band of disciples now stand out together as a distinct religious community, their mutual manner of life claims our attention. It was through these disciples that the work of the great reformer was carried on and made permanently fruitful; they were the "living stones" which he shaped into a lasting edifice. Of his relations to them we have only a few glimpses, but they are sufficient to set his work in a more genial and human light than that of the mere teacher or leader. We are told that he "always displayed much affection towards his disciples." In addressing any one of them he habitually said Beradar, the Persian word for brother. They, however, usually addressed him as Dewanji, the title of respect borne by the collector. Nor did he limit this fraternal appellation to his own following. He used it to all whom he met. And the brotherhood he believed in was no mere matter of names. It was Oriental in its warmth of demonstrativeness. It was Western in its equal freedom. It is said that "if any cause of joy arose he immediately embraced his followers. And he was not above receiving kindly words of rebuke from them, as we shall see later.

Rammohun made no secret of the strong theistic passion which ruled his life. A favourite disciple remarked that whenever he spoke of the Universal Theism, to the advocacy of which he had devoted himself, he was moved even to tears. Hearing of a man who from theist turned atheist, Rammohun rejoined, "And later he will become a beast. Yet intense as was his religious zeal and his aversion to disbelievers in deity, he could tolerate men of sceptical opinions even among his intimate friends. "Babu Prusunnu Coomar Thakur, had a great affection for Rammohun Roy, and for the Brahmo Samaj, but he was a sceptic. For this reason Rammohun Roy, called him a rustic philosopher. Hume and the French school of deniers were known urbi et orbi; Babu Prusunnu was a sort of country cousin aping the cut of their philosophic habit. Thus the master would banter and condemn, without alienating an unbelieving disciple.

"When not engaged in benevolent works," says Babu A. C. Bose," he was constantly advising his disciples." One disciple smitten with a fair Rachel had palmed upon him an ill-favoured Leah. Naturally wroth with his father, "The in-law, he was about to avenge himself for the deception by taking another wife. Rammohun dissuaded him. tree which bears excellent fruit is beautiful," said he. "If your wife bears you a fine child, you must consider her to be in all respects beautiful." The anecdotist adds that, as it actually turned out, "the sons of that disciple were the most forward in promoting widow-marriage and all the most excellent features in Rammohun Roy's beloved work in the Brahmo Samaj."

Like many other religious reformers, Rammohun introduced changes in dress. He adopted the costume of the Mussulmans. "He directed that a closely twisted turban should be worn instead of a loose one, and a choga instead of a skirt. He tried zealously to keep this style of dress in fashion."+ He made it a rule for himself and his disciples always to wear it when attending the Samaj. He was very particular about the observance of this rule. He asked a friend to reprove a disciple who had come to worship in his office clothes, the ordinary dhuti and chadar. He held that "handsome apparel should be worn in God's durbar." He was very careful in other ways to show respect to the act of Divine service. Thus he would never go to the Samaj save on foot; he only returned in his carriage. He did not usually reprimand a faulty follower, but when it was no longer a case of minor transgression but an offence of a serious nature, he did not hesitate to exercise discipline. "For excess in drinking he has refused to see the offender for six months. Thus the disciple was corrected."*

"Rammohun could not," as has been observed, " rebuke his followers for ordinary faults. But if he committed a fault himself, and a disciple reproved him he received the rebuke with great gentleness. According to the custom of the time, Rammohun Roy wore long hair. After his bath he was somewhat long in dressing. Observing this his plain spoken disciple, Tara Chand Chakravrati, quoted the first line of a song running,' How much longer will you please yourself studying your face in the glass?' and added. 'Is this song only for other people, Mahashoi?' Confounded, Rammohun Roy replied, Ha! brother, you are quite right."'+

Of the daily habits of the master, the following interesting account is furnished by Mr. G. N. Tagore, on the authority of his father, who was an intimate friend and disciple :-

Rammohun Roy was an early riser, and regularly took his morning walk. He used to oil his body every morning before bathing. Two big fellows used to oil him and shampoo him. While engaged in this process he would read by rotation and day-by-day in parts the Sanskrit grammar 'Moogdhabodha.' After bath he would have his breakfast in the Indian fashion, squatting on the ground, surrounded by Indian utensils for food. His breakfast consisted of fish and rice and perhaps milk too. He never took any meals between his morning and evening meal. He generally used to work till two and then go out and see his European friends in the afternoon. His evening meal was between seven and eight, and that as in the English fashion but the dishes were Mohammedan dishes, Pillan, Kofta, Korma, etc.

He never went out without his shawl turban, not like the present Bengalis with a French smoking cap. When at home he was always dressed in the Mohammedan fashion, Chupkan, Ungaga, Pyjama, and a skull cap on his head. He never sat bareheaded, following in this instance the Mohammedan custom. He never gave up his Brahmanical thread. His spoken Bengali was highly classified in structure. His English was good, but he spoke with great hesitancy lest he should commit some verbal error or other.

Another and slightly different account of Rammohun's day is gathered by a friend of the author, R. D. H., from conversation with Ramhari Das, "the old and faithful servant of Rammohun Roy," at Burdwan in 1863

He used to rise very early, about 4 a. m., to take coffee, and then to have his morning walk, accompanied by a few persons. He would generally return home before sunrise, and when engaged in morning duties Golokdas Napit would read to him newspapers of the day. Tea would follow; gymnastics; after resting a little he would attend to correspondence; then have his daily bath; breakfast at 10 a. m.; hearing newspapers read an hour's siesta on the bare top of a table; getting up he would pass his time either in conversation or in making visits. Tiffin at 3 p.m.; dessert 5 p.m. Evening walk; supper at 10 p.m. He would sit up to midnight conversing with friends. He would then retire to bed again eating his favourite cake, which he called "Halila." When engaged in writing he would be alone.

If no man is a hero to his valet, just as little should we expect a man to be a saint to his cook. Yet Rammohun's cook who accompanied his master to England and knew him in his decadence as well as in his prime, bore witness to his punctual piety: "The worship of God was Rammohun Roy's first daily work.

A pretty little incident is preserved by babu R. N. Bose,* who had it from his father, which sets the dignified Brahman in a new and attractive light.

Rammohun Roy was one morning walking in Bow Bazaar. He perceived a vegetable-seller looking in vain for some one to place his load of vegetables on his head. Although dressed in nice clothing, Rammohun Roy did not hesitate to place the basket on the man's head. Many gentlemen walk in the early morning in handsome garments, but how many among them would show their benevolence by an act of this kind?

It was in this circle of disciples that "The Hymns of Rammohun Roy" were mostly born. He lacked not, it seems, "the accomplishment of verse." He had cherished ambitions as a poet, but as he playfully remarked, Bharat Chandra's achievements in Bengali poetry were such as forbade any competition. But he did not shrink from employing the still plastic Bengali as the metrical vehicle of his religious life. All the hymns in the volume quoted above, except those marked by author's initials, are from his pen. By those who know the language they are said to belong to a very high order of religious poetry, the sublimity of the thought being admirably sustained by the dignity and music of the words. A translation of one of Rammohun's hymns by A. Tosh, may be cited here as illustrative of its purport:

> Think of that final day on earth, Appalling thought!
>
> When friends and neighbors all will speak,
>
> But thou wilt not.
>
> When with thy wife and little babes,
>
> To thee so dear, To part shall sure thy bosom rack
>
> With pain severe.
>
> When piercing eyes their strength shall lose,
>
> The pulse be still,
>
> The vital warmth for ever fled,
>
> The limbs be chill.
>
> Thy friends shall mourn,
>
> the friends shall weep most bitterly;
>
> And for thy hoards of cherished wealth
>
> Anxious thou'lt be.

Then, yet be wise, thy pride abjure,

Thyself resign

To that Eternal Source of Truth

His Will Divine!

Prose versions of two other hymns by Rammohun Roy may also be given:

Meditate on the Only One

Who pervades land, water, and air,

Who has created this Universe of which there is no bound.

He knows all, but none can know Him.

He is Lord of Lords, the God of Gods, and the Master of Masters:

Let us know this Adorable One.

A thing that surpasses speech,

How can it be described in words?

Of Him the Universe is a Shadow:

He is without likeness as the Scriptures declare:

 Where can we find His likeness?

If thou wouldst know, meditate with singleness of mind.

Then thou shalt attain true knowledge, and shalt be free from error.

 I know no other way.

The spirit of sacred song extended from the master to the disciples. They brought him their verses, and when the hymn pleased him, he would reward the author with a joyous embrace. Several of their compositions are included in his collection where they are distinguished from his by appended initials.

Of the founder at the close of this memorable epoch an interesting picture is presented by Col. Young, who writes from intimate personal knowledge, in a letter dated Calcutta, Sept. 30, 1828, to Jeremy Bentham. It gives quite another aspect of these eventful years. This is what the Colonel says:--

His whole time almost has been occupied for the last two years in defending himself and his son against a bitter and vindictive persecution which has been got up against the latter nominally, but against himself and his abhorred free opinions in reality - by a conspiracy of his own bigoted countrymen, protected and encouraged, not to say instigated, by some of ours - influential and official men who cannot endure that a presumptuous "black" should tread so closely upon the heels of the dominant white class, or rather should pass them in the march of mind. Rammohun Roy, after an arduous and prolonged battle through gradations of tribunals, has at length by dint of talent, perseverance, right, got the better in the last resort; but the strife and the magnitude of the stake and the long despairs of justice have shattered his nerves and bodily health and his energies of mind. It is now over, and I hope most fervently that he will recover himself again. Not only has he no equal here among his countrymen, but he has none that at all approach to equality, even among the little "sacred squadron" of disciples whom he is slowly and gradually gathering around him in despite of obstacles. But he perseveres, and does make a distinct and visible progress, slow as it is very slow. It must increase in geometrical ratio if he is only spared long enough to organize the elements he is gathering together of resistance to superstition and fanaticism.

It is strange that such a man should be looked upon coldly, not to say disliked by the mass of Europeans, for he is greatly attached to us and our regime. Not that he loves our churches, or priests, or lawyers, or politicians, but because he considers the contact of our superior race with his degraded and inferior countrymen as the only means and chance they have of improving themselves in knowledge and energy.

One regrets to record this indictment of Anglo-Indian sentiment, all the more that it is so well substantiated. The native champion of English civilization deserved better treatment from our countrymen.

The ominous reference to Rammohun's health will not escape the reader's notice.

The Abolition of Suttee (1828 -1830)

The concluding stages of the Anti-Suttee movement form a highly instructive chapter in the history of the British government of India. It is interesting to watch the slow and cautious steps with which the official mind approached the decision which was at last precipitated by the resolute action of one strong personality. The feeling of the authorities had been, as we have seen, opposed to forcible repression of the rite. They preferred to hope that the influence of European education and the efforts of native reformers like Rammohun Roy would lead to its gradual desuetude. Out of this otiose optimism they were startled by the sudden increase of victims in 1825. The annual tale of suttees rose at a bound from 577 to 639, an advance of more than ten per cent. And the increase was not least rapid in and around Calcutta, the very district where European culture was most strongly entrenched. The Nizamat Adalat considered the matter afresh (in Nov. 1826). Judge Smith again insisted on immediate and entire prohibition; and he was supported in this demand by Judge Ross who expressed the belief that it would not, as had been feared, cause any disaffection among the native troops. These minutes coming before the Council, Vice-President Bayley (Jan. 13, 1827) could not commit himself to so peremptory a policy, but recommended that suttee should be prohibited in the territories where the earlier regulations were not in force, and where the British sway had been recently introduced, viz. in the districts of Delhi, Saugor, Nerbudda, Kumaoon, and Rungpore. Mr. Harington (Feb. 18, 1827) drafted a Minute for the suppression of suttee, against the time when that measure should be decided on. On March Ist, Vice-President Combermere strongly advocated the immediate adoption of Mr. Bayley's proposals. Lord Amherst (Mar. 18) declined the taking of this step, as he did not believe the practice prevailed in the districts specified, or that half measures would be productive of goed; and he was not prepared to enact its total suppression. He trusted to the diffusion of knowledge among the natives for the gradual eradication of the "detestable superstition." He "would rather wait a few years" for this desirable consummation. At the end of 1827 the Judges reiterated their convictions on the matter, and Mr. Bayley urged his plea once more. On Jan. 4, 1828, Lord Amherst again declined to legislate, looking to "general instruction and the unostentatious exertions of our local officers" to bring about the diminution, and, "at no very distant period the final extinc- tion of the barbarous rite." This is practically his last word on the subject. Two months later he left India.

He was succeeded in the Governor-Generalship by a man of very different character. Lord William Bentinck was one of those resolute Englishmen, of slight culture but re-

markable practical insight, who, seeing that a certain thing needs to be done, do it, and by the fact accomplished dissipate a thousand fears and difficulties. Faced with an ugly deficit and charged with unpopular commissions from the Directors, he cheerily undertook one fresh measure after another of dreaded reform, and showed how much stronger one man in earnest is than a whole crowd of conventional obstacles. He found the suttee problem confronting him. He was not content, like Lord Amherst, to "wait a few years." He proceeded to grapple with it at once. He was well aware that the ultimate sanction of British sway was the sword; and his first quest was to know how far the army would support him. Confidential inquiries from forty-nine experienced officers elicited the gratifying information that the Sepoy would be scarcely if at all affected by the prohibition of the practice. Twenty-four out of the forty-nine officers declared in favour of its immediate and entire abolition; only five were opposed to change of any kind. The army was safe.

The judiciary was daily becoming more pronounced. The humane zeal of local British magistrates outran their legal powers. Cases occurred where they interfered to prevent suttees which the law allowed; and the Supreme Court was forced, on appeal, to sanction the perpetration of the horrid deed. But the English gentlemen who formed the Nizamat Adalat winced under the charge of "unnecessarily authorizing suicide"; and we are not surprised to find that in 1828 before the reports of the military officers had been presented four judges out of five declared for putting a stop at once and forever to the hateful custom. A year later all five judges were agreed. The Superintendents of Police for both Upper and Lower Provinces emphatically vouched for the complete safety of the step. Nine-tenths of the public functionaries in the interior were reported to be in its favour. Anglo-Indian opinion was practically unanimous.

Native opinion was more difficult to sound directly. But the Governor-General had too keen an eye for the material facts of the situation to overlook the value of the man who had been a life-long mediator between Hindu and European civilizations; and he was still less likely to omit consulting the great native champion of the Anti-Suttee movement. Lord William took counsel of Rammohun Roy. There is an interesting story of the way their first interview was arranged, which we transcribe from the Rev. Principal Macdonald's lecture on the Hindu Reformer * :--

* Published at the Herald Press, Calcutta, 1879. The lecturer gives the incident on the authority of m_{2} Bengali friend." Essentially the same account was communicated in writing to the Commemoration of Rammohun Roy in January, 1879, by Rammohun's "oldest pupil," Ananda Chandra Basu. His version of his Master's declinature runs: "I am withdrawn from worldly affairs and am devoted to the reading of the Shastras and the study of religion," etc.

Lord William Bentinck, the Governor-General, on hearing that he would likely receive considerable help from the Rajah in suppressing the pernicious custom of widow-burning, sent one of his aide-de-camp to him expressing his desire to see him. To this the Rajah replied, "I have now given up all worldly avocations, and am engaged in religious culture and in the investigation of truth. Kindly express my humble respects to the Governor-General and inform him that I have no inclination to appear before his august presence, and therefore I hope that he will kindly pardon me." These words the aide-de-camp conveyed to the vice roy, who enquired, "What did you say to Rammohun Roy?" The aide-de- camp replied, "I told him that Lord William Bentinck, the Governor- General, would be pleased to see him." The Governor-General answered, "Go back and tell him again that Mr. William Bentinck will be highly obliged to him if he will kindly see him once." This the aide-de-camp did and Rammohun Roy could no longer refuse the urgent and polite request of his lordship.

The incident sheds light on the character of both the illustrious reformers. Rammohun's refusal may at first cause some surprise. He might have been expected to welcome conference with a ruler so able and willing to accelerate reform. But it must be observed that the invitation gave no hint of the particular purpose for which it was issued. Ram- mohun did no more than decline an invitation to Court; he pleaded a distaste for its worldly pageantry and frivolous ambitions; and perhaps he was unwilling to give colour to the charge of his being a tool of the conquerors. When he found it was the man and not the Court functionary who appealed to him, he straightway waived all scruple and agreed to come.

A more official and less picturesque account of the matter is given by the India Gazette, of July 27, 1829:-

An eminent native philanthropist who has long taken the lead of his countrymen on this great question has been encouraged to submit his views of it in a written form, and has been subsequently honoured with an audience by the Governor-General, who, we learn, has expressed his anxious desire to put an end to a custom constituting so foul a blot.

The Gazette goes on to mention three courses as open to the Government, either rigidly to enforce existing regulations; or to suppress suttee in the provinces of Bengal and Behar where it was most prevalent, but where British rule was longest known and best appreciated; or to abolish it throughout the Presidency.

The purport of Rammohun's advice to the Governor-General has been preserved in Lord William Bentinck's Minute of Nov. 8. And here another surprise awaits us. We naturally suppose that the leader of the revolt against the burning of widows would eagerly grasp at the prospect of its prompt and forcible suppression by Government. But Rammohun positively endeavoured to dissuade Lord Bentinck from this drastic project. The Governor-General, after detailing Mr. Horace Wilson's arguments against abolition, wrote on:

I must acknowledge that a similar opinion as to the probable excitation of a deep distrust of our future intentions was mentioned to me in conversation by that enlightened native, Rammohun Roy, a warm advocate for the abolition of sati and of all other superstitions and corruptions, engrafted on the Hindu religion, which he considers originally to have been a pure deism. It was his opinion that the practice might be suppressed quietly and unobservedly by increasing the difficulties and by the indirect agency of the police. He apprehended that any public enactment would give rise to general apprehension; that the reasoning would be: 'While the English were contending for power they deemed it politic to allow universal toleration and to respect our religion, but having obtained the supremacy their first act is a violation of their profession, and the next will probably be, like the Muhammadan conquerors, to force upon us their own religion.'

We may explain Rammohun's attitude by recalling his constitutional aversion to coercion; and any one who had undergone the bitter persecution which had fallen to his lot might be pardoned for over-estimating the strength of popular antagonism to reform. The man of force argued differently from the man of suasion. He observed that out of 463 suttees 420 took place in the Lower Provinces and 287 in the Calcutta Division. The figures for suttees in the Bengal Presidency during the last four years in which the practice was tolerated are given thus:-

DIVISIONS	1825	1826	1827	1828
CALCUTTA	398	324	337	309
DACCA	101	65	49	47
MURSHIDABAD	21	8	2	10
PATNA	47	65	55	55
BENARES	55	48	49	33
BARELLY	17	8	18	10
TOTAL	639	518	510	464

The people in these districts had through the centuries been so habituated to submission that "insurrection or hostile opposition to the ruling power may be affirmed to be an impossible danger." Had suttee been prevalent among "the bold and manly people" of the Upper Provinces, the problem would have been fraught with much graver peril. But, as the faculty of resistance had all but died out of the chief practicers of suttee, their apprehensions and suspicions might be safely disregarded.

So Lord William Bentinck cut the Gordian knot; and on the 4th of December, 1829, the Regulation was passed which declared the practice illegal and punishable as a criminal offence. All persons convicted of aiding and abetting in the sacrifice of a Hindu widow, whether she were a willing victim or not, whether she requested them or not, were pronounced guilty of culpable homicide; and where violence or other means of overpowering the victim's will were employed, the death sentence might, at the discretion of the Court, be inflicted. Suttee was abolished. The reputation of the British Government and the fair fame of religion itself were redeemed from one of the foulest stains.

It would not be just to describe this result as a triumph of principle over policy. The toleration of suttee hitherto had been due to a conflict of principles. On the one side was the plain principle of humanity, which demanded the instant suppression of the rite. On the other side was the sacred principle of religious liberty, which forbade the conqueror to interfere with the religious practices of a subject race. One cannot but admire the sensitive magnanimity which mingled with the calculating prudence of the British rulers and made them shrink from doing violence even to the most barbarous and outrageous dictates of the native conscience.

It is Rammohun's distinctive glory that he relieved the British Government from this deadlock. He proved from the authoritative standards of Hinduism that suttee was not a religious duty. He did more than this. He showed that not religious devotion, but the avaricious desire of relatives to avoid the cost of supporting the widow, had a great deal to do with the perpetuation of suttee. Its suppression would therefore do no wrong to the faith which British honour had pledged itself to tolerate and respect. The principles of humanity and of religious liberty no longer clashed. The atrocity could consistently be put down. This solution of the difficulty was set in the forefront of the prohibitory regulation:-

The practice of suttee, or of burning or burying alive the widows of Hindoos, is revolting to the feelings of human nature; it is nowhere enjoined by the religion of the Hindoos as an imperative duty; on the contrary, a life of purity and retirement on the part of the widow is more especially and preferably inculcated, and by a vast majority of that people throughout India the practice is not kept up nor observed; in some extensive districts it does not exist; in those in which it has been most frequent it is notorious that in many instances acts of atrocity have been perpetrated which have been shocking to the Hindoos themselves, and in their eyes unlawful and wicked. The measures hitherto adopted to discourage and prevent such acts have failed of success, and the Governor- General in Council is deeply impressed with the conviction that the abuses in question cannot be effectually put to end without abolishing the practice altogether.

But for the researches and the agitation carried on by Rammohun Roy, it is a question whether this preamble could have been written. Certain it is that the sentences which we have italicised would have fallen almost powerless but for the way Rammohun had driven home the truths they contained by speech and newspaper and pamphlet to the native mind.

But the old custom was not to be surrendered without a strong protest. The 'Sumachar Chundrika,' the organ of Conservative Hinduism, sounded the alarm; and the India Gazette of Nov. 30th announced that a petition against the abolition of widow-burning was already in progress. The Gazette expressed the hope that the Sambad Kaumudi and the Bungu

Doot, as representing the more liberal portion of the native public, would correct current misconceptions and set the action of the Government in the right light. This deserves notice, as tribute to the value of Rammohun's journalistic work. The petition against the new regulation found little support, the Gazette said, among the respectable and influential classes. Signatures were procured with difficulty, having to be extorted by threats and taunts. So stated the Asiatic Journal of June 1830, which even went so far as to declare that "the Government had satisfied itself that the majority of the native community was decidedly opposed to the practice."

At last on January 14th (1830), "a numerous and respectable body of petitioners," as the Governor-General described them, consisting of 800 inhabitants of Calcutta, laid before him their prayer for the abandonment of the prohibition. The main purpose of their representations was to overthrow the position which Rammohun, and after him the Government, had taken up, that the practice of suttee was not required by the laws of Hindu religion. This they denounced as "a doctrine derived from a number of Hindoos, who have apostatized from the religion of their forefathers, who have defiled themselves by eating and drinking forbidden things in the society of Europeans and are endeavouring to deceive your Lordship in Council." They humbly submitted that "in a question so delicate as the interpretation of our sacred books and the authority of our religious usages none but pandits and Brahmins, and teachers of holy lives and known learning and authority ought to be consulted," not "men who have neither any faith nor care for the memory of their ancestors." They suggested with a touch of rather pungent irony that if his Lordship in Council would assume to himself "the difficult and delicate task of regulating the conscience of a whole people. on the authority of its own sacred writers," he should trust to recognized and accredited and orthodox experts. To assist him in this direction, they appended a paper of citations from legal authorities, signed by 120 pandits, and intended to show that suttee was a religious duty. They were obliged to quote the decisive sayings of Vishnu and Manu, which allowed a widow either to practise austerities or to ascend her husband's pyre. By tortuous exegesis and by liberal appeal to immemorial usage, the effort was made to transmute the option between alternatives into a demand for self-immolation. Lord Bentinck, in reply, was unkind enough to say that the authorities they cited "only confirmed the supposition that widows are not by the religious writings of the Hindoos commanded to destroy themselves. "No attack on Hindu religion was committed or intended. If they disputed his interpretation of

Hindu and British laws, they might appeal to the King in Council. Another petition, of similar purport and signed by 346 "respectable persons" from the interior, was presented at the same time, with legal opinions signed by 28 pandits. Counter demonstrations were speedily forthcoming. Two days afterwards two addresses were presented to the Governor-General in support of his anti-Suttee policy. One was from the Christian inhabitants of Calcutta, and bore some signatures. The other was signed by 300 native inhabitants of the same city and presented by Rammohun Roy and several of his well-known comrades. This address (Jan. 16th), of which Rammohun is the reputed and probable author, refers the introduction of suttee to jealousy and selfishness, acting under the cloak of religion, but in defiance of the most sacred authorities. It rehearses the yet more barbarous abuses of this barbarous rite, and rejoices at the prospect of "the most ancient and purest system of Hindu religion" being "no longer set at nought by the Hindus themselves." It expresses "the deepest gratitude" and "the utmost reverence" to his Lordship in Council "for the everlasting obligation" he had "graciously conferred on the Hindu community at large." The signatories finally confess themselves "at a loss to find language sufficiently indicative even of a small portion of the sentiments" they desire to express. Rammohun's joy at so unexpected an erasure of this historic blot from the Hindu escutcheon might well be too great to be altogether articulate.

Next day the opponents of the measure met and resolved to appeal to the authorities in England. Feeling the need of some permanent organization, they formed themselves into a Dharma Sabha, or Religious Society, in evident contrast to the Brahmo Sabha of Rammohun and his friends. They subscribed 11,260 rupees on the spot, and decided to erect a meeting place. The purpose of the association was manifestly militant. It was to enable "the excellent and the noble" so ran the explanation of their own organ to "unite and continually devise means for protecting our religion and our excellent customs and usages." At its first meeting the treasurer significantly remarked with "the concurrence of all present" that "those Hindus who do not follow the rites of Hindu religion should be excluded from the Hindu society." "No names, however, were mentioned," a reticence which the Chundrika hoped would ere long be laid aside. Rammohun was made to feel how much mischief lurked behind these threats.

The Abstract of the Arguments regarding the Burning of Widows considered as a Religious Rite, which was issued in 1830, may be taken as his rejoinder to the manifesto of the 128 pandits. He wished to gather into a clear and concise epitome for popular use the points which had been scattered through many essays and tracts. These he grouped under three heads. According to the sacred books of Hindus, Con-cremation was (1) not obligatory but at most optional; (2) not the most commendable but the least virtuous act a widow could perform; and (3) must be a voluntary ascending of the pile and entering into the flames - a mode never practised in the conventional suttee. The tract concludes with devout "thanks to Heaven, whose protecting arm has rescued our weaker sex from cruel murder," and "our character as a people" from international opprobrium.

While his campaign against suttee was drawing to this triumphant conclusion, Rammohun Roy was busily engaged in other directions as champion of Indian rights and interests. We find him writing on August 18th, 1828, to Mr. J. Crawford, and entrusting to him petitions for presentation to both Houses of Parliament, signed by Hindus and Mohammedans, against the new Jury Act which came into operation in the beginning of 1827. He thus concisely states the grounds of grievance:-

In his famous Jury Biil, Mr. Wynn, the late President of the Board of Control, has by introducing religious distinctions into the judicial system of this country, not only afforded just grounds for dissatisfaction among the Natives in general, but has excited much alarm in the breast of everyone conversant with political principles. Any natives, either Hindu or Mohammedan, are rendered by this Bill subject to judicial trial by Christians, either European or Native, while Christians, including Native Converts, are exempted from the degradation of being tried either by a Hindu or Mussulman juror, however high he may stand in the estimation of society. This Bill also denies both to Hindus and Mussulmans the honor of a seat in the Grand Jury even in the trial of fellow- Hindus or Mussulmans. This is the sum total of Mr. Wynn's late Jury Bill, of which we bitterly complain.

In this letter Rammohun shows once more how deeply the analogy between Ireland and India and the prospects of nationalism in both countries had impressed him. Had not Mr. Wynn seen misery enough result in Ireland from making civil discriminations between different religious beliefs? Why should he want to reproduce the same calamities in India? Rammohun goes on to suggest a possibility which is by no means so remote now as when he wrote:-

Supposing that some 100 years hence the native character becomes elevated from constant intercourse with Europeans and the acquirements of general and political knowledge as well as of modern arts and sciences, is it possible that they will not have the spirit as well as the inclination to resist effectually unjust and oppressive measures serving to degrade them in the scale of society? It should not be lost sight of that the position of India is very different from that of Ireland, to any quarter of which an English fleet may suddenly convey a body of troops that may force its way in the requisite direction and succeed in suppressing every effort of a refractory spirit. Were India to share one fourth of the knowledge and energy of that country, she would prove from her remote situation, her riches and her vast population, either useful and profitable as a willing province, an ally of the British Empire, or troublesome and annoying as a determined enemy.

In common with those who seem partial to the British rule from the expectation of future benefits arising out of the connection, I necessarily feel extremely grieved in often witnessing Acts and Regulations passed by Government without consulting or seeming to understand the feelings of its Indian subjects and without considering that this people have had for more than half a century the advantage of being ruled by and associated with an enlightened nation, advocates of liberty and promoters of knowledge.

In default of other means of making their voice heard, the natives of India resolved to petition, and invoked the help of friends like Mr. Crawford.

We have quoted this letter at some length because of the far-sighted glance into the future it reveals. There is here in germ the national aspiration which is now breaking forth into cries for "representation of India in the Imperial Parliament." "Home Rule for India," and even "India for the Indians.' The prospect of an educated India, of an India approximating to European standards of culture, seems to have never been long absent from Rammohun's mind; and he did, however vaguely, claim in advance for his countrymen the political rights which progress in civilization inevitably involves. Here again Rammohun stands forth as the tribune, and prophet of the New India.*

* It is interesting to note that the petition in question was presented to the House of Commons, June 5, 1829, by Mr. Wynn, and the promise of the Government to direct its attention thereto was made by Lord Ashley, then a Commissioner of the Board of Control, and afterwards Lord Shaftesbury. The young philanthropist "acknowledged the advan- tages which had been derived from admitting the natives of India to take a part in the administration of justice."

But his nationalism was of no narrow type. It was not bound up with the interests of a few well-to-do classes. It was ready to welcome in the interests of the labouring masses, an extensive importation of European settlers and European capital. An outcry of the baser order of nationalism having been raised against the indigo planters of Bengal, Rammohun came boldly to the defence of those aspersed Europeans. His Sambad Kaumudi pointed out that indigo plantations had led to waste lands being cultivated, and to the freedom and comfort of the lower classes being increased. The peasants receiving a higher salary from the planters were no longer "victims to the whims of zamindars and great banias." The more numerous and permanent the settlement of European gentlemen, the better for the soil, the better also for the poor and middle classes. Writing (Nov. 12, 1829) in answer to certain inquiries on the subject from Mr. Nathaniel Alexander, and speaking from investigations he had instituted for the purpose, Rammohun said:--

The advances made to ryots by the indigo planters have increased in most factories in consequence of the price of indigo having risen, and in many, better prices than formerly are allowed for the plant.......I am positively of opinion that upon the whole the indigo planters have done more essential good to the natives of Bengal than any other class of persons. This is a fact which I will not hesitate to affirm whenever I may be questioned on the subject either in India or Europe. I at the same time must confess that there are individuals of that class of society who either from hasty disposition or want of due discretion have proved obnoxious to those who expected milder treatment from them. But, my dear sir, you are well aware that no general good can be effected without some partial evil, and in this instance I am happy to say that the former greatly preponderates over the latter. If any class of the natives "would gladly see them all turned out of the country," it would be the zamindars in general, since in many instances the planters have successfully protected the ryots against the tyranny and oppression of thir landlord.

Rammohun also attended a public meeting in the Calcutta Town Hall on the 15th of December, 1829, which was called to petition Parliament "to throw open the China and India trade, and to remove the restrictions against the settlement of Europeans in India." He reiterated the strong statements of his letter, and prefaced them with the weighty remark:-

From personal experience, I am impressed with the conviction that the greater our intercourse with European gentlemen, the greater will be our improvement in literary, social, and political affairs; a fact which can be easily proved by comparing the condition of those of my countrymen who have enjoyed this advantage with that of those who unfortunately have not had that opportunity; and a fact which I could to the best of my belief declare on solemn oath before any assembly.

In suggestive contrast with this defence of the European settler against the propertied classes of Bengal, we may set Rammohun's vindication of the Bengali law of the trans- mission of property against the findings of the British Court. British judges had wavered in their interpretation of the Hindus' power of alienation over ancestral property. About this time (1829-1830) Sir C. E. Grey, then Chief Justice of the Supreme Court, declared in favour of limiting the power in question. Rammohun accordingly brought out a book in 1830 on 'The Rights of Hindus over Ancestral Property' according to the law of Bengal. This essay showed that of the two great treatises on the law of Hindu inheritance, the 'Mitakshara' was accepted through the greater part of India, while the

'Dayabhaga' had been long established as paramount authority in Bengal. Numerous instances were quoted to indicate the difference and even contrariety of the two codes; and on the crucial point it was shown that the Mitakshara limited the disposal of ancestral property by requiring the consent of son and grandson, whereas the Dayabhaga left a man free to alienate it as he pleased. Recent decisions in British Bengali Courts had ignored the distinctive and established Bengali law and had followed the teachings of the Mitakshara. This breach of loyalty to Bengali institutions could not be excused by appeals to sayings in the Hindu scriptures, which imposed moral limits on power of alienation. These were ethical precepts, not legal enactments; and a vast amount of learning is expended in maintaining the legal validity of the Bengali digest along with the ethical authority of the sacred writings. In disputing the principle that "we ought to make that invalid which was considered immoral," Rammohun suggested a number of testing cases, one of which reads curiously in the light of later agitation:-

To permit the sale of intoxicating drugs and spirits, so injurious to health, and even sometimes destructive of life, on the payment of duties publicly levied, is an act highly irreligious and immoral. Is the taxation to be, therefore, rendered invalid and payments stopped?

This essay involved its writer in a lengthy correspondence in the Hurkaru, with a critic who signed himself "A Hindu" ; which led to a plentiful display of legal lore and casuistry, but did not modify Rammohun's main contention. That was indeed confirmed by the Sudder Dewany Adawlut in 1831, and still later by the Privy Council. Jogendra Chunder Ghose thinks this result to have been in large measure due to Rammohun's treatise.

Amid the multiplicity of these pursuits, philanthropic political, economic and legal, Rammohun never lost sight of his central vocation, to purify and elevate the faith of his countrymen. In 1829 he published a tract entitled, 'The Universal Religion'; religious instructions founded on sacred authorities. This is a short catechism, with proof texts from the sacred writings of Hinduism. It describes worship as "a contemplation of the attributes of the Supreme Being." It styles the object of worship "the author and Governor of the Universe," "imperceptible and indefinable," but by His creation and government of the universe known to exist. Worship is to be performed "by bearing in mind that the Author and Governor of this visible Universe is the Supreme Being and comparing this idea with the sacred writings and with reason." Furthermore, "it is proper to regulate our food and conduct agreeably to the sacred writings." For this worship "a suitable place is certainly preferable, but not necessary"; "in whatever place, towards whatever quarter or at whatever time the mind is best at rest, that place, that quarter, and that time is the most proper." This kind of worship cannot be hostile to any other kinds, nor can they reasonably be hostile to it; "for all believe the object whom they adore to be the Author and Governor of the Universe."

This is a bold statement to make in face of the facts of fetishism and kindred cults. The infinitely diverse religions of the world will scarcely yield as their common denominator a theism so pure and lofty as Rammohun's "Universal Religion." But Rammohun believed in it intensely and the progress of the Brahmo Sabha was witness to his faith.

The time had in fact arrived for providing the new community with a permanent home of its own. The growth in the funds at its disposal soon rendered possible the purchase of a site in Chitpore Road and the erection of a building (a "brick-built messuage.") The Trust Deed, which is dated January 8th, 1830, sets forth the transfer of the property as fr om Dwarkanath Tagore, Kaleenath Roy, Prussunnocoomar Tagore, Ramchunder Bidyabagish, and Rammohun Roy, to the three trustees, Boykontonath Roy, Radapersad Roy, and Ramanath Tagore. The sum paid to the vendors for the site and building is stated to be ten sicca rupees (about one guinea) and for the appurtenances five sicca rupees more.

Whether this nominal sale followed on a prior and more costly purchase, or was tantamount to a real gift does not appear. Possibly the five vendors did make a present of the house and ground; and the funds which had been gathered were invested as an endowment on the place. Certainly, "the sum of rupees 6,080, was kept in the custody of the late well-known firm of Messrs. Mackintosh & Company as a permanent fund, from the interest of which the ordinary expenses of the church were to be met."

The Trust Deed of this place of worship is a notable theological document. It is the one legal statement of the original creed of the Brahmo Samaj; and being inspired by Rammohun Roy, it falls to be quoted here as the formal deliverance of the purpose of his life-work. The terms of the Trust are that the trustees shall at all times permit the said building, land, tenements, hereditaments and premises, with their appurtenances, to be used, occupied, enjoyed, applied and appropriated, as and for a place of Public Meeting, of all sorts and descriptions of people, without distinction, as shall behave and conduct themselves in an orderly, sober, religious, and devout manner; for the worship and adoration of the Eternal, Unsearchable, and Immutable Being, who is the Author and Preserver of the Universe, but not under, or by any other name, designation, or title, peculiarly used for, and applied to, any particuar Being, or Beings, by any man, or set of men, whatsoever; and that no graven image, statue or sculpture, carving, painting, picture, portrait or the likeness of any thing, shall be admitted within the messuage, building, land, tenements, hereditaments, and premises; and that no sacrifice, offering, or oblation of any kind or thing, shall ever be permitted therein; and that no animal or living creature shall, within or on the said messuage, building, land, tenements, hereditaments and premises, be deprived of life, either for religious purposes or for food; and that no eating or drinking (except such as shall be necessary, by any accident, for the preservation of life), feasting or rioting be permitted therein or thereon; nd that, in conducting the said worship or adoration, no object, animate or inanimate, that has been, or is, or shall hereafter become, or be recognized, as an object of worship, by any man, or set of men, shall be reviled, or slightingly or contemptuously spoken of, or alluded to, either in preaching, praying, or in the hymns, or other mode of worship that may be delivered or used in the said messuage or building;and that no sermon, preaching, discourse, prayer or hymn be delivered, made or used in such worship, but such as have a tendency to the promotion of the contemplation of the Author and Preserver of the Universe, to the promotion of charity, morality, piety, benevolence, virtue, and the strengthening the bonds of union between men of all religious persuasions and creeds;

and also, that a person of good repute, and well-known for his knowledge, piety, and morality, be employed by the said trustees . . as a resident superintendent, and for the purpose of superintending the worship so to be performed, as is hereinbefore stated and expressed; and that such worship be performed daily, or at least as often as once in seven days.

On January 23rd, 1830, the building was solemnly set apart to the purposes of public worship. Mr. Montgomery Martin, in his 'History of the British Colonies' gives this account of the ceremony: "The institution was opened by the late Rajah Rammohun Roy, accompanied by the writer (the only European present) in 1830. There were about five hundred Hindus present and among them many Brahmins who, after the prayers and singing of hymns had been concluded, received gifts in money to a considerable extent."

Rammohun must have taken part in this inauguration with a devoutly thankful heart. It was a sign that the movement of religious reform to which he had given his life had attained something like permanency. The society he had founded was showing itself to be no evanescent group of atoms, but a veritable Church. It had passed from the stage of dream and hope, through a series of tentative and preliminary experiments, into a solid materialized fact; an institution legally in possession of property; and the endowment settled upon it suggested a prospect of perpetuity. The decisive significance attached to the acquisition of this "local habitation" is shown in its annual celebration by all branches of the Samaj. The Society itself was founded, as we have seen, on the 20th of August, 1828. The building was opened on the 23rd of January, 1830. Yet, though at first the earlier event was yearly commemorated as the Church's birthday, the 23rd of January, soon came to be observed as the proper anniversary, and Brahmos have generally reckoned from 1830 as the era of the Samaj.

The same year shows us the founder assisting, with characteristic breadth of sympathy, at the beginning of another and widely different religious movement. The great educational departure in Indian missions which is for ever associated with the name of Alexander Duff may boast of Rammohun Roy as its co-initiator. It will be remembered that six years previously the Hindu had, as an attendant on St. Andrew's Kirk, supported a petition to the General Assembly of the Church of Scotland, begging it to send out missionaries to British India. In response to this plea, the young

Scotsman, hereafter so famous, arrived in Calcutta and was soon directed by his friends to the "pleasant garden house in a leafy suburb of Calcutta" where dwelt the "Erasmus of India."* Duff having unfolded his plans, Rammohun expressed general approval. "All true education," he said, "ought to be religious, since the object was not merely to give information but to develop and regulate all the powers of the mind, the emotions of the heart, and the workings of the conscience. Though not himself a Christian by profession, he had read and studied the Bible and declared that, as a book of religious and moral instruction, it was unequalled. As a believer in God, he also felt that everything should be begun by implor- ing His blessing. He recommended the opening of the proposed school with the recitation of the Lord's Prayer, for in all his reading he "nowhere found any prayer so brief and all-comprehensive" as it. A very significant remark must be quoted entire:-

"As a youth," he said to Mr. Duff, "I acquired some knowledge of the English language. Having read about the rise and progress of Christianity in apostolic times, and its corruption in succeeding ages, and then of the Christian Reformation which shook off these corruptions and restored it to its primitive purity, I began to think that something similar might have taken place in India, and similar results might follow here from a reformation of the popular idolatry."

On the young missionary saying that he was at a loss where or how to get a school-house in the native city, Rammohun offered the small hall in Chitpore Road, which the Brahmo Sabha was on the point of leaving for the new building; and driving off at once to the spot secured it for Duff at a rental of £4 a month, one pound less than he himself had been paying. He removed other difficulties from Duff's path. By personal influence among his enlightened Hindu friends, he secured their children for Duff's first pupils. On the day of opening, the 13th of July, 1830 Rammohun Roy was present from the first to explain away prejudices. Duff's repetition of the Lord's Prayer in Bengali passed without remark, but a murmur arose among the pupils, when he put copies of the Gospels into their hands and bade them read. Rammohun straightway intervened :-

"Christians like Dr. Horace Hayman Wilson have studied the Hindu Shastras and you know that he has not become a Hindu. I myself have read all the Koran again and again; and has that made me a Mussulman? Nay, I have studied the whole Bible, and you know I am not a Christian. Why then do you fear to read it? Read it and judge for yourselves."

This quieted the remonstrants; but Rammohun was careful to attend every day at ten when the Bible lesson was taken, for the whole of the next month and frequently afterwards, a very signal evidence of his determination to promote the success of Duff's work. His powerful example soon told. For instance, one of his principal followers, Kaleenath Ray Chowdhery, offered buildings and appliances at Taki, forty miles from Calcutta, for a school to be supervised by Duff and taught on his lines by his teachers, who would be paid by the Chowdhery family, for Bengali and Persian instruction. This was the beginning of a thriving mission school. Duff might well say in a letter intended to introduce Rammohun Roy to Dr. Chalmers, "He has rendered me the most valuable and efficient assistance in prosecuting some of the objects of the General Assembly's Mission."

While these events were proceeding, Rammohun was making arrangements for his long expected journey to Europe. It was a somewhat unlooked-for occurrence which precipitated his intentions of travel. The Emperor of Delhi, nominal successor to the traditions of the Great Mogul, had a grievance against the real possessors of empire, the Directors of the British Company. The allowance they granted His Majesty was, he considered, neither equal to the amount guaranteed to him by treaty, nor sufficient for his needs; and strangely exaggerated stories were circulated about the straits to which the Imperial household was reduced. Having possibly heard of his intended visit to England, the aggrieved potentate decided to appoint Rammohun as his envoy to the British King, to plead for measures of substantial redress. At the same time - apparently about the beginning of August, 1829 - he conferred on him the tittle of 'rajah.' Rammohun, after accepting these honours, took as his assistant in the Imperial service Mr. Montgomery Martin. This gentleman was editor of the Bengal Herald, an English newspaper, of which Dwarkanath Tagore, N. R. Haldar and Rammohun Roy became, in 1829, the proprietors. This journalistic venture, it seems, did not prosper. Rammohun, as proprietor, was obliged to plead guilty in the Supreme Court of Calcutta to a libel on an attorney, and the paper soon afterwards ceased to appear, Mr. Martin relinquishing his editorship for new duties under the Imperial envoy. According to a facetious and decidedly malicious but evidently well informed writer in the John Bull of Feb. 27, 1830, the envoy and ex-editor had first arranged to leave for Europe about the beginning of September, 1829. A month later they decided to go overland via Allahabad, but for three months Mr. Martin waited in daily readiness to depart. Meantime the Regulation abolishing suttee had been passed, and Rammohun was busily engaged, as we have seen, in supporting the action of the Governor-General.

The threatened appeal to England of the infuriated supporters of the doomed rite furnished another reason for Rammohun's contemplated journey. His presentation of counter memorials and personal influence in the capital of the Empire would help to circumvent their machinations. A further ground, doubtless present to his mind from the first, was the approaching expiry of the East India Company's Charter. His presence on the spot might help the House of Commons to shape the new Charter more favourably to Indian needs. Rammohun thought the time propitious for approaching the Governor-General on the subject of his errand. On January 8, 1830, while petitions were being actively promoted on both sides of the suttee question, he wrote to Lord Bentinck as follows:-

I beg leave to submit to your Lordship that some months ago I was informed by His Majesty, Manussur Moinuddin Mohamed Uk- bur Badshah, that His Majesty had apprised your Lordship of my appointment as his Elchee (Envoy) to the Court of Great Britain, and of his having been pleased to invest me as His Majesty's servant with the title of Rajah, in consideration of the respectability attached to that situation, etc. Not being anxious for titular distinction, I have hitherto refrained from availing myself of the honour conferred on me by His Majesty.

His Majesty, however, being of opinion that it is essentially necessary for the dignity of His Royal House that I, as the representative thereof to the most powerful Monarch in Europe, and Agent for the settlement of His Majesty's affairs with the Honourable East India Company, should be invested with the title above mentioned, has graciously forwarded to me a seal engraved for the purpose at Delhi. I therefore take the liberty of laying the subject before your Lordship, hoping that you will be pleased to sanction my adoption of such title accordingly. This measure will, 1 believe, be found consistent with former usage as established by a Resolution of Government on the subject in 1827, when, at the recommendation of the then Resident, Sir Charles Metcalfe, in his report of 26th June of that year, His Majesty's power of conferring honorary titles on his own servants was fully recognized.

Answer to this request was sent by Secretary Stirling on the 15th of January, to the effect that the Governor in Council could not sanction his acceptance of the title of Rajah nor recognize him as envoy from the Court of Delhi. We can hardly wonder at this reply, when we remember that Rammohun's mission was at once a deviation from the usual official channels of communication with the Home Government and a reflection upon the conduct of officials. Both as to form and substance it stood condemned in the official eye. It is pleasant to find that this rebuff did not hinder Rammohun appearing next day at the Governor-General's with the Anti-Suttee address of congratulation.

With the beginning of the last year which Rammohun was to spend on Indian soil, the resentment which his reforming career had been steadily accumulating in the breasts of orthodox Hindus broke out into threats and plots of mortal violence. It was the abolition of suttee which let loose the floods of reactionary fury. Avarice and bigotry, two of the strongest passions of human nature, had been hard hit; and they demanded a victim. Rammohun was marked out as the guilty party. He was the traitor within the gates, who had sold the keys to the infidel oppressor. Therefore, he must die.

So doubtless argued his enemies. Their intentions were, however, conveyed to Rammohun. About the new year he informed Mr. Martin that "his life was seriously threatened by a gang of assassins." Mr. Martin accordingly took up his abode at his patron's house and armed the household. "Firearms, gunpowder, and daggers were immediately procured and burkandazes employed to guard the premises." These last were daily exercised in firing. Whenever Rammohun went into town, he took with him dagger and swordstick, and was accompanied by Mr. Martin, who carried swordstick and pistols, and by other armed attendants. We learn from other sources that twice attempts * were made on his life, and he was dogged about by spies, who even dared to tear holes in his walls to watch him in his privacy, in the hope of detecting some act which would render him an outcaste.

The militant forces of reaction were organized by the Dharma Sabha, started, as we have seen, only six days before the opening of the Brahmo Sabha building; and the

antagonism between the two societies, each with an influential following, each with its popular newspaper, made a great stir, of which Siva Nath Sastri in his history of the Brahmo Samaj gives us this lively picture:

The common people became participators in this great conflict; for the tracts of the reformers, mostly written in the simplest Bengali, appeals to them as much as to the enlightened classes. In the bathing-ghats of the river side, in market-places and public squares, in the drawing-rooms of influential citizens, everywhere the rivalry between the two associations became the subject of talk. Lines of comical poetry caricaturing the principles of the great reformer were composed by the wags of the time, and passed from mouth to mouth until the streets rang with laughter and ridicule. The agitation spread from Calcutta to the interior, and everywhere the question was discussed between the two parties. A large number of Brahmins who accepted presents from the members of the Brahmo Sabha, were excommunicated by the other party on that account, and the duty of supporting them devolved upon the rich of Rammohun's friends, who cheerfully undertook it. It was in the midst of these furious party contests that Ram- mohun opened his church in 1830.

One of the favourite subjects of satire and ridicule was Rammohun's intended visit to Europe.

It is no small tribute to the character of our hero that amid all this storm of obloquy and in peril of his life he calmly pursued his reforming course. Charges of cowardice and of time-serving have been plentifully hurled against him: but they find slight room for lodgement in the conduct of a man who, surrounded by virulent calumny and mortal menace, went on presenting addresses and publishing books and preparing memorials against suttee, housed and endowed his Sabha, and even dared to launch Duff's great scheme of Christian education.

Nevertheless the "hatred, scoffing and abuse" to which he was subjected must have made him less sorry to leave India. How his plans for departure had matured appears from the following letter, in which the Hindu Reformer bids a stately farewell to the British ruler, whose name the abolition of suttee has linked with his own in everlasting conjunction:-

From the kindness I have so often experienced from your Lordship, I trust to be pardoned for my present intrusion in a matter solely concerning myself, but in which your Lordship's condescension has induced me to persuade myself that you are pleased to take some interest.

Having at length surmounted all the obstacles of a domestic nature that have hitherto opposed my long cherished intention of visiting England, I am now resolved to proceed to that land of liberty by one of the vessels that will sail in November, and from a due regard to the purport of the late Mr. Secretary Stirling's letter of 15th January last, and other considerations, I have determined not to appear there as the Envoy of His Majesty Akbar the Second, but as a private individual.

I am satisfied that in thus divesting myself of all public character, my zealous services in behalf of His Majesty need not be abated. I even trust that their chance of success may be improved by being thus exempted from all jealousy of a political nature to which they might by misapprehension be subjected.

As public report has fixed an early day in October for your Lordship's departure to examine personally into the condition of the inhabitants of the Upper Provinces, I take the present occasion as the last that may offer in this country for the expression of my sincere wishes for your Lordship's success in all your philanthropic designs for the improvement and benefit of my countrymen. I need not add that any commands for England with which your Lordship may honour me shall receive from me the most respectful attention, and I beg to subscribe myself your Lordship's most humble and grateful servant.

The "obstacles of a domestic nature" may, perhaps, be the suit of the Rajah of Burdwan, which was not finally dismissed by the last Court of Appeal - the Sudder Dewanee Adaulut until November of next year, but the issue of which may have now been confidently foreseen. It is interesting to know that, on leaving, Rammohun charged his sons to forget the conduct of their cousins who had shared in this forensic persecution.

Having completed all arrangements for his departure, Rammohun sailed from Calcutta by the Albion on the 19th of November. Careful even in this daring innovation on Brahman custom, to observe the laws of caste, he took with him Hindu servants to prepare his food and two cows to supply him with milk. Rammohun also took with him an adopted son, a boy of about twelve years, who was known as Ram Roy or Rajaram. Malicious gossip did not spare this lad's origin. Chunder Sekhar Deb, the disciple who, it will be remembered, suggested the formation of the Brahmo Samaj - stated in conversation with a friend, R. D.H, at Burdwan, so late as January, 1863, that "rumour had it that at one time he [Rammohun] had a mistress; and people believed that Rajaram was his natural son, though he himself said Rajaram was the orphan of a darwan of some Saheb, and Rammohun Roy brought him up."

This scandalous insinuation emerges here in our sources for the first and only time, and then some thirty years after Rammohun's death. We have not come across the remotest semblence of evidence to sustain the charge.* True, Mr. Deb was an intimate disciple; but the rest of his reported conversation shows him to be no loyal admirer of the deceased master. And even he advanced no scintilla of proof. He merely repeated the gossip as "rumour" and what "people believed." There is no need to question his veracity. Ortho- dox Hindus of the Dharma Sabha type were thirsting to show up the great apostate, as they regarded him, in the blackest of colours. The fact that his wives had deserted him, and the presence of this adopted son, offered a combination of circumstances which eager malice could scarcely fail to construe in its own way. Men who made attempts on Rammohun's life were not likely to scruple about attacking his reputation. And against this rumour, so easily explained, we have to set the unanimous testimony of British missionaries to Rammohun's pure moral habits. An intimate friend like Mr. William Adam, who was closely questioned by Unitarian correspondents about Rammohun's domestic relations, could scarcely have been mistaken in his uniformly high estimate of the reformer's character. And his aggrieved Trinitarian opponents, even in the heat of controversy, never breathed a whisper against his fair fame. The reputation that has passed scatheless and stainless the ordeal of criticism by missionaries, Baptist and Unitarian, Presbyterian and Anglican, hostile as well as sympathetic, may afford to ignore stale Hindu gossip served up a generation afterwards.

* The true history of Rajaram was supplied to Dr. Carpenter in the following letter from India in 1835," you ask me to give you any corrections (of Dr. C.'s Sermon and Review) that may appear necessary.

One has been suggested to me by his native friends, as desirable to be made for the sake of Rammohun's Roy's character. The boy Rajah whom he took with him to England is not his son, not even an adopted son according to the Hindoo form of adoption; but a destitute orphan whom he was led by circumstances to protect and educate. I have a distinct recollection of the particular circumstances under which he stated to me how Raja came into his hands. And my recollection is confirmed by that of others. Mr. Dick, a civil servant of the company found the child helpless and forsaken at one of the fairs at Hurdwar, where from two to three hundred thousand people annually congregated. It is not known whether the parents lost or forsook him, but Mr. Dick had him clothed and fed, and when he was under the necessity of leaving the country for the recovery of health, he consulted with Rammohun Roy how the child should be disposed of. I well recollect our late friend's benevolent exclamation: 'When I saw an Englishman, a Christian, thus caring for the welfare of a poor orphan, could I, a native, hesitate to take him under my care and provide for him?' Mr. Dick never returned to India, having, died, I believe, on the passage to England and the child remained with Rammohun Roy."

Rammohun was also accompanied by two Hindu servants, by name Ramhurry Doss and Ramrotun Mukerjee. The latter as cook was entrusted with the duty of providing his master with food prepared in accordance with caste regulations.

Some extracts from Mr. J. Young's letter of introduction to Jeremy Bentham (of date Nov. 14, 1830) may fitly close this chapter:-

If I were beside you, and could explain matters fully, you would comprehend the greatness of the undertaking - his going on board ship to a foreign and distant land, a thing hitherto not to be named among Hindoos, and least of all among Brahmins. His grand object, besides the natural one of satisfying his own laudable spirit of inquiry, has been to set a laudable example to his benighted countrymen; and every one of the slow and gradual moves that he has made preparatory to his actually quitting India, has been marked by the same discretion of judgment. He waited patiently until he had by perseverence and exertion acquired a little but respectable party of disciples. He talked of going to England from year to year since 1823* to familiarize the minds of the orthodox by degrees to this step, and that his friends might in the meantime increase in numbers and in confidence. . . He now judges that the time is come, and that the public mind is pretty well ripe for his exploit. . .

The good which this excellent and extraordinary man has already effected by his writings and example cannot be told. But for his exertions suttee would be in full vigour at the present day, and the influence of the priesthood in all its ancient force; he has given the latter a shake from which, aided by education and the spirit of bold inquiry gone forth among the Hindoos, it can never recover. Modest men I have ever met with he is withal one of the most.

It is no small compliment to such a man that even a Governor-General like the present, who, though a man of the most honest intentions, suspects everyone and trusts nobody, and who knows that R. M. R. greatly disapproves of many of the acts of the Government, should have shown him so much respect as to furnish him with introductions to friends of rank and political influence in England.

Embassy to Europe (1830-1833)

The significance of Rammohun Roy's visit to Europe can scarcely be exaggerated. At first sight indeed it is in some danger of being overlooked. We are tempted to consider the last three years of the reformer's life a mere appendix or postscript to a career already complete. We are apt to suppose the full tale of his great services for India made up when he left her soil. He had initiated the Hindu Theistic movement, He had given it permanent literary expression. He had selected or indicated the order of Scriptures more peculiarly its own. He had seen it finally housed and endowed. He had moreover successfully inaugurated native journalism. He had launched Dr. Duff's great educational enterprise. The cause of English education which he had championed was now on the eve of official victory. And he had witnessed the abolition of suttee. What follows these achievements may wear to the unreflective observer a semblance of anti-climax, or at best of mere stage pageant after the real work was done. But a deeper discernment will soon dissipate this impression. Rammohun's three years in the West form the crown and consummation of his life-work. They were spent away from the scene of his regular labours and under widely different conditions; they were shadowed by failing health and saddened by misplaced confidence; but they follow in strict logical and genetic succession. They complete the continuity. They supply the dramatic culmination of Rammohun's half century of service to his country and his kind.

The epoch they mark in Hindu development only confirms and extends his religious record. He was the first Brahman to cross the ocean. He was the first Hindu of eminence who dared to break the spell which for ages the sea had laid on India. He set a conspicuous precedent to the host of educated Hindus who have since studied and travelled in Europe. The consequences for his countrymen are such as to make this act alone sufficient to secure for its author a lasting distinction. Its Imperial importance is not less striking. Rammohun Roy's presence in this country made the English people aware, as they had never been before, of the dignity, the culture, and the piety of the race they had conquered in the East. India became incarnate in him, and dwelt among us, and we beheld her glory. In the court of the King, in the halls of the legislature, in the select coteries of fashion, in the society of philosophers and men of letters, in Anglican church and Non-conformist meeting-house, in the privacy of many a home, and before the wondering crowds of Lancashire operatives, Rammohun Roy stood forth the visible and personal embodiment of our Eastern empire. Wherever he went, there went a stately refutation of the Anglo-Indian insolence which saw in an Indian fellow-subject only a "black man" or a "nigger." As he had interpreted England to India, so now he interpreted India to England. He was the first great representative of the Hindu race at the Seat of Empire, and the contrast between official London and official Calcutta in their treatment of him showed the effect of his personal presence at headquarters.*

* [Miss Carpenter gives the following general summary of the impression of Raja's visit to England:-

"The arrival of the illustrious Hindu Reformer in our country was anxiously anticipated by all who had become acquainted with him through the various channels which have been laid before the reader. The nature of his labours, and the distance of the scene of them, naturally prevented his being an object of popular enthusiasm; nor if that had been excited in his favour, would he have desired the public demonstrations of admiration and respect which were recently accorded to the great Italian patriot. But the reception given to him though of a widely different kind, must have been no less gratifying to him, at the time, and to his countrymen since his departure. The highest honours were publicly accorded to him, and a place was awarded to him among the foreign ambassadors at the coronation of the sovereign; persons the most remarkable for their social standing and literary eminence sought his society, and highly esteemed the privilege of intercourse with him; he was received into our English homes not only as a distinguished guest, but as a friend and when he was prostrated on the bed of sickness and of death in a foreign land, he was surrounded with the most loving attentions, tended with the most anxious solicitude, and finally laid in the grave surrounded with true mourners, who felt him akin to them in spirit, if not connected with him by the ties of earthly relationship."]

He came, too, at a time of crucial transition in the political history of the United Kingdom. He was an eager and sympathetic spectator of the stupendous revolution achieved by the first Reform Bill. The process then began which has by successive extentions of the franchise transformed the government of this nation in fifty years from a close oligarchy to a democracy. While he was here, he saw the East India Company changed by statute from a trading concern into a political organization: and that was practically the last renewal of its charter, prior to its replacement, in 1858, by the Imperial Government. He saw the Act pass which abolished slavery throughout the British dominions. The period of his visit also covers the passing of the Factory Act and the beginnings of the Tractarian movement. The Manchester and Liverpool railway had been opened only a month or two before he left India. He was here, in a word, when the New England was being born out of the heart of Old England, the New England of democracy, of social and industrial reform, of Anglican revival, and of Imperial policy tempered by Non-conformist Conscience. And at that decisive era, he was present as the noble and precocious type of the New India which has been growing up under British rule. In him the New England first became acquainted with the New India. That is a connection which has already borne much fruit, and which seems destined to play a greater part in the near future. And if we glance beyond the limits of India and of Empire, we can hardly fail to see in Rammohun's visit a landmark in the general history of modern civilization. The West had long gone to the East. With him the East began to come to the West. India has followed in his wake, and Japan and even China have followed in the wake of India. Leading scions of the hoariest civilizations are now eager pupils in the schools of the youngest civilizations. As a consequence the East is being rapidly occidentalized; and there are signs not a few of a gradual orientalizing of the West. This movement towards the healing of the schism which has for ages divided mankind, and the effort to intermingle more thoroughly the various ingredients of humanity, are rich in promise for the humanizing and unifying of man. The role which Rammohun Roy had played in this world-drama among his own countrymen was fitly crowned by his appearance in the chief city of the globe.

We are anticipating, it is true, but in following the kaleidoscopic variety of the reformer's European experiences we need to keep clearly in mind the world-historic import of the entire event. Otherwise the unity and continuity of a great lifework might seem to be dissipated in a crowd of details.

The cosmopolitan character of the man received fresh and striking illustration from the direction of his mind during the time of his departure. He was not weighed down with the thought of separation from home and friends, or with vague forebodings as to the outcome of his momentous enterprise. He was simply full of the latest French Revolu- tion. News had just reached Calcutta of the famous Three Days (July 27-29, 1830): and, "so great was his enthusiasm that," we are told, "he could think and talk of nothing else!" He viewed it as a triumph of liberty and rejoiced accordingly.

This is the testimony of James Sutherland, a friend of Rammohun, who sailed with him to England. His narrative of the voyage sheds so interesting a light on the conduct of the great Hindu that we cannot do better than reproduce portions of it here.

On board ship Rammohun Roy took his meals in his own cabin, and at first suffered considerable inconvenience from the want of a separate fireplace, having nothing but a common choola on board. His servants, too, fell desperately sea-sick, (though, as if his ardour supported him against it, he himself never felt this malady at all) and took possession of his cabin, never moving from it, and making it as may easily be conceived, no enviable domicile; in fact they compelled him to retreat to the lockers; but still the kindness of his nature would not allow him to remove them. The greater part of the day he read, chiefly I believe, Sanskrit and Hebrew. In the forenoon and the evening he took an airing on deck, and always got involved in an animated discussion. After dinner when the cloth was removed and the dessert was on the table, he would come out of his cabin also and join in the conversation and take a glass of wine. He was always cheerful and so won upon the esteem of all on board that there was quite a competition who should pay him the most attention, and even the sailors seemed to render him any little service in their power... His equanimity was quite surprising. In more than one case everything in his cabin was quite afloat owing to the sea washing in but it never disturbed his serenity. If anything threw him off his equilibrium of temperament, it was the prevalence of contrary winds, because of his anxiety to get on, and his alarm lest the great question of the Company's charter should come on before he arrived in England.

He put ashore at the Cape for only an hour or two. Returning on board, he met with a nasty accident. The gangway ladder had not been properly secured and he got a serious fall," from which he was lame for eighteen months afterwards" and indeed never finally recovered.

But no bodily suffering could repress his mental ardour. Two French frigates, under the revolutionary flag, the glorious tricolour, were lying in Table Bay; and lame as he was, he would insist on visiting them. The sight of these colours seemed to kindle the flame of his enthusiasm, and to render him insensible to pain. . His reception was, of course, worthy of the French character and of him. He was conducted over the vessels and endeavoured to convey by the aid of interpreters how much he was delighted to be under the banner that waved over their decks, an evidence of the glorious triumph of right over might; and as he left the vessels he repeated emphatically, "Glory, glory, glory to France !"

Some of the most distinguished people at the Cape left their cards for him at the Hotel, and some called on board, but not the Governor ... As we approached England, his anxiety to know what was passing there became most urgent, and he implored the captain to lose no opportunity of speaking any vessel outward. At length near the equator, we fell in with a vessel which supplied us with papers announcing the change of Ministry* and his exultation at the intelligence may be easily conceived. We talked of nothing else for days. . It was in its probable beneficial effect on the fate of India that he regarded the event as a subject of triumph. When we got within a few days' sail of the Channel we fell in with a vessel only four days out, that brought us intelligence of the extraordinary circumstance of the second reading of the Reform Bill being carried in the House in which the Tories had so long commanded majorities, by a single vote ! . . Rammohun Roy was again elated with the prospect. A few days afterwards, at that . eventful crisis in our history Rammohun Roy first landed in Great Britain. .

The effect of this contagious enthusiasm of a whole people in favour of a grand political change upon such a mind as his was of course electrifying, and he caught up the tone of the new society in which he found himself with so much ardour that at one time I had fears that this fever of excitement would prove too much for him.

Mr. Sutherland gives a vivid description of the first days of Rammohun Roy in England. He tells us, his arrival was no sooner known in Liverpool than every man of any distinction in the place hastened to call upon him, and he got into inextricable confusion with all his engagements, making half a dozen sometimes for the same evening. He was out morning, noon, and night... On all occasions, whether at breakfast or dinner, a number of persons was assembled to meet him; and he was constantly involved in animated discussions on politics or theolgy.

The first public place Rammohun Roy attended was fitly enough a Unitarian Chapel, where Mr. Grundy delivered a sermon "rather too metaphysical" for Mr. Sutherland, but greatly appreciated by the illustrious

Hindu. It was a homily on the duty of unlimited charity in regard to other men's creeds.

"When the sermon was over the scene that ensued was curious. Instead of dispersing as usual, the congregation thronged up every avenue in crowding to get a near view of him as he passed out." On his way out, Rammohun was moved to sudden grief by the sight of a mural tablet in memory of a Mr. Tait whom he had known in India. On recovering from the shock, he attempted to express his feelings, and as he did so with propriety, though with hesitation, the surprise and excitement of the crowd at hearing a native of India address them in their native tongue was extreme, and it was near an hour after the service terminated ere we could make our way out of church. He had to shake hands with many who had waited for that purpose. To some his adopted son was scarcely less an object of curiosity, and to him it was fine fun; he seemed to enjoy being stared at amazingly.

At night Rammohun Roy went to an Anglican church, and heard the Rev. Mr. Scoresby, formerly a sailor, and now a man of great scientific reputation, and a good Evangelical. Of this discourse, too, the distinguished hearer expressed his admiration.

Among the earliest invitations received by Rammohun after his arrival was one to the house of William Roscoe. The venerable historian, who had been a prisoner though paralysis for many years, and was now within a few weeks of his end, had previously corresponded with Rammohun, read his writings, and earnestly longed to see him. The interview which resulted is described as exceedingly affecting.*

* [An account of this interesting interview is happily preserved in the Memoir of Roscoe by his son, Henry Roscoe, and is worth reproducing.]

The first impression produced by the Hindu in the drawing-rooms of Liverpool magnates, as well as in more public places, seems to have been one of profound surprise.

To hear a Brahman zealously advocating Reform, and, with an earnestness and emphasis that bespoke his sincerity, expatiating on the blessings of civil and religious liberty, of course amazed our countrymen; and perhaps they were not less surprised, if the discussion took a religious turn, to find him quoting text upon text with the utmost facility,and proving himself more familiar with their sacred books than themselves.

"It will be recollected," says the biographer, "that at a very early period of his life Mr. Roscoe had collected the moral precepts of the New Testament into a small volume, to which he gave the title of 'Christian Morality, as contained in the Precepts of New Testament, in the language of Jesus Christ.' In the decline of life this youthful attempt was recalled to his mind by a work of a similar character proceeding from a very unlooked for quarter. This was the 'Precepts of Jesus' collected, arranged and published at Calcutta by a learned Brahmin Rammohun Roy....The character and history of this extraordinary man excited in the highest degree the interest and the admiration of Mr. Roscoe. It is not surprising that with a man of this high and enlightened character Mr. Roscoe should be desirous of communicating; and accordingly he took advantage of the opportunity of one of his friends proceeding to India, to transmit to Rammohun Roy a small collection of his works, which he accompanied with the following letter....... Before this letter could reach its destination, Mr. Roscoe had the unexpected gratification of hearing that the extraordinary person to whom it was addressed was already on his voyage to Europe. This intelligence was quickly followed by his arrival at Liverpool, where his character and striking appearance excited much curiosity and interest. The interview between him and Mr. Roscoe will never be forgotten by those who witnessed it. After the usual gesture of eastern salutation, and with a mixture of oriental expression, Rammohun Roy said, 'Happy and proud am I - proud and happy to behold a man whose fame has extended not only over Europe, but over every part of the world.' 'I bless God,' replied Mr. Roscoe, that I have been permitted to live to see this day.' Their conversation chiefly turned upon the objects which had led Rammohun Roy to this country, and in the course of it he displayed an intimate acquaintance with the political and commercial state of England."]

Two wealthy Quaker families, Cropper and Benson by name, paid him special attention, and brought him into social fellowship with persons of all faiths. At one of these Quaker parties "there were present High Churchmen, Baptists, Unitarians, and Deists, all meeting in perfect harmony and Christian charity." At the house of Mr. William Rathbone he met the phrenologist Spurzheim, with whom personally he was on excellent terms, but for whose "science" he had only good-humoured ridicule. Theology and politics were, as has been said, the favourite themes of colloquy; but an attempt at Mr. Rathbone's to draw Rammohun into confession of his own precise religious conviction ended in failure.

The Rajah stayed only a few days in Liverpool. He was eager to be present in the House of Commons on the second reading of the Reform Bill. So he hurried on to London about the end of April. But his stay in Liverpool was a fitting prelude to the general tenour of his visit, and has therefore claimed slightly fuller notice.

The eclat of his first reception followed him on his way to the metropolis says Mr. Sutherland:-

The scene at Manchester, when he visited the great manufactories, was very amusing. All the workmen, I believe, struck work, and men, women, and children rushed in crowds to see "the King of Ingee! Many of the great unwashed insisted upon shaking hands with him; some of the ladies who had not stayed to make their toilets very carefully wished to embrace him, and he with difficulty escaped. The aid of the police was required to make way for him to the manufactories, and when he had entered, it was necessary to close and bolt the gate to keep out the mob. After shaking hands with hundreds of them he turned round and addressed them, hoping they would all support the King and his Ministers in obtaining Reform; so happily had he caught the spirit of the people. He was answered with loud shouts, "The King and Reform forever!" On the road to London, wherever he stopped the inn was surrounded.

On the night of his arrival in the capital a rare honour awaited him. He got into London late in the evening, and being dissatisfied with the rooms assigned him in "a filthy inn in Newgate Street," went on to the Adelphi Hotel which he reached about ten o'clock. He had not told his friends when he was coming, but they had learned from other sources, and had prepared rooms for him at an hotel in Bond Street.

Yet, strange to say, long after he had retired to rest, the venerable Bentham, who had not for many years called on anyone or left his house, I believe, except to take his habitual walk in the garden, found his way to the hotel, and left a characteristic note for him.

This signal compliment from the leading British philosopher of the time must have greatly gratified the stranger. Rammohun took up his residence at 125, Regent Street, and for some months held court there as real, if informal, Ambassador from the people of India.

As soon (says Sutherland) as it was known in London that the great Brahman philosopher had arrived, the most distinguished men in the country crowded to pay their respects to him; and he had scarcely got into his lodgings in Regent Street, when his door was besieged with carriages from eleven in the morning till four in the afternoon; until this constant state of excitement (for he caught the tone of the day and vehemently discussed politics with everyone) actually made him ill, when his physicians gave positive orders to his footman not to admit visitors.

He became, in short, the lion of the season, and the Dowager Duchess of Cork, a noted lion-hunter, early marked him out for her prey. Mr. Sutherland comments with surprise upon Rammohun's being "for a considerable time much more in Tory than in Whig circles," even being introduced into the House of Lords by the Duke of Cumberland. It was his urgent solicitations which prevented the Tory peers voting against the Indian Jury Bill. Considering the round terms in which he rated the Tories to their face for opposing the Reform Bill, their hospitable behaviour towards him does them no small credit. "With Lord Brougham," Sutherland tells us, "he was on terms of the closest and most confidential intimacy * and, in short, he was honoured and esteemed by men of the most opposite opinions."

* [Mr. William Roscoe introduced Rammohun Roy on his arrival in England to Lord Brougham with the following letter:- "I have the great honour and very singular pleasure of introducing to your Lordship's kind notice and attention the bearer of this, the clebrated and learned Rammohun Roy, who has just arrived here from Calcutta, and of whom you must already have frequently heard as the illustrious convert from Hinduism to Christianity, and the author of the selections from the New Testament of "The Precepts of Jesus;" by the publication and diffusion of which amongst the natives of the East reasonable hopes are now entertained, that in a short time the shocking system and cruel practices of Paganism will be abolished, and the people of those populous regions be restored to the pure and simple precepts of morality and brotherly love. Amongst the many and important motives which have induced him to leave his country and connections, and visit this island, I under- stand he is induced to hope he may be of some assistance in promoting the cause of the natives of India in the great debate which must ere long take place here, respecting the Charter of the East India Company; but I have yet seen so little of him, from his numerous engagements here, that I must leave your Lordship to learn his intentions from himself, which you will find him very capable of explaining in his own strong and appropriate English idiom. One great reason, as I understand, for his haste to leave this for London, is to be present to witness the great measure that will be taken by your Lordship and your illustri- ous colleagues for promoting the long-wished for reform of his native country. On the present occasion, I will not

trouble you farther than to request, that, if it should not be inconsistent with your Lordship's station and convenience, you would obtain for our distinguished visitor the benefit of a seat under the gallery in the House of Commons on the debate on the third reading of the Reform Bill, which favour I am anxious he should owe rather to your Lordship (if you have no objection to it) than to other individuals, to whom, I understand, he has letters of introduction.]

That he should have been in great demand among the Unitarians, with whose leaders he had corresponded for years, and whose cause at home and abroad he had done so much to promote, was of course inevitable. He had not been long in London before a special meeting of the Unitarian Association was held in his honour. He was welcomed by Dr. Carpenter and others as 'brother' and 'fellow-labourer.++Rammohun had not yet recovered from the illness which his excessive popularity had brought on him, and responded with manifest exhaustion. A few sentences may be quoted from his brief speech:-

'With respect to your faith I may observe that I too believe in one God, and that I believe in almost all the doctrines that you do; but I do this for my own salvation and for my own peace.' 'I have honour for the appellation of Christian.' 'Scripture seconds your system of religion, common sense is always on your side.' 'I am convinced that your success sooner or later is certain.'

++[The full report of this meeting, as recorded in the Monthly Repository is as follows :-

"Just at this period (after the proceedings had commenced) the Rajah Rammohun Roy made his appearance on the platform, and was greeted with the cordial applause of the meeting.

The Rev. Chairman (Robert Aspland) Our illustrious friend (for such I trust he will allow me to call him) will permit me to state that his presence creates among us a sensation which he perhaps will hardly understand. It does so, because in his person and example we see an instance of the power of the human mind in recovering itself from the errors of ages; and because we conceive that we see in him, with his intelligence and character, one of the best and most disinteresed judges of the claims of Unitarianism to be the original Christian doctrine.

Dr. Bowring (afterwards Sir John Bowring) I feel it as a very signal honour to have entrusted to my care a resolution, the object of which is to welcome our illustrious oriental friend, and to communicate all we feel and hope towards him. I ought not to say all how we feel and hope, for I am sure that it is impossible to give expression to those sentiments of interest and anticipation with which his advent here is associated in all our minds. I recollect some writers have indulged themselves with inquiring what they should feel if any of those time-honoured men whose names have lived through the vicissitudes of ages, should appear among them. They have endeavoured to imagine what would be their sensation if a Plato or a Socrates, a Milton or a Newton were unexpectedly to honour them with their presence. I recollect that a poet, who has well been called divine, has drawn a beautiful picture of the feelings of those who first visited the southern hemisphere, and there saw, for the first time, that beautiful constelltation, the Golden Cross. It was with feelings such as they underwent, that I was overwhelmed when I stretched out in your name the hand of welcome to the Rajah Rammohun Roy. In my mind the effect of distance is very like the effect of time; and he who comes among us from a country thousands of miles off, must be looked upon with the same interest as the illustrious men who lived thousands of years ago. But in the case of our friend, his coming may be deemed an act of heroism of which the European cannot form a just estimate. When Peter the Great went forth to instruct himself in the civillzation of the South, when he left the barbarous honours of his own court to perfect himself in shipbuilding at Saardam, he presented himself to the public eye in a more illustrious manner than after any of his most glorious victories. But Peter had to overcome no prejudices, he had to break down no embarrassments, for he knew that he had left those who were behind him with an enthusiasm equal to his own, and he knew that he would be received by them, when he should return, with the same display of enthusiasm. Our illustsious friend, however, has made a more severe experiment: he has ventured to accomplish that which perhaps none other, connected as he is, with the highest honours of the Brahmanical race, ever attempted: he has ventured to do that which would have been regarded with incredulity ten years ago, and which hereafter will crown his name with the highest honour. He will go back to his friends in the East and tell them how interested we are in them, and how delighted we are to communicate to them through him all our desires to do everything in our power to advance their improvement and felicity. Time would fail me if I were to attempt to go over the history of our illustrious guest, if I were to tell how eminently and constantly he has exerted himself for the removal of misery, and the promotion of happiness.

If at this moment Hindoo piles are not burning for the reception of widows it is owing to his interference, to his exhortations, to his arguments. Can we look on such benefits as those without considering him our brother? Can he come here without hearing our enthusiastic voices telling him how we have marked his progress, and without our professing to him, if not our note of triumph, at least our accents of gratitude? It was to us a delightful dream that we might on some occasion, welcome him here; but though it was a hope, it was but a trembling one of which we scarcely dared to anticipate the fruition. But its accomplishment has produced recollections so interesting, that this day will be an epoch in our history, and no one will forget the occasion when the Brahmin stood among us to receive our welcome, and the assurance of the interest we take in all he does and in all he shall do; to which I may add that our delight will be too great if we can in any way advance those great plans, the progress of which is the grand object of his exertions. Sir, I move with great pleasure, "that the members of this Association feel a deep interest in the amelioration of the condition of the natives of British India; that we trust their welfare and improvement will never be lost sight of by the Legislature and Government of our country; that we have especial pleasure in the hope that juster notions and purer forms of religion are gradually advancing amongst them; and that our illustrious visitor from that distant region, the Rajah Rammohun Roy, be hereby certified of our sympathy in his arduous and philanthropic labours, of our admiration for his character, of our delight in his presence amongst us, and of our conviction that the magnanimous and beneficent course which he has marked out for himself and hitherto consistently pursued, will entitle him to the blessings of his countrymen and of mankind, as it will assuredly receive those of future generations.

Dr. Kirkland (late President of Harvard University, United States) In the absence of the Hon. Henry Wheaton, who was to have seconded this motion but is prevented by indisposition, I have great pleasure in seconding the motion. It is well-known that the Rajah is an object of lively interest in America; and he is expected there with the greatest anxiety.

The Rev. Chairman, in proposing this resolution, I beg to suggest that the assembly should rise in unanimous approbation of its object.

Rammohun continued to the last in close communication or personal fellowship with the chief Unitarian families of the time, the Estlins, the Carpenters, the Foxes, and the like. We have a letter of his to Rev. W. J. Fox, dated May 31, 1831, acknowledging with truly Oriental courtesy certain books which the author had sent him, and hoping for an interchange of visits "as soon as I am fully recovered" ; and on June 10th, a note assuring Mr. Fox "it will give me more real gratification to visit you in your cottage, as you call it, than to visit a palace. But as I happen to be engaged for dinner every day till the 19th, I would prefer seeing you at breakfast. "This shows us something of the throng of social engagements which claimed Rammohun. The visit to breakfast was finally arranged, as we learn from a note of June 13th, in which the Rajah says, "I shall endeavour to bring my little youngster with me, agreeably to your kind request." He also thanks Mr. Fox for the sermon sent him, adding,"After the discourse which I had the supreme gratification of hearing delivered by you, I must read anything that comes from your pen both with interest and instruction. "

A note to his booksellers, of May I, 1832, shows that he was a regular subscriber to the Monthly Repository, the Unitarian organ. He frequently attended Unitarian places of worship. But Unitarians found, to their considerable surprise that he was by no means prepared to identify himself wholly with their cause. His first Sunday in England was typical. He divided his attendance between Unitarian and Anglican churches. In fact the balance seemed latterly to turn in favour of the Anglican. It was no Unitarian divine, but the Rev. Dr. Kenney, the "Established" incumbent of St. Olaves Southwark, whom Rammohun Roy came to style "his parish priest." The ground assigned for this choice is the Hindu's admiration for Dr. Kenney's "benignity, charity, liberality to the creeds of others, and honesty in the great political struggle for Reform." There is a dash of humour about the fact of the author of 'Reasons for frequenting a Unitarian place of worship instead of the numerously attended established Churches' coming round in the end to style an established clergyman his "parish priest." But of this more anon.

Rammohun's political sagacity in supposing that his influence would tell more decisively for India through his personal if unofficial presence in London than through the usual official channels connecting the subject race with the supreme government was abundantly confirmed by the event. Whatever flaw official etiquette might find in the validity of his credentials was more than covered by the acceptance which the ultimate authority accorded to his mission. It is said that Ministers of the Crown "recognised his embassy and his title" as the ennobled representative of the Emperor of Delhi. But the much more important fact was that the people of England, in their own spontaneous way, acknowledged him as

Ambassador from the people of India. And this fact, however trying to official nerves, could not be ignored. The East India Company did indeed adhere stiffly to its refusal to recognise him either as Envoy from Delhi or as Rajah. But it could no longer afford to treat him as cava- lierly as it had treated him in Calcutta. Mr. Sutherland remarks somewhat sardonically on the striking alteration in their demeanour to Rammohun Roy which his receptlon in England effected among the Anglo-Indian officials. The very same men who had treated him with scorn in India now eagerly courted his acquaintance. The change of attitude was conspicuously signalized on the 6th of July, 1831, when a dinner was given to the distinguished stranger by the East India Company. "It was what was called a family dinner in contradistinction to the grand feast given upon the eve of the departure of a Governor for India."* It was nevertheless quite a State affair. The Chairman and Deputy Chairman of the Company presided, and some four-score guests were present. In proposing the toast of the evening the Chairman chiefly indulged in personal eulogy, but added the hope that Rammohun's reception would encourage other 'able and influential' Hindus to visit England. Rammohun in reply was equally discreet. 'That day was one,' he said, 'to which he had looked forward with the greatest degree of expectation. It rejoiced him to be seated amongst a body of gentlemen who had with such humanity and kindness carried on the government of India.' He contrasted the sanguinary anarchy which had prevailed in India prior to the advent of the British with its present peace and progress. 'He felt most grateful to the various illustrious persons who had filled from time to time the office of Governor-General,- to Lords Cornwallis, Wellesley, and Hastings' (he is careful not to mention Lord Amherst), and to Lord William Bentinck, who had done all in his power to gain the good opinion of the natives of India and so raise them in the scale of nations. He felt proud and grateful at what India was experiencing, and hoped she would ever enjoy a government equally popular, kind, conciliatory, and humane.

The meeting accordingly rose and carried the resolution by acclamation.

Rammohun Roy. I am too unwell and too much exhausted to take any active part in this meeting; but I am much indebted to Dr. Kirkland and to Dr. Bowring for the honour they have done me by calling me their fellow-labourer, and to you for admitting me to this society as a brother, and one of your fellow-labourers. I am not sensible that I have done anything to deserve being called a promoter of this cause; but with respect to your faith I may observe, that I too believe in one God, and that I believe in almost all the doctrines that you do: but I do this for my own salvation and for my own peace. For the objects of your Society, I must confess that I have done very little to entitle me to your gratitude or such admiration of my conduct. What have I done? I do not know what I have done! If I have ever rendered you any services, they must be very trifling - very trifling I am sure. I laboured under many disadvantages. In the first instance, the Hindoos and the Brahmins, to whom I am related, are all hostile to the cause; and even many Christians there are more hostile to our common cause than the Hindoos and Brahmins. I have honour for the appelation of Christian; but they always tried to throw difficulties and obstacles in the way of the principles of Unitarian Christianity. I have found some of these here; but more there. They abhor the notion of simple precepts. They always lay a stress on mystery and mystical points, which serve to delude their followers; and the consequence is, that we met with such opposition in India that our progress is very slight; and I feel ashamed on my side that I have not made any progress that might have placed me on a footing with my fellow-labourers in this part of the globe. However, if this is the true system of Christianity, it will prevail notwithstanding all the opposition that may be made to it. Scripture seconds your system of religion, common sense is always on your side; while power and prejudice are on the side of your opponents. There is a battle going on between reason, scripture, common sense, and wealth, power and prejudice. The three have been struggling with three; but I am convinced that your success, sooner or later, is certain. I feel overexhausted, and therefore conclude with an expression of my heartfelt thanks for the honour that from time to time you have conferred on me, and which I shall never forget to the last moment of my existence.

The Rajah will now allow me, as the representative of this assembly, to take him once more by the hand, and to repeat in your name our deep and heartfelt thanks for his presence on this occasion."

The chronicler observes thal "it was rather curious to see the Brahman surrounded by hearty feeders upon turtle and venison and champagne, and touching nothing himself but rice and cold water."

This public honour would certainly not lessen the influence which Rammohun possessed as an authority on all Indian questions. It was only natural that the Select Committee of the House of Commons which was appointed in February and re-appointed in June to consider the renewal of the Company's Charter should invite him to appear before it. This request

Rammohun declined, but tendered his evidence in the form of successive "Communications to the Board of Control," which besides duly appearing in the Blue Books were published by him in a separate volume.† The first of these was dated August 19, 1831, and dealt with the Revenue. It consists of two parts, one setting forth the facts and remedies proposed in question and answer, the other a summary paper of proposals. Rammohun here appears as the champion of the rack-rented ryot, or cultivator. While the Zamindars or landholders had been greatly benefited by the Permanent Settlement of 1793, while their wealth and the wealth of the community generally had increased, the poor cultivator was no better off. "Such is the melancholy condition of the agricultural labourers," he wrote, "that it always gives me the greatest pain to allude to it." The remedy he asked for was in the first place the prohibition of any further rise in rent, and secondly, rents being now so exorbitantly high as to leave the ryot in a state of extreme misery, a reduction in the revenue demanded from the zamindar so as to ensure a reduction in the ryot's rent. The decrease in revenue he would meet by increasing taxes upon luxuries, or by employing as collectors low-salaried natives instead of high-salaried Europeans. He also approved of the settlement in India of a few model landlords from England, but was careful to stipulate that they should not be drawn from the lower classes. He concluded with an earnest appeal "to any and every authority to devise some mode of alleviating the present miseries of the agricultural peasantry of India.".

In an appendix he urged the Imperial utility of this policy to recognise the indefeasible rights of the ryot in the soil that would make him loyal to the power that secured them. "The saving that might be effected by this liberal and generous policy, through the substituting of a militia force for a great part of the present standing army, would be much greater than any gain that could be realized by any system of increasing land revenue." This argument was backed up by a quotation from Saadi, which puts Rammohun's ideal for British rule in India in a nutshell:-

Be on friendly terms with thy subjects,

And rest easy about the warfare of thine enemies;

For to an upright prince his people is an army.

Throughout this communication the spokesman of the New India showed himself once more to be no mere advocate of the moneyed and educated classes, but the real tribune of the toiling and oppressed poor.

In his 'Questions and Answers on the Judicial System of India,' which was dated September 19, 1831, he proposed many and extensive reforms. Among the principal measures he advocated were the substitution of English for Persian as the official language of the courts of law; the appointment of native assessors in the civil courts; trial by jury, of which the Panchayet system was the native parallel; separation of the offices of judge and revenue commissioner; separation of the offices of judge and magistrate; codification of the crimi- nal law and also of the civil law of India; and consultation with the local magnates before enacting laws.

His additional queries respecting the condition of India, dated September 28, 1831, contained much valuable information. He recommended at the outset that "if the people of India were to be induced to abandon their religious prejudices and thereby become accustomed to the frequent and common use of a moderate proportion of animal food, the physical qualities of the people might be very much improved." The moral condition of the people he found to be good at a distance from large towns and head-stations and courts of law; bad among townsfolk; and still worse among clerks of courts, zamindars' agents, and the like. The people generally possessed "the same capability of improvement as any other civilized people." Those about the courts of princes rather carried their politeness to an inconvenient extent. He declared the ancient families to be "decidedly disaffected" to British rule, and urged that the only policy which could ensure the attachment of the intelligent natives was to make them eligible for gradual promotion, by merit and ability, to situations of trust and respectability in the State.

In this same month of September, Rammohun Roy was presented to the King and added to his other distinctions that of being the first Brahman received at the British court. The incident is one that lends itself to the art of a great historical painter. The ceremony was the picturesque token of a significant moment in the evolution of empire.

Rammohun was now a fully fledged member of the highest circles of society. Perhaps it was at this time that he was induced to depart from the "perfectly unostentatious" style of living which was to him habitual. "For a short time, about three months," according to Sutherland, "he had yieled to advice that was anything but disinterested, and taken up his residence in a most magnificent abode in Cumberland Terrace, Regent's Park, where he lived extravagantly. +*

Under the advice that was not disinterested, Mr. Sutherland is evidently referring to a man of whom we have heard before and who comes into unpleasant prominence in connection with the closing scenes of Rammohun's career. Mr. Sandford Arnot was acting as assistant editor to Mr. Buckingham on the staff of the Calcutta Journal in 1823, when that newspaper roused the wrath of Acting Governor-General Adams, and when consequently he had to follow his chief into banishment from India. On Rammohun's arrival in England, Mr. Sandford Arnot, doubtless on the strength of old acquaintance, was engaged as his secretary, and seems to have generally accompanied him. ++

+*The Indian Gazette, February 18, 1834. We have letters of Rammohun, Roy, dated 125, Regent Street, up to June 13, 1831, and letters of his dated from 48, Bedford Square, from January 27, 1832; so that this interval of extravagant residence must have fallen between those dates. Arnot says that most of Rammohun Roy's papers on the Judicial and Revenue System were written in Regent Street; which points to the removal to Cumberland Terrace taking place in or about September.

++ "As I may be accompanied by a European friend and two servants, I will lodge at some hotel in your immediate neighbourhood." R. Roy to J. B. Estlin, in a letter dated May 10, 1831.

Unless this quondam journalist has been shamefully, traduced, he was a low, cunning parasite. Having fastened on a rich and generous patron, whose position in a strange land made him peculiarly dependent on the guidance of British friends, he turned the opportunity without scruple to his own sordid account. In this as in other instances Rammohun showed himself - probably through excess of good nature - lacking in a wise choice of friends.

Not that he was by any means a slave to the caprice of those he had chosen; as was shown in this very matter of residence. Sutherland tells us that "his good sense soon prevailed over this folly of an extravagant establisment.

He abandoned this splendid mansion and went to live with Mr. Hare, the brother of Mr. David Hare* of Calcutta, in Bedford Square, where he continued while he was in London. He kept a plain chariot, with a coachman and footman in neat liveries; in fact adopted and adhered to the style of a private gentleman of moderate fortune, though still courted by the first men in the kingdom.

Of the stately figure which so much impressed London society, it may be well to reproduce here two portraits drawn by different hands. The first is by his friend Mr. Sutherland, writing in the Indian Gazette, Feb. 18, 1834. He says:-

Rammohun Roy surpassed the generality of his countrymen in his personal appearance almost as much as in his mental powers. In his prime of manhood his figure was beyond the common height, and was stout and muscular in proportion. His countenance wore an expression of blended dignity and benevolence that charmed at first sight and put his visitors at their ease, while it checked an irreverent familiarity. In the latter part of his life, which closed in his sixtieth year, his manly figure began to droop, perhaps not so much from age as the weight of thought and the toil of study. But his fine dark eye, though it lost some- thing of its fire, retained its intelligence and amenity to the last.

*The old comrade of Rammohun in Calcutta, in the struggle for the higher education of the natives.

The other sketch is by "R. M. M.," and appeared in the Court Journal for Oct. 5, 1833:

The Rajah, in the outer man, was cast in nature's finest mould: his figure was manly and robust: his carriage dignified: the forehead towering, expansive and commanding the eye dark, restless, full of brightness and animation, yet liquid and benevolent, and frequently glistening with a tear when affected by the deeper sensibility of the heart; the nose of Roman form and proportions: lips full and indicative of independence; the whole features deeply expressive, with a smile of soft and pecular fascination which won irresistibly the suffrages to whom it was addressed. His manners were characterized by suavity blended with dignity, verging towards either point according to the company in which he might be placed. To ladies his politeness was marked by the most delicate manner, and his felicitous mode of paying them a compliment gained him very many admirers among the high-born beauties of Britain. In conversation with individuals of every rank and of various nations and professions, he passed with the utmost ease from one language to another, suiting his remarks to each and all in excellent taste, and commanding the astonishment and respect of his hearers.

It was in argument, however, that this exalted Brahmin was most conspicuous: he seemed to grapple with truth intuitively, and called him invective, raillery, sarcasm, and sometimes a most brilliant wit, to aid him in confuting his opponent; if precedent were necessary, a remarkably retentive memory and extensive reading in many languages supplied him with a copious fund; and at times with a rough, unsparing, ruthless hand he burst asunder the meshes of sophistry, error and bigotry, in which it might be attempted to entangle him.

Of Rammohun's social life in London, as of his entire European visit, very much is told in Miss Mary Carpenter's Last Days in England of the Rajah, which need not be repeated here. We catch glimpses of him at sundry sorts of society functions, always the centre of admiring attention, always, too, the thorough Oriental gentleman, versatile, emotional, yet dignified.* His gracious manners and his especial deference to woment greatly ingratiated him with the fair sex, several of whom have left on record warmly appreciative reminiscences. Mrs. Le Breton ‡ who was a near neighbour of the Hares, tells of her aunt frankly confessing that "his feelings for women, still more his admiration of the mental accomplishments of English ladies, won our hearts." Mrs. Le Breton goes on-

I often met him in London.. at large parties and even balls, where he would converse on subjects that seemed rather unsuitable to the place, the Trinity and other sacred things which were occupying his own thoughts.

The same lady has preserved an instructive incident which explains better than volumes of analysis the fatuous failure of the baser sort of Anglo-Indian:-

At a party at a friend of ours - Captain Mauleverer, who had known the Rajah in India and was very much attached to him, we overheard one of the guests, an Indian officer of rank, say angrily, "What is that black fellow doing here?" A shocking speech to those who loved and honoured him so much!

Such is the folly which pride works in the less worthy members of a conquering race. Rammohun might be - and was - scholar and statesman, philanthropist and religious reformer, the friend and superior of many a Governor and Minister; yet to this military bully he was only 'that black fellow'; and therefore to be chevied out of genteel society.

We nevertheless find Rammohun thoroughly at home among the young Tory bloods, not hesitating to rate them soundly as "vagabonds" and worse for impeding the progress of Reform.

Fanny Kemble was one of the celebrities who have left on record appreciative reminiscences of their meeting with the Rajah. She was introduced to him at the house of Mr. Basil Montagu, a mutual friend. He was delighted to find her already acquainted with the Hindu drama, but was surprised to learn that she did not know 'Sakuntala,' which he regarded as the most remarkable play which India had produced, and which Goethe called "the most wonderful production of human genius." The Rajah subsequently sent her a copy of Sir William Jones' translation, but she failed to find in it the beauty and sublimity he attributed to it. Rammohun was evidently profoundly susceptible to dramatic impressions, as may be seen from an entry in Mrs. Kemble's diary for December 22, 1831:-

In the evening the play was "Isabella"; the house very bad. I played very well. The Rajah Rammohun Roy was in the Duke of Devonshire's box, and went into tits of crying, poor man!

This is a fact in a many-sided character which we are glad to have preserved. It is pleasant to know that the great reformer was not above tears, even over a well-acted play. We owe another instructive glimpse of the man to the same keen and kindly eye. The young actress records her presence at 'a pleasant party' at the Montagus' on March 6, 1832, where for an hour she 'recovered her love of dancing,' and where she met the Rajah.

We presently began a delightful nonsense conversation, which lasted a considerable time, and amused me extremely. His appearance is very striking. His picturesque dress and colour make him, of course, a remarkable object in a London ballroom. His countenance, besides being very intellectual, has an expression of great sweetness and benignity.

After a threatened break "we resumed our conversation together and kept up a brief interchange of persiflage which made us both laugh very much." Three days later she notes receiving "a charming letter and some Indian books from that most amiable of all the wise men of the East." One smiles to imagine what the good Baptists at Serampore Mission would think now of their quondam associate and literary combatant. These visits to the playhouse in the society of one of the first peers of the realm, and these gay frivolities with an actress would doubtless only confirm their theological misgivings as to the future fate of the "intelligent heathen." Rammohun had certainly no scruples about theatre going. On June 12, 1833, we find him writing to Miss Kiddell offering to accompany that lady and her friends to Astley's in the evening.

Among other celebrities which Rammohun met about this time was Robert Owen, the father of British Socialism The religious and the economic reformers were guests of Dr. Arnot, and Owen did his best to convert

Rammohun to Socialism. As the Scot finally lost his temper, the Hindu was considered to have had the best of the argument. It is interesting to remember that Mr. John Hare could call himself in a letter to Mr. Estlin (of March 25, 1834) "a poor Owenite."

The broad humanness of the Rajah's character is further shown in a little incident recorded by Miss Carpenter. The infant son of the Rev. D. Dawson was named after him 'Rammohan Roy'. The Rajah was actually present at the baptismal ceremony, and subsequently evinced a lively interest in the little fellow, calling frequently to see him. In fact, Mrs. Dawson wrote, "His visits to me were generally paid to me in my nursery, as he insisted on coming up so as to visit his namesake at the same time and not to interrupt me." Whatever the measure of perpetuity vouchsafed to the religious movement begun by Rammohun, this glimpse of the stately and courtly Brahman in the nursery, eager to see the baby and thoughtful of the mother's convenience, will, one may hope, be treasured by his followers to the very last of them as one of the sweetest and most beautiful memories of their Founder. Probably no index of character is so decisive as the attitude assumed to mother and child; and especially of religious leaders does this rule hold. Rammohun Roy in the nursery will be remembered by Brahmo mothers and Brahmo children much more vividly and endearingly than in any of his appearances in Court, or Senate-house, or Church, or even in the group of loving disciples.

Amid these varied social experiences, Rammohun never seems to have forgotten the scrutiny to which his conduct would be subjected by public opinion in India. We find him on January 27, 1832, writing to a friend who had invited him to attend a Unitarian Anniversary dinner, on Feb. 8th, in terms which reveal his constant watchfulness and sensitive regard to Indian criticism. He says:

It is truly mortifying for me to hesitate even for a moment to comply with a request of one whom I so highly esteem and respect. But I have before explained to you how much attending public dinners might be injurious to my interest in India and disagreeable to the feeling of my friends there. When you recollect, my dear Sir, that I attended the anniversary of the Unitarian, Association in defiance of the positive advice of my medical attendants, who declared that my joining so large an assembly while I was troubled with inflammation would endanger my life, I feel satisfied that you will not attribute my absence to indifference about your success.

I was induced to attend Dr. Williams' anniversary dinner under an assurance from the Rev. Mr. Aspland that the party would consist of friends who felt a warm interest on my behalf. But even then I felt all the time disquiet and low spirited. However should there be any divine service before dinner at the meeting or at your Chapel, I shall be very happy to attend at the service and return home. I sincerely feel the absence of our esteemed friend Dr. Bowring.

He finally consented to join the party "after dinner at 9 o'clock......at the London Tavern," so we learn from a note of his of Feb. 7. This dislike of his to public dinners was evidently due to their publicity. We have already observed the readiness with which he accepted invitations to private dinner parties - at one time dining out nine successive days; but these not being reported in the newspapers would not be so likely to reach the ears of his Hindu opponents, who were eagerly seeking occasions to prove against him breach of caste.

But about this time Rammohun's chief pre-occupation was political rather than social or ceremonial. The agitation for Reform was sweeping on to the final crisis. The First Bill introduced by Lord John Russell as Rammohun was nearing England (March 1, 1831), and defeated in Committee in April, had been followed by an immediate Dissolution. The Second Bill was carried through the new House of Commons by Sept. 22, but on Oct. 8 was rejected by the Lords, and the country was brought to the verge of civil war. The Third Reform Bill was carried through all its stages in the Lower House before the end of the following March (1832); and the nation awaited the action of the Lords in a wild fever of excitement. Rammohun shared in the general agony of suspense. He felt that it was no mere British business, but that it vitally affected the fortunes of mankind, and in no place more than in India. In a letter to Miss Kiddell, of date "48, Bedford Square, March 31," he says:-

I had lately the pleasure of seeing the Rev. Dr. Carpenter, and hearing from that truly venerable minister that Miss Castle and yourself were perfectly well and deeply interested in the cause of Reform, on the success of which the welfare of England, nay of the world, depends. I should have long ere visited Bristol and done myself the honour of paying you my long promised visit, but I have been impatiently waiting in London to know the result of the Bill. I feel very much obliged by your kind offers of attention to my comforts while I am in that part of the country, of which I hope to be able to avail myself as soon as my mind is relieved on this subject.

It wil! be remembered that on the momentous measure being introduced in the Upper Chamber, the peers showed signs of yielding to the storm of popular agitation. The Second Reading was carried on April 14th by 9 votes. On the 27th Rammohun was sending to a lady friend in the country, Mrs. Woodford by name, copies of his Remarks on India and a pamphlet on the abolition of suttee; and in the accompanying letter he referred to Lord W. Bentinck's Anti-Suttee administration and then to the victory over the peers, as follows:-

You will, I am sure, be highly gratified to learn that the present Governor-General of India has sufficient courage to afford them [Hindu widows] protection against the selfish relations, who cruelly used to take advantage of their tender feelings in the name and under the cloak of religion.

It must have afforded Mr. Woodford and yourself much gratification to learn by the first conveyance the division on the second reading of the Reform Bill. The struggles are not merely between the reformers and anti-reformers, but between liberty and oppression throughout the world; between justice and injustice, and between right and wrong. But from a reflection on the past events of history, we clearly perceive that liberal principles in politics and religion have been long gradually but steadily gaining ground, notwithstanding the opposition and obstinacy of despots and bigots. I am still unable to determine the period of my departure from London and my visit to you in the country. I may perhaps do myself that pleasure.

After the peers had shown fight for the last time, and had at last (in June) been cowed into finally passing the Bill, which was followed by similar measures for Ireland and Scotland, the Rajah wrote to Mr. Wm. Rathbone under date of July 31st:-

I am now happy to find myself fully justified in congratulating you and my other friends at Liverpool on the complete success of the Reform Bills, notwithstanding the voilent opposition and want of political principle on the part of the aristocrats. The nation can no longer be a prey of the few who used to fill their purses at the expense, nay, to the ruin of the people, for a period of upwards of fifty years. The ministers have honestly and firmly discharged their duty and provided the people with means of securing their rights. I hope and pray that the mighty people of England may now in like manner do theirs, cherishing public spirit and liberal principles, at the same time banishing bribery, corruption, and selfish interests from public proceedings.

As I publicly avowed that in the event of the Reform Bill being defeated I would renounce my connection with this country, I refrained from writing to you or any other friend in Liverpool until I knew the result. Thank Heaven, I can now feel proud of being one of your fellow subjects, and heartily rejoice that I have the infinite happiness of witnessing the salvation of the nation, nay, of the whole world.

Pray remember me kindly to Mr. Cropper and Mr. Benson, and present my best respects to Mrs. Rathbone and my love to the children....

P.S.- If the German philosopher is still at Liverpool, be good enough to remember me kindly to him, and inform him that we have succeeded in the Reform question wirhout having recourse to the principles of phrenology.

One is glad to see that the Rajah did not forget the children when he wrote, and that he could not resist the chance of poking fun at the good-humoured Spurzheim. His public threat of renouncing British allegiance in case the peers triumphed might perhaps seem amusing to the lower type of Anglo-Indian mind, the type that thought of him as only "that black fellow." The spectacle of a solitary Hindu renouncing the British Empire and all its works because of its refusing a wider franchise, not to his Eastern countrymen, but to the people of England, might be so construed as to look positively funny. But Rammohun was conscious of being virtually Ambassador for India; and if the sympathies of the progressive Hindus whom he typified were estranged from an unreformed England, and given, say, to a more democratic France, the Oriental memories and aspirations of the French might find less difficulty in making trouble for us in India. In any case, it was the most pronounced protest the Hindu reformer could make; and at a time of world crisis, as he conceived it, he must strike his heaviest stroke. It was stated, indeed, that should the Bill be defeated, he was resolved on leaving England and transfering himself and his allegiance to the United States. But we remember the intense enthusiasm he displayed for the tricolour when he first saw it at the Cape; and a further proof of his French sympathies was supplied by his visit to Paris in the autumn of the year.

While the people of England were thus successfully re-modelling their own system of Government, the Select Committee of the House of Commons was busily employed, amid all the storm of semi-revolutionary agitation, in considering how the government of the people of India might be in its turn - though on a widely different plane - advantageously remodelled. Rammohun, alive to the fingertips with the significance of both phases of imperial reconstruction, was naturally most concerned with what directly affected his own countrymen. We have from his hand under date July 14th, 1832, a highly suggestive document which appeared in the General Appendix to the Report of this Select Committee, and was so submitted to Parliament. It consists of Remarks on Settlement in India by Europeans.*

* [In the the midst of his absorbing political labours and social engagements the Raja, while in England, made time to publish several books, some of them new editions of old writings. The Christian Register for February 1832, announced the following publications from the pen of Rajah Rammohun Roy. "An essay on the Rights of Hindus over ancestral property according to the Law of Bengal, with an append containing Letters on the Hindoo Law of Inheritance" and "Remarks on East India Affairs; comprising the evidence to the Committee of the House of Commons on the Judicial and Revenue systems of India, with a dissertation on its Ancient Boundaries; also suggestions for the future government of the country illustrated by a map and further enriched with notes." A volume of his theological writings was published in 1832 by Allen and Co. under the title "Translation of several principal books, passages and texts of the Vedas, and of some controversial works on Brahminical Theology." The Raja intended to publish the journal of his visit to Europe, which would certainly have been very interesting, but evidently the work did not make much progress.]

It is a paper of rare personal and national importance. It supports the plea, which he had previously put forward both in speech and writing, for the removal of the restrictions imposed by the old Charter on the lease or purchase of lands by Europeans. He now enumerates nine advantages which he expects from the freedom asked for. European settlers would improve the agriculture and industry of the country, would help to dispel native superstitions and prejudices, would more readily secure improvements from Government, would be a check on oppression, native or British, would diffuse education through the land, would acquaint the public at home with what was going on in India as it appeared to other than official eyes, and would be an additional strength to the Government in case of invasion. The two remaining "advantages" must be quoted in full because of their daring forecast of remote possibilities:-

The same cause would operate to continue the connection between Great Britain and India on a solid and permanent footing; provided only that the latter country be governed in a liberal manner, by means of Parliamentary superintendence and such other legislative checks in this country as may be devised and established. India may thus for an unlimited period enjoy union with England, and the advantage of her enlightened Government; and in return contribute to support the greatness of this country.

If, however, events should occur to effect a seperation between the two countries, then still the existence of a large body of respectable settlers (consisting of Europeans and their descendants, professing Christianity, and speaking the English language in common with the bulk of the people, as well as possessed of superior knowledge, scientific, mechanical and political) would bring that vast Empire in the East to a level with other large Christian countries in Europe, and by means of its immense riches and extensive population, and by the help which may be reasonably expected from Europe, they (the settlers and their descendants) may succeed sooner or later in enlightening the surrounding nations of Asia.

Certain disadvantages are then specified, with their remedies. The insolence, over-reaching, and discredit to the British name, which were feared, might be obviated by allowing to settle, for the first twenty years at least, only "educated persons of character and capital," by equal laws, and by the appointment of European pleaders in country courts. Then follows a strange look ahead:-

Some apprehend as the fourth possible danger, that if the population of India were raised to wealth, intelligence, and public spirit by the accession and by the example of numerous respectable European settlers, the mixed community so formed would revolt (as the United States of America formerly did) against the power of Great Britain, and would ultimately establish independence. In reference to this, however, it must be observed that the Americans were driven to rebellion by misgovernment, otherwise they would not have revolted and separated themselves from England. Canada is a standing proof that an anxiety to effect a separation from the Mother country is not the natural wish of a people, even tolerably well ruled. The mixed community of India in like manner, so long as they are treated liberally and governed in an enlightened manner, will feel no disposition to cut off its connection with England, which may be preserved with so much mutual benefit to both countries. Yet as before observed, if events should occur to effect a separation (which may arise from many accidental causes. about which it is vain to speculate or make predictions), still a friendly and highly advantageous commercial intercourse may be kept up between two free and Christian countries, united as they will then be by resemblance of language, religion, and manners.

The fifth obstacle mentioned is the prejudicial effect of the climate on the health of Europeans. This, it is suggested, might be obviated to some extent by selecting the more salubrious spots for settlement. The paper concludes with a plea for at least a trial of the experiment.

The prospects unfolded here in close and rapid succession are almost enough to take one's breath away. The means by which the anticipated results should be attained is a matter of minor importance. The hope of an extensive and permanent settlement of Europeans on Indian soil may have proved in the present stage of civilization utterly fallacious. The remarkable thing is the vision of the eventual condition of his country, however arrived at, as it disclosed itself to the mind of Rammohun Roy. He shows here with ample clearness the kind of India he desired, and to some extent at least expected to arise. It is an English-speaking India. He anticipates that the settlers and their descendants will "speak the English language in common with the bulk of the people." It is, moreover, and this is a matter of yet greater surprise - a Christian India. He looks to it being raised to a level with "other large Christian empires," and speaks of England and India as prospectively "two free and Christian countries.. united..by resemblance of religion." It is, in a word, generally Anglicized India, possessing the opulence, intelligence and public spirit, and also the language, religion and manners of the English race. Nor is the Rajah in the slightest degree indisposed to contemplate the prospect of India as a nation politically independent. In any case he evidently desires to accept as her destiny the sublime role of the Enlightener of Asia.

These five points constitute a singularly daring programme. Never has the spokesman of the New India been so outspoken before. Never has he drawn so liberally on the future. Yet, most of the points are in the right line of his previous development. He had been throughout a consistent advocate for Europeanizing the Hindu intellect and the Hindu civilization. His sympathy with the struggle for national independence all over the world takes from his anticipation of a free and independent India any element of surprise. His hope that India would become a light to lighten the nations of the East was a natural product of his patriotism and love of rational culture. The one puzzling thing in this forecast is the prospect of a Christianized India. The cynic may be ready with the jibe that this part of the programme was srtictly for British comsumption. The Evangelical and Non-conformist public were shortly to show their strength by carrying through Parliament the abolition of West Indian Slavery; and the lure of a converted East Indies might be supposed to secure their powerful support for Rammohun's less distant projects. This explanation, quite apart from its slur on the Rajah's character, scarcely fits the case. The reform Rammohun is asking for is by no means of the dimensions to justify so tremendous a concession; and even if such a concession were intended, it would hardly be veiled in those indirect and allusive sen- tences. No one can suppose that the rest of the forecast is disingenuous. Indian independence was not exactly a prospect most agreeable to British susceptibilities; yet it is calmly advanced as a future possibility. The other points are quite of a piece with all we have known of Rammohun Roy. The imputation of insincerity in this one point of religion is surely gratuitous. The whole forecast bears the appearance of being genuine and in good faith. But we must in fairness point out that to anticipate as possible the conversion of India to Christianity is not necessarily to regard that as the most desirable result, or to accept Chris- tianity as one's own religion. In the struggle which must ensue between Hinduism and the Christian faith Rammohun may have foreseen that the latter would conquer as being the more fit, without himself believing it to be the most fit. It was certainly nearer his pure theism than the agglomerate of beliefs which went under the Hindu name; and its triumph would certainly be more acceptable to him than its defeat. But he still may have looked beyond the victory of Christiantty and hoped for the subsequent ascendency of his own theistic faith. Nevertheless, however we may explain his forecast, the fact remains that the founder of the Brahmo Samaj did anticipate the eventual Christianization of India. This is a fact the significance of which ought to be at no time overlooked either by Brahmos or by Christians.

Its importance is vastly increased when we remember that this is the last publication of Rammohun Roy. His career as author closes here; and closes with this truly colossal outlook. The document may not unfitly be held to embody the Last Will and Testament of Rammohun Roy to the People of India. His final literary deliverance holds up to them the five-fold prospect of

India speaking English,

India Christian,

India socially Anglicized,

India possibly independent,

India the Enlightener of Asia.

Among all the permutations and combinations of the Eastern and the English-speaking worlds, may these large hopes of the first Brahman who visited the English capital be reverently remembered!

Within a few months of penning this high tribute to the worth of English civilization, we find Rammohun Roy resident in the metropolis of our traditional rival in the East. Of his stay in Paris we have very scanty information. Between the letter cited above and dated Bedford Square, July 31st, and a letter of Miss Aikin written in October (1832), in which she speaks of Rammohun Roy being then in Paris, we have no account of his movements. We do not know when he went or when he returned. In an Appendice to M. Garcin de Tassy's Rudiments de la Langue Hindustani, published in 1883, there are twenty-one original Hindustani letters from various authors, one of whom is Rammohun Roy. Whether this was a fruit of his Parisian visit we have no knowledge. The next that we do know of him is given in a letter of his written after his return to England, and dated January 31st, 1833. It is addressed to Mr. Woodford and reads in full:-

My dear Sir,

I had on the 27th the pleasure of receiving your obliging communication, and beg to offer you and Mrs. W. my best thanks for this mark of attention towards me. I rejoice to observe that the translation of the Vedas, etc., which I presented to Mrs. W. before my departure for the continent of Europe, has proved interesting to her and yourself. I am now confirmed in the opinion that her good sense and her rational devotion to religion will not induce her to reject any reasonable sentiments on the ground that they are not found in this book, or in that volume.

I was detained in France too late to proceed to Italy last year; besides, without a knowledge of French, I found myself totally unable to carry on communication with foreigners, with any degree of facility. Hence, I thought, I would not avail myself of my travels through Italy and Austria to my own satisfaction. I have been studying French with a French gentleman, who accompanied me to London, and is now living with me.

I shall be most happy to receive your nephew, Mr. Kinglake, as I doubt not his company and conversation, as your relative and a firm friend of liberal principles, will be a source of delight to me. I thank you for the mention you made of Sir Henry Strachey. His talents, acquirements and manners, have rendered his name valuable to those who know him and can appreciate his merits. To the best of my belief and recollection, I declare that I do not know a native of Persia or India who could repeat Persian with greater accuracy than this British-born gentleman.

RAMMOHUN ROY.

It appears that he broke his return journey at Dover, for in a letter from 48, Bedford Square, of February 7, 1833, he writes to Miss Kiddell, of Bristol:-

I intended to pay you both [you and Miss Castle] a visit while residing in Dover, but was informed that it was necessary to pass London on my way to Bristol. My health is, thank God, thoroughly re-established.

He adds that he hopes to visit Bristol within a month's time, and begs them to "present my best respect to Dr. Carpenter, who truly stands very high in my estimation."

The public ends which brought Rammohun to England were being one by one attained. For two years after his arrival he had been prosecuting his mission from the King of Delhi, and bringing the claims of his royal master before influential personages. Mr. Arnot, in the Asiatic Journal for 1833, p. 208, thus states the result:-

A short time before his death he had brought his negotiations with the British Government on behalf of the King of Delhi to a successful close, by a compromise with the Ministers of the Crown, which will add £30,000 a year to the stipend of the Mogul, and of course make a proportionate reduction in the Indian revenue. The deceased ambassador had a contingent interest in this large addition to the ample allowance of the Mogul pageant, and his heirs, it is said, will gain from it a perpetual income of £3,000 or £4,000 a year.

A denial of this version of the facts appeared, evidently from an official source, in the Journal for January, 1834. The writer, "A.B.," did, however, allow that "Rammohun Roy delivered into the Court" of Directors "and partially circulated a statement regarding the claims of the King"; and that he "also framed a letter in English and Persian from the King of Delhi to his late Majesty George the Fourth, corresponding in substance with the former"; but "no answer was returned to either of these representations, and no negotiation on the subject of them carried on with Rammohun Roy."

The Court of Directors had indeed granted an augmentation of the King of Delhi's income, but solely on the representation of the Governor-General in Council, and would have made the addition although Rammohun Roy had never set foot in England. The writer concludes by regretting that any portion of the Directors' bounty to their royal beneficiary should have been diverted to Rammohun or his heirs. From these admissions the non-official reader will probably conclude that Rammohun's mission, however ignored officially, had really succeeded. An impecunious monarch, is not likely to bestow a pension of three to four thousand pounds a year except in return for solid service rendered.*

During his last summer Rammohun had the satisfaction of witnessing the final blow administered to the cause of suttee. The Appeal against the abolition of that inhuman rite was brought before the imperial authorities at home and was by them decisively rejected. Rammohun was present when the decision was announced on July 11, 1833.

Meantime the deliberations connected with the renewal of the East India Company's Charter were proceeding towards legislation. The Report of the Special Committee had been completed and presented to Parliament in August, 1832. It was before the Court of Directors in the months of March and April, 1833, and its recommendations agreed to. It was then drafted as a Bill and presented in the House of Commons in June. During these momentous negotiations Rammohun was doubtless very busy. In a letter to Miss Kiddell, of date May 14th, 1833, he again speaks of his intention to visit Bristol.

But (he adds) important matters passing here daily have detained me and may perhaps detain me longer than I expect. I, however, lose no time in informing you that the influenza has already lost its influence in London, a circumstance which justifies my entertaining a hope of seeing you and your friends in the metropolis within a short time, * perhaps by the 25th instant.

P.S. I sincerely hope that you all have escaped the complaint. So the influenza and the puns its name suggests were a malady common in the year of the first reformed Parliament. On June 22 he writes to Miss Castle, who with Miss Kiddell had charge of the education of his adopted son.

I hope you will excuse my boldness when I take upon myself to remind you of your promise to read the publication of a certain learned Brahmin which I have brought to your notice.

As we have seen, Rammohun was always eager to introduce Hindu books to the knowledge of English people, and this desire was naturally greater in regard to his son's teachers. About the same time, he wrote Miss Kiddell, begging her acceptance of a volume containing a series of sermons preached by Dr. Channing, which, he added, "I prize very highly." The following letter to Miss Kiddell gives another glimpse of the Rajah's varied character:

(48, Bedford Square, July 9th, 1833.)

Dear Madam,

I had yesterday the pleasure of receiving your letter of the 6th, and rejoice to learn that you find my son peaceable and well-behaved. I however entreat you will not stand on ceremony with him.

Be pleased to correct him whenever he deserves correction. My observation on, and confidence in, your excellent mode of educating young persons, have fully encouraged me to leave my youngster under your sole guidance. I at the same time cannot help feeling uneasy now and then at the chance of his proving disrespectful or troublesome to you or to Miss Castle.

Miss Daniel is not going to Bristol today. She will probably leave us on Friday next, when I intend to send a parcel of books, etc., in her charge. I hope I shall be able to have the peasure of visiting you at your country residence next week, and not before, a circumstance which I fear will prevent us from joining the meeting in your neighbourhood. Dr. Carpenter (I think) left London on Saturday last. I doubt not you will take my youngster every Sunday to hear that pious and true minister of the Gospel.

I will write again by Friday next. In the meantime I remain, dear Madam,

Yours very sincerely,

RAMMOHUN ROY.

Private convenience was, however, still further interfered with by the slow progress of public business, as is shown by this letter to Miss Ann Kiddell:-

48, Bedford Square, July 19th, 1833.

Dear Madam,

I know not how to express the eager desire I feel to proceed to Bristol to experience your further marks of attention and kindness, and Miss Castle's civil reception and polite conversation. But the sense of my duty to the natives of India has hitherto prevented me from fixing a day for my journey to that town, and has thus overpowered my feeling and inclination. It is generally believed that the main points respecting India will be settled by Wednesday next, and I therefore entertain a strong hope of visiting you by Friday next. I shall not fail to write to you on Wednesday or perhaps on Tuesday next. I feel gratified at the idea that you find my youngster worthy of your company. Nevertheless, I entreat you will exercise your authority over him, that he may benefit himself by your instructions. If you find him refractory, pray send him back to London. If not, you may allow him to stay there till I supply his place. With my best wishes for your uninterrupted health and happiness, I remain, dear Madam.

Yours very sincerely,

RAMMOHUN ROY.

P.S. All the active members of the East India Company having been incessantly occupied by the Charter question, I have not yet brought the subject relative to your young nephew to the notice of any of them.

R. R.

The following letter to Miss Castle is on the same sheet:-

Friday, dispatched on Saturday.

Ma chere Demoiselle,

Many thanks for your obliging and polite communication, which by mistake, bears no date. I am glad to observe that you are pleased with your late journey, and with your visit to Windsor. The account which Miss Kiddell and yourself have given of my son, gratifies me very much. Miss Hare received a letter from him this morning which she read to me, expressing his utmost joy and satisfaction with his present situation. I beg you will accept my best thanks for your kind treatment of him. Instead of thanking me for the little tract I had the pleasure to send you last week, I wish you had said only that you would pay attention to it.

You will perceive from my letter to Miss Kiddell that I am to be detained here a week longer at the sacrifice of my feelings. I however cannot help reflecting that to entertain a hope of enjoying the society of friends though for a short time, say one month, is more pleasant than bringing it to a termination by the completion of it. Adieu for the present.

I remain, Yours very sincerely and obliged,

RAMMOHUN ROY.

Impatience of protracted parliamentary delay appears again in the following to Miss Ann Kiddell ;-

48, Beford Square, July 24th, 1833.

Dear Madam,

From my anxiety to proceed to Bristol, heavy duties appeared to me light, and difficult tasks had seemed easily manageable.

The consequence was that I met with disappointments from time to time, which I felt severely. Today is the third reading of the Indian Bill in the House of Commons, after long vexatious debates in the Committee, impeding its progress under different pretensions. After the Bill has passed the Lower House, will lose no time in ascertaining how it will stand in the Upper Branch, and will immediately leave London without waiting for the final result. I will proceed direct to Bristol next week, and on my way to London, I will endeavour to visit my acquaintances at Bath and its vicinity. I deeply regret that I should have been prevented from fulfilling my intention this week, by circumstances over which I had no control.

I feel very much obliged by your kind suggestions contained in my son's letter. You may depend on my adhering to them. I intend to leave this place a little before ten A. M., that I may arrive there on the morning of the following day. Before I leave London I hope to be able to procure the situation for your young relative. Pray present my kindest regards to Miss Castle, and believe me, dear Madam.

Yours very sincerely,

RAMMOHUN ROY.

Three days after this letter (July 27th) we find Rammohun writing to Miss Mary Carpenter, "happy to observe from the communications of his son and his friends at Bristol that Dr. Carpenter is perfectly well, and has been discharging his duty as a faithful minister of Christ with his usual zeal and piety."

The delay attending his Bristol visit is further explained in another note to Miss Kiddell, dated 48, Bedford Square, August 16th, 1833:—

Dear Madam,

I have now the pleasure of informing you that I feel relieved, and will proceed to Stapleton Grove on Thursday next. I beg you will excuse this short letter as I am incessantly engaged in making preparations, particularly in writing letters to India and in different parts of this country. Pray give my love to my son and my kind regards to Miss Castle and believe me, dear Madam.

Yours very sincerely,

RAMMOHUN ROY.

At last the great measure which legalized the twenty odd years, transition of Indian government from a trading company to an Empire was finally enacted. The East India Bill received the Royal Assent on August 20. The Charter, then and thus renewed, made the Company less than ever a commercial agency and more more than ever a political. It was virtually the last Charter. A precarious renewal in 1853 ended in the Government of India being taken over by the Queen in 1858. But Rammohun was not pleased with the legislative activity of the Reformed Parliament, as may be seen from this letter to Mr. Woodford.

48, Bedford Square, August 22nd, 1833.

My dear Sir,

I was glad to hear from Mr. Carey some time ago that you and Mrs. W. were in good health when he saw you last; and Sir Henry Strachey, whom I had the pleasure of seeing about three weeks ago, has confirmed the same information. He is indeed an extraordinary man; and I feel delighted whenever I have an opportunity of conversing with that philosopher. I have been rather poorly for some days past; I am now getting better, and entertain a hope of proceeding to the country in a few days, when I will endeavour to pay you a visit in Taunton. The reformed Parliament has disappointed the people of England; the ministers may perhaps redeem their pledge during next session. The failure of several mercantile houses in Calcutta has produced much distrust both in India and England. The news from Portugal is highly gratifying, though another struggle is expected. I hope you will oblige me by presenting to Mrs. W., with my best respects, the accompanying copy of a translation, giving an account of the system of religion which prevailed in Central India at the time of the invasion of that country by Alexander the Great.

RAMMOHUN ROY.

A singular pathos attaches to this letter, which is the last we have preserved from Rammohun's pen. Its wide outlook, personal, political, historical, is characteristic of the man, but his disappointment with the new Parliament is more difficult to explain. The Session had given birth to Lord Ashley's first Factory Act, and decreed the abolition of West Indian slavery, no small achievements even for a reformed legislative machine. Possibly the terms of the new Charter were not to Rammohun's mind. Yet perhaps in this connection it would be well to recall what Mr. Arnot said in his obituary sketch in the Asiatic Journal before referred to:

Though a decided reformer, he was generally a moderate one. For his own country he did not propose even an Indian legislative council like Mr. Rickards', and he deemed the English more capable of governing his countrymen well than the natives themselves. A reference of measure of internal policy to a few of the most distinguished individuals in the European and native community, for their suggestions, previous to such measures being carried into law, was the utmost he asked in the present state of the Indian public mind. He not only always contended, at least among Europeans, for the necessity of continuing British rule for at least forty or fifty years to come, for the good of the people themselves; but he stood up firmly against the proposals of his more radical friends, for exchanging the East India Company's rule for a Colonial form of Government.

The reasons he adduced for this position are not wanting in shrewdness. "A Colonial Form of Government," be it remembered, did not then mean colonial self-government. Mr. Arnot continued:

His argument was, that in all matters connected with the colonies, he had found from long observation that the Minister was absolute, and the majority of the House of Commons subservient, there being no body of persons who had any adequate motive to thwart the Government in regard to distant dependencies of the British Crown. The change proposed was, therefore, in his estimation, a change from a limited Government, presenting a variety of efficient checks on any abuse oi its powers, for an absolute despotism.

His suggestions for the reform of Indian Government were thus of no extreme type. Yet mild as they were, they were not embodied in the East India Bill. His elaborate recommendations submitted to the Parliamentary Committee and to the British public had not obtained legislative endorsement.

But whatever may have led to his estrangement from the Grey Ministry, which he had at first applauded with enthusiasm, it need not now specially concern us. For Rammohun's political career was over. The series of brilliant services which mark him out as the pioneer of Indian freedom may be said to have ended when King William gave his assent to the East India Bill. The less than forty days which remained to Rammohun Roy after that event were spent outside of the arena of public questions.

About the closing weeks of his life there gathered many shadows. His was a sunset not of flaming sky and gorgeous cloud-wreath, but of struggling beams and weeping mist. Sandford Arnot insisted that "during the last period of his life his manners were much changed and the powers of his mind seemed to be decaying." This charge was stoutly denied by his staunch Unitarian friends, and may have been due only to Arnot's disappointed rapacity. The bluntest statement of the Rajah's difficulties is given in a private letter from the Sanskrit scholar, Horace Hayman Wilson, to Babu Ram Comul Sen, written 21st December, 1833 - three months after Rammohun's death - but published in the Indian Mirror, July 15, 1872.

Rammohun had grown very stout, and looked full and flushed when I saw him. It appears also that mental anxiety contributed to aggravate his complaint. He had become embarrassed for money, and was obliged to borrow of his friends here; in doing which he must have been exposed to much annoyance, as people in England would as soon part with their lives as their money. Then Mr. Sandford Arnot, whom he had employed as his secretary, importuned him for the payment of large sums which he called arrears of salary, and threatened Rammohun, if not paid, to do what he has done since his death-claim as his own writing all that Rammohun published in England. In short, Rammohun had got amongst a low, needy,unprincipled set of people, and found out his mistake, I suspect, when too ate, which preyed upon his spirits and injured his health.

As this letter was written after conversation with Mr. Hare's brother, it may be taken for trustworthy testimony. Pecuniary embarrassment was a misfortune from which Rammohun had never suffered before. His sons in India, according to the letter of Babu Nagendra Nath Chatterjee of Jan. 2,

1883, reporting the testimony of Babu Nanda Kishore Bose, neglected to send him money latterly," a neglect which seems the less excusable in the light of the large pension he had secured for the family from the King of Delhi. His wealth, actual or prospective, being in India, he could not realize it in England. Babu N. Bose declares (in a letter cited above) that owing to the lack of remittances from India, Rammohun, who had previously "refrained from dining with Englishmen," "was compelled from sheer necessity to dine with the Carpenters." The revolt of his parasites, however, only throws into clearer contrast the firm loyalty of his Unitarian friends. He had been living for some time now at the house of Mr. Hare, and the daughter [sister] of Mr. David Hare - his educational ally in Calcutta - was his devoted attendant to the end.

The long-lookedfor journey to Bristol was taken at last. Early in September the Rajah arrived at Stapleton Grove* on the outskirts of that city, the hospitable home of Miss Kiddell and Miss Castle, where his adopted son was being educated. With Rammohun came his two Hindu servants Ramhurry Doss and Ramrotun Mukerjee, neither of whom proved models of domestic loyalty, and the ever faithful Miss Hare. Dr. Carpenter was in Bristol at the time, and Mr. Estlin was Rammohun's medical adviser and friend.

Doubtless the Rajah, however worried by the claims of the extortionate Arnot, and however anxious about his future, would feel Stapleton Grove to be something like a haven of rest. He was among cultured religious people whose fidelity was beyond question. He was entertained and accompanied by admiring and sympathetic women. And his adopted boy was with him. It is pleasant to reflect on this little lull, of less than a fortnight, between a career full of conflict and what Browning calls "the last fight and the best." One menace to the tranquility of his stay at the Grove was perhaps offered by the religious eagerness of the hospitable circle in which he moved. On the two Sundays he was able to do so, he worshipped with his friends at Lewin's Mead Chapel; and they showed no slight desire to secure from him a confession of Christian faith. Mr. Estlin recorded in his diary for Sept. 9 that Rammohun had in his hearing declared "he denied the Divinity of Christ," but "distinctly asserted his belief in the Divine Mission of Christ." Rev. John Foster* bore witness to the fact that on the 11th of September the Rajah "avowed unequivocally his belief in the resurrection of Christ and in the Christian miracles generally.

*[Stapleton Grove is an agreeable and commodious mansion, which might well be selected as an example of an English gentleman's country residence. It had belonged to Mr. Michael Castle, a highly esteemed Bristol merchant, and one of Dr. Carpenter's congregation. On the death of that gentleman, and shortly after that of his wife, Dr. Carpenter undertook the charge (they had requested him to fulfil) of being one of the guardians of their only child, a young lady of great promises. As neither Dr. Carpenter's professional engagements, nor the nature of his own establishment, authorised his seeking the privilage he would so greatly have valued of receiving his distinguished friend in his own house, it had been arranged soon after the Raja's arrival in England, that whenever he was able to visit Bristol he should take up his abode at Stapleton Grove, where Miss Kiddel and Miss Castle esteemed it a high honour to receive him, and would do all in their power to render agreeable his stay in the neighbourhood. Last Days in England.]

At the same time he said that the internal evidence of Christianity had been the most decisive of his conviction." Mr. Estlin's diary for the 11th attests that the Rajah gave an account of the process which he went through in arriving at his present religious conclusions: "his belief in the resurrection of Christ, as the foundation of his faith in the general resurrection, he firmly declared."

The Rev. William Jay, of Bath, confesses to receiving a similar impression. He preached on June 17th, 1832, in Rowland Hill's chapel, a sermon on "The Riches of His Goodness," and among his hearers were the Lord Mayor of London and the Rajah. Mr. Jay says in his advertisement dated 1843* :

"When the service was over the Rajah came into the chapel house and pressed for leave, at his own expense, to print the sermon for distribution among his friends." "The author, with regard to this very extraordinary man, cannot help remarking that not only from the circumstance of his espousing this sermon (which, though not highly doctrinal, has allusions and intimations which would not accord with some theology), but from subsequent intercourse, as also from the testimony of others, he is persuaded that though at his first embracing Christianity he was Unitarian in his views, he was after he came to this country a sincere and earnest enquirer after evangelical truth, and would have professed his adoption of it had he not been prematurely removed by death.'+

* Works of William Jay, vol. vii., page 1oo (London, 1843).

+ A glimpse of the heart of the man is given in an incident mentioned by Mr. Jay. The worthy divine had told the old story: "When Dr. Doddridge asked his little daughter, who died so early, why everybody seemed to love her, she answered, 'I cannot tell, unless it be because I love everybody.'" He adds in a footnote: "Around this anecdote the Rajah, in the copy he sent the preacher, had drawn a pencil line."

In this connection we may mention another witness. The Rev. Richard Warner, Rector of Great Chalfield, Wilts., published in 1832 a sermon on "Charity, the Greatest of the Christ- ian Graces," with a Dedication to Rammohun Roy ‡, (‡ Quoted in pp. 22 and 23 of "A learned Indian in search of a Religion," by William Hamilton Drummond, D.D., London, 1833.) in which the Rajah is extolled "for the labours in which he exercises himself for the diffusion of the Light of Christianity and the promotion of Evangelical Love among an hundred millions of his countrymen." The worthy Rector proceeds:

Rajah, never shall I forget the long and profundly interesting conversation which passed between us a few days ago. Nor will the noble declaration fade from my recollection, that you were not only ready to sacrifice station, property and even life itself to the advancement of a religion which (in its genuine purity and simplicity proved its descent from the God of Love,.. but that you should consider the abstain- ing from such a course as the non-performance of one of the Highest Duties imposed upon rational, social, and accountable man!. May God prosper your benevolent endeavours to spread......the knowledge of Christ and the practice of Christian Charity !

This enthusiastic clergyman signs himself "Your friend and brother in Christ."

The diary of Mr. Estlin, published in Miss Marry Carpenter's work cited above, furnishes the fullest account of the last days of Rammohun Roy. On Thursday, the 19th, he found the Rajah ill in fever. From Mr. H. W. Wilson we learn that "it was thought he had the liver complaint, and his medical treatment was for that, not for determination to the head." But it was, after all, the overworked brain that was giving out. Mr. Estlin (on the 19th) noted the headache which accompanied the fever, and that he slept with his eyes much open. He needed a nurse. The medical man suggested that Miss Hare be allowed to attend to him. The sick Hindu objected on the score of propriety. Mr. Estlin reassured him as to British notions on that head, and David Hare's daughter was forthwith installed as nurse to her father's friend and her own. Mr. Estlin on the 22nd remarked on Miss Hare's weariless watchfulness and great influence with the Rajah: "He is evidently much attached to her, and her regard for him is quite filial," a pleasing fact to remember of the lone Hindu's last days. Next day (the 23rd) "the head appearing the organ most affected, leeches were applied." But the illness moved on towards its fatal issue.

The Rajah seemed to pass much of his waking time in prayer. What special burdens weighed on his mind and pressed out his entreaties, we have no means of knowing. His utterance of the sacred "AUM" one of the last words he was heard to utter - suggested that at the solitary gate of death as well as in the crowded thoroughfare of life the contemplation of Deity was the chief pre-occupation of his soul. Soon he began to lose all power of consciousness and speech, and yet he occasionally recovered sufficiently to express his deep thankfulness to the kind friends about him.

On Friday, the 27th September, the final crisis came. Mr. Estlin thus describes it -

The Rajah became worse every few minutes, his breathing more rattling and impeded, his pulse imperceptible. He moved about his right arm constantly and his left arm a little a few hours before his death It was a beautiful moonlight night; on one side of the window, as Mr. Hare, Miss Kiddell and I looked out of it, was the calm rural midnight scene; on the other, this extraordinary man dying. I shall never forget the moment. Miss Hare, now hopeless and overcome, could not summon courage to hang over the dying Rajah as she did while sooth- ing or feeding him ere hope had left her, and remained sobbing in the chair near; the young Rajah was generally holding his hand. . . . At half-past two Mr. Hare came into my room and told me it was all over. His last breath was drawn at 2.25.

So passed the soul of the great Hindu. His was a life of transition, from the time when he broke with his boyish faith and his father's house, all through the stormy years of his manhood; and now the greatest transition of all had come. The restless and valiant seeker after truth had at last arrived and attained. The pathos and poetry of that death-scene will linger long in the wistful imagination of India. The strange and distant western region, the rich rural landscape sleeping under the glamour of an autumn moon, the solitary country house standing out distinct in the silvery mystery of the moonlight, eveything wrapped in tranquillity and hushed to perfect stillness, nature and night combining to suggest the presence of the eternal calm; and within, the spirit of the great emancipator struggling to burst the fetters of mortality, and at last achieving the freedom and peace of the mystery which he had given his life to apprehend:--ere is a weirdly-mingled memory for the spiritual descendants of Rammohun, the myriad millions yet to be of an enlightened and enfranchised East.

On the day after death the body was subjected to a medical examination by Mr. Estlin, assisted by several friends. The cause of death was found to be "fever producing great pros- tration of the vital powers, and accompanied by inflammation of the brain." The fact that the brain was inflamed, of which the usual symptoms had not appeared, was ascertained only by this post-mortem inspection. Brain fever, brought on by financial and other worry, following on a life of intense mental activity, was thus the natural termination of the Rajah's career.

Mr. Estlin's diary records of the deceased that "his Brahminical thread was over the left shoulder and under the right, like a skein of common brown thread." The same evening the body was placed in the shell and leaden coffin under the superintendence of Mr. Estlin, who took care that the "Brahminical thread was never removed." One of Rammohun's servants, Ramrotun, was compelled -- "much against his will"- to attend as witness of these facts.

The interment of the great Brahman was characteristic of his career. In a postscript which is attached to Dr. Lant Carpenter's funeral Review, (London and Bristol, 1833) we have at once the narrative and explanation of Rammohun's singular obsequies:

The knowledge that the Rajah had in various ways manifested solicitude to preserve his caste with a view both to his usefulness and to the security of his property, and the belief that it might be endangered if he were buried among other dead or with Christian rites, operated to prevent the interment of his remains in any of the usual cemeteries. Besides this the Rajah had repeatedly expressed the wish that in case of his dying in England, a small piece of freehold ground might be purchased for his burying place, and a cottage be built on it for the gratuitous residence of some respectable poor person, to take charge of it. Every difficuly, however, was removed by the offer of Miss Castle, in which she had the warm accordance of all her intimate friends, to appropriate to the object a beautifully adapted spot in a shrubbery near her lawn, and under some fine elms. There this revered and beloved person was interred, on the 18th of October, about 2 p.m. The coffin was borne on men's shoulders, without a pall, and deposited in the grave, without any ritual and in silence. Everything conspired to give an impressive and affecting solemnity to his obsequies, Those who followed him to the grave and sorrowed there were his son and his two native servants, the members of the families of Stapleton Grove and Bedford Square, the Gurdians of Miss Castle and two of her nearest relatives, Mr. Estlin, Mr. Foster, and Dr. Jerrard, together with several ladies connected with the attendants already enumerated; and as there could be no regular entry of the interment in any official registers, those who witnessed it have signed several copies of a record drawn up for the purpose, in case such a document should be needed for any legal purposes.

So he was buried. Alone in his death as in his life, in alien soil, but carefully protected to the last from violation of his native customs. The silence that fell at the grave which closed so active and vocal a life is strangely suggestive. Rammohun's last word remains unspoken.

The grave in which he was laid was not, however, to be the final resting place. Ten years later a new home was found for his earthly remains in the cemetery of Arno's Vale near Bristol. There the Rajah's great friend and comrade, Dwarkanath Tagore, who had come over from India on pious pilgrimage to the place where the Master died, erected a tomb of stone. It was in 1872 - nearly forty years after Rammohun had passed out of the region of sensuous existence.

As was to be expected, the demise of the Hindu theist led to the delivery of many eloquent and impressive funeral discourses.* Among these many be mentioned Dr. Lant Carpenter's at Bristol, and Rev. W. J. Fox's at Finsbury Chapel, London, both of which contain much valuable biographic material. They display an easily explicable desire to identify the late Brahman with Christianity, but bear also striking witness to the power the Rajah had shown of inspiring warm personal affection. It is the ardent and admiring friend, not the spiritual undertaker, which appears in the preacher. That Rammohun should have rivetted to himself Hindu souls, of the same clime and blood as he was, and groping as he had groped after the light behind the cloud of ancient Indian religion, was not to be wondered at so much as the devoted friendships which he created among foreigners, of alien ways of thinking and believing, whom he had known only for a comparatively short period. It is no small testimony to his character that even a slight acquaintance with him was enough to stir stolid and phlegmatic Englishmen to something very nearly a passin of love for him. There must have been much love in the man to evoke evoke such devotion.

*[There were notices of the mournful event in many pulpits. The Rev. Dr. Kenney, of St. Olav's, Southwark whose ministrty Rammohun Roy

had frequently attended, preached a funeral sermon at the request of his parishoners. Five sermons were printed, viz, those by Dr. Carpenter preached in Lewin's Mead Chapel, Bristol, by Rev. R. Aspland in the New Gravel Pit Meeting, Hackney, by Dr. W. H. Drummond in the Presbyterian Church of Strand Street, Dublin, by the Rev. J. Scott Porter in the Meeting House of the first Presbyterian Congregation, Belfast, and the one by Rev. W. J. Fox in Finsbary Chapel, London,]

A jarring note in the general chorus of eulogy was struck by the biographic writings of M. Sandford Arnot, who had been Secretary to the Rajah from his arrival in England until a few months prior to his death. This man contributed a sketch of his deceased master to the November number of the Asiatic Journal (1833), in which besides speaking some- what harshly of the change that came over the mind and manners of the Rajah in the last months of his life, he suggested that the Rajah's literary work in English owed more than was generally supposed to his secretary's assistance. Dr. Lant Carpenter replied with some severity to this charge, in his published memorials of the great Hindu, as did also Mr. John Hare in the Times and other public prints. Arnot made rejoinder in the January number of the Asiatic Journal, specifying his services to the Rajah, and remarking, "I did no more than I suppose every other secretary does, that is, ascertains from his principal what he wishes to say or prove on any given subject, receives a rough outline, and works it out in his own way, making as many points and giving as much force of diction as he can." We may readily admit that Rammohun made free use of secretarial help, without impairing to any extent worth considering the genuineness of his authorship, or the reality of his singular command of the English language.* Subeditors and secretaries may lender most valuable aid, but their minor labours may never be mistaken for the work of the Chief. If he be a foreigner, it is their duty to preserve his English from lapses into foreign idiom and to suggest idiomatic utterances in their native tongue in place of his more colourless expressions. But editing is not composing. This Arnot as a journalist very well knew, and his effort to magnify his secretarial functions at the expense of his patron's literary reputation ought never to have been made. The pecuniary claims with which it was preceded and accompanied betray the extortionate purpose of the whole miserable business.

* [Dr. Carpenter has left on record the following authentic information on the subject on the authority of the Hare family: "Possessed of the Raja's unbounded confidence, acquainted with all his movements, and

enabled to judge with complete accuracy of his habits and dispositions, the unhesitating and unequivocal testimony of this (Hare) family, one and all, to the unvarying purity of his conduct and the refined delicacy of his sentiments, is as decisive as it is valuable. I had myself, repeated opportunities of observing with what earnest respect he appreciated the true delicacy in the female character: and I learnt that, while he always maintained his habitual politeness to the sex, and may therefore have misled the superficial observer, he manifested a very prompt and clear discrimination as to individuals; and that he commonly expressed strong dislike, and even disgust, where they seemed to him to depart from that true modesty which is essential to its excellence.

Mr. Joseph Hare - his brother fully agreeing with him-assures me that the Rajah was constantly in the habit of dictating, to those who were for the time acting as amanunses, in phraseology requiring no improvement, whether for the press or for the formation of official document--such verbal amendments only excepted, as his own careful revision supplied before the final completion of the manuscript: that he often hal recourse to friends to write from his dictation; among others to himself and the members of his family: that it is his full conviction, that from the day of the Raja's arrival in this country, he stood in no need of any assistance except that of a mere mechanical hand to write: and that he has often been struck-and recollects that he was particularly so at the time the Raja was writing his 'Answers to the queries on the Judicial and Revenue departments'- with his quick and correct diction, and his immediate perception of occasional errors when he came to revise the matter. These facts I and others have repeatedly heard from the Hares; and I rest with conviction upon them." Last days of Rammohun Roy.].

A controversy of a nobler kind arose concerning the religious position which the Rajah finally adopted. There was a very natural desire on the part of his Christian friends to claim him as in the end a decided Christian. Reverends W. Jay and Richard Warner did, we have seen, declare him a signal convert to Evangelical religion. In a conversation on the Lord's Prayer with the father of Mr. G. N. Aitchison (as reported in a letter from the latter to Prof. Max Muller, of date Sept. 27, 1883) Rammohun is stated to have declared his conviction that "that prayer was never made by man: its author could have been nothing less than Divine." Rev. John Foster held him to have made virtual confession, a few days before he died, of the Divine authority of Christ. Mr. Estlin, as already recorded, reported more precisely Rammohun's disbelief in the Divinity, but acceptance of the Divine mission of Jesus. Both these friends of his assert the Rajah's unequivocal conviction of the Resurrection of Jesus. We cannot wonder at Unitarian Christians regarding him as an illustrious champion of their views. But we may not accept offhand the testimony of these eager witnesses. Their differing estimates of his faith had been anticipated by him. Babu N. Bose used to tell how "Rammohun Roy before leaving for England, told him that the followers of every prevailing religion would reckon him, after his death, as one of their co-religionists. The Mohammedans would call him a Mohammedan, the Hindus would call him a Vedantic Hindu, the Christians a Unitarian Christian." But Babu N. Bose added, "he really belonged to no sect. His religion was Universal Theism." As he believed this principle to be the quintessence of every religion, he was able to approach the advocates of the most different creeds with a sympathy and an emphasis on points of agreement which they could only interpret as complete adhesion. The impression thus made was deepened by his extreme Oriental courtesy which seemed to not unfriendly Westerns to pass into over-great complaisance. Mr. James Sutherland, who was warmly attached to the Rajah, could write (in the Indian Gazette, Feb. 18, 1834):-

On questions of religious faith Rammohun Roy was in general too pliant, perhaps from his excessive fear of giving offence, or wounding the feelings of anybody, which accounts for the controversy which has arisen about his religious opinions. In fact, no matter what the creed of the parties with whom he conversed on such a subject, he was sure to impress them with an idea, either that he was of their peculiar faith, or that they had converted him to it. A lady once observed to me that she was rejoiced to find that he was a sincere Trinitarian, and that he had merely gone to Unitarian places of worship from curiosity, as he had attended Quakers' meetings, the Jewish Synagogue, etc.

Full weight must be given to these considerations. But they are not sufficient to account for the impression that the mind of the Rajah was in his later days moving towards more positive religious convictions. Sandford Arnot, whose testimony is not without value after allowance has been made for his one distorting motive roundly asserts that "in regard to religious belief" he saw "no reason to think that the slightest change took place in the Rajah's mind for the last forty or fifty years, that is, since the period when about sixteen years of age he began to doubt Hinduism." But this statement is no sooner made than Arnot-apparently quite unconsciously

-goes on to show how the Rajah's mind was actually changing. Arnot's scornful disbelief in Rammohun's reputed movement towards Christianity makes the following remarks of his all the more striking evidence:-

As he advanced in age, he became more strongly impressed with the importance of religion to the welfare of society, and the pernicious effects of scepticism. In his younger years, his mind had been deeply struck with the evils of believing too much, and against that he directed all his energies; but in his latter days he began to feel that there was as much, if not greater, danger in the tendency to believe too little.

Friends and believers in the New India growing up under British rule will warmly sympathise with the observations which next follow:-

He often deplored the existence of a party which had sprung up in Calcutta, composed principally of imprudent young men, some of them possessing talent, who had avowed themselves sceptics in the widest sense of the term. He described it as partly composed of East Indians, partly of the Hindu youth, who, from education had learnt to reject their own faith without substituting any other. These he thought more debased than the most bigoted Hindu, and their principles the bane of all morality.

His sense of this, the gravest danger of the Indian people, was only deepened by his experiences in the West :-

His strong aversion to infidelity was by no means diminished during his visit to Englahd and France; on the contrary, the more he mingled with society in Europe, the more strongly he became persuaded that religious belief is the only sure ground work of virtue. "If I were to settle with my family in Europe," he used to say, "I would never introduce them to any but religious persons, and from amongst them only would I select my friends: amongst them I find such kindness and friendship that I feel as if surrounded by my own kindred."

Next comes still more impressive evidence-from such a witness-as to the Rajah's changed mental attitude:-

He evidently now began to suspect that the Unitarian form of Christianity was too much rationalized (or sophisticated, perhaps, I may say) to be suitable to human nature. He remarked in the Unitarians a want of that fervour of zeal and devotion found among other Sects, and felt doubts whether a system appealing to reason only was calculated to produce a permanent influence on mankind.

Revulsion from the rationalism of Unitarians is a very decided portent of religious evolution. A kindred reaction affected him in regard to the philosophy then prevalent in England. Arnot continues:-

He perceived the same defect in the Utilitarian philosophy, and ridiculed the notion that man, a being governed by three powers, reason imagination and the passions, could be directed by those who addressed themselves only or chiefly to the first of these powers, overlooking the importance of the two other elements of human nature, which must continue to exert an everlasting influence.

There is much to confirm, there is nothing to impugn, these statements of Arnot. They bear every mark of being thoroughly veracious and are made still less open to question by Arnot's own contemptuous disbelief in Rammohun's supposed Christianity. They present additional indications of a kind which have been numerous throughout Rammohun's whole career, and which have grown more numerous towards its close. We have seen him lean increasingly towards fellowship with Anglicans, claiming an Anglican clergyman as his "parish priest." We have observed his remarkable anticipation that India would eventually become Christian. We may discount, but cannot wholly disallow, the witness of John Foster and J. B. Estlin concerning Rammohun's faith in the Resurrection.

To what do these things points? To Rammohun having gradually glided into Unitarian or even Evangelical Christianity? By no means. Rammohun was no Evangelical Christian, like Mr. Kenney or Mr. Jay. He was no Christian even of the type of Dr. Carpenter.* The conscious and com- plete surrender of the will to the authority of Jesus which is involved in conversion to either of these forms of Christian life is an experience through which, according to the evidence before us, Rammohun never passed. With the awful demand, "If any man would come after Me, let him deny himself and take up his cross and follow Me." we have no adequate ground for supposing that Rammohun complied. But a dispassionate view of the marvellous history of the man discredits the fancy that his convictions showed no change throughout his career of reform, even more utterly than it discredits the idea that he was a Christian. It points con-clusivly to the fact that Rammohun's awakened life was one of continuous transition. From the time when he left his father's house in revolt against conventional Hinduism to the last days in Stapleton Grove, his mind was moving on. It was driven forward by the imperious personal problem: Given an intensely religious nature, with profound emotions, large imagination and fine ethical sense, how to find expression for the same consonantly with the claims of a keen and comprehensive intellect.

The solution involved in the first instance a resolute break with the traditional polytheism. The process was to begin with chiefly negative. The youthful Reformer was for showing up the mistakes of all the religions. To gain the freedom demanded by his religious impulses, he was glad to welcome the destructive aid of rationalism. But rationalism was to him ever a means, never an end. His end was persistently religious, and therefore eventually positive. So he soon passed from an attitude towards all religions that was critical if not hostile, to an attitude that was sympathetic. He would extract the rational elements out of Hinduism and appropriate the ethical contents of Christianity. He tried to find a common denominator for Hindu and Christian Unitarianism. The device might please his intellect' but European Unitarianism left little room for the development of his warmblooded Oriental passion for religion. The founding of the Brahmo Samaj showed an effort not merely to satisfy the large ambitions of a devout and comprehensive intellect, but to meet the more specifically religious needs of a genuine fellowship and of social "morality touched with a Intellectualism emotion." was ascendent, but the driving power still in the was religion. With his arrival in England the process of evolution was naturally vastly accelerated. His knowledge of religious and philosophic systems was fertilized by close contact with the life out of which they grew or with which they were supposed to correspond. In especial, he came to know Christianity, not through its books or through isolated persons or groups as in India, but in its collective life and in its domestic civilization. He came to adopt a more positive and concrete, and perhaps a less merely speculative view of religion.

For the negative and disintegrating influence of the analytic intellect he developed an increasing horror. He denounced its effects in the scepticism of Calcutta and still more of Paris. He felt the barrenness and impotence of the Utilitarian philosophy. Man was much more than an intellectual machine. He had an imagination and a heart, and unless these were stirred creed or calculus or code were of slight avail. The need of religion, as distinguished from plausible speculations, became ever more paramount in Rammohun's eyes. Religion kindled imagination, roused passion, set the conscience in motion, as well as appeased the reason. But judged by these standards, Unitarian Christianity with which he had once hoped to effect much, was seriously lacking. It was too exclusively intellectual.

In the other Christian sects there might be less of reason and reasoning, but there was manifestly more of religion. Rammohun was coming to recognise more and more that religion was a whole-human thing: it was a force: it was a vital soul-kindling soul-begetting power: it was infinitely more than any causal theory of the Universe: it was never to be confounded with an arid rationalism or a bloodless ethicism. The primal religious impulse of Rammohun's nature was at last disentangling itself from the intellectualism under which it had long been working, at first joyously, but latterly with painful sense of oppression.

It will not do, therefore, to dub Rammohun Roy "Universal Theist" with Babu N. Bose, and pass on as though that formula could express his ever-changing career. At the outset his Theism was intellectually not far from the Deism of last century, in the end it was religiously not far from the spirit of Christianity. In the earlier stages of his emancipa- tion, his faith seemed to differ little from the fictitious "natural religion" of the eighteenth century philosophers, save for a strong infusion of Oriental passion. Towards the close, we see him turning with weary disgust from the fanciful abstractions of the speculative intellect to the dynamic facts of human nature and of human history. How much further he would have moved in the direction of positive religion if his life had been prolonged for any considerable period, it is idle to conjecture. The theological transition which lasted all his life was at his death left incomplete. We may not guess at its completion. It is enough for us to observe its direction.

These conclusions to the inner movement of Rammohun's mind suggest his place in history. The life is the life work. His own career of constant but incomplete transition constituted him the leader and the instrument of a kindred transition among his fellow-countrymen. The path he trod they seem destined to follow; more or less rapidly as opportunity and inducement vary, but perhaps none the less surely because the goal towards which he was moving was never by him visibly attained. Rammohun stands in history as the living bridge over which India marches from her unmeasured past to her incalculable future. He was the arch which spanned the gulf that yawned between ancient caste and modern humanity, between superstition and Science, between despotism and democrocy, between immobile custom and a conservative progress, between a bewildering polytheism and a pure, if vague, Theism. He was the mediator of his people, harmonizing in his own person often by means of his own solitary sufferings, the conflicting tendencies of immemorial tradition and of inevitable enlightenment.

The impact of Christian civilization, with its wide freedom and strong tolerance, upon the unreconciled juxtaposition of Islam and Hinduism, introduced into the life of the people of India a painful crisis. There were new and fierce revulsions, there were attractions, powerful though hidden: there was an intense mental effervescence: there was the sudden generation of strange and composite ideas: there was, in short, a sort of silent explosion within the spiritual frame, which sent thrills of agony through every shattered and lacerated fragment. But the misery caused by the destructive consequences, although more obvious at first, cannot conceal the sympathetic and constructive forces at work. Of the result of this impact we may regard Rammohun as the personal type. He embodies the new spirit which arises from the compulsory mixture of races and faiths and civilizations, he embodies its freedom of inquiry, its thirst for science, its large humane sympathy, its pure and sifted ethics; along with its reverent but not uncri- tical regard for the past, and prudent even timid disinclination towards revolt. But in the life of Rammohun we see what we hope yet to have shown us in the progress of India, that the secrect of the whole movement is religious. Amid all his wanderings Rammohun was saved by his faith. From the perfervid piety of his Pagan boyhood to the strong leanings which, in his latest years, he evinced towards Christianity he was led by his faith, the purpose and passion of belief which he inherited from all the ages of India's history. He was a genuine outgrowth of the old Hindu stock; in a soil watered by new. influences, and in an atmosphere charged with unwonted forcing power, but still a true scion of the old stock. The Rajah was no merely occidentalized Oriental, no Hindu polished into the doubtful semblance of a European. Just as little was he, if we may use the term without offence, a spiritual Eurasian. If we follow the right line of his development we shall find that he leads the way from the Orientalism of the past, not to, but through Western culture, towards a civilization which is neither Western nor Eastern, but something vastly larger and nobler than both. He preserves continuity throughout, by virtue of his religion, which again supplied the motive force of his progressive movement. The power that connected and restrained, as well as widened and impelled, was religion.

Rammohun thus presents a most instructive and inspiring study for the New India of which he is the type and pioneer, He offers to the new democray of the West a scarcely less valuable index of what our greatest Eastern dependency may yet become under the Imperial sway of the British commonalty. There can be little doubt that, whatever future the destinies may have in store for India, that future will be largely shaped by the life and work of Rammohun Roy. And not the future of India alone. We stand on the eve of an unprecedented intermingling of East and West. The European and the Asiatic streams of human development, which have often tinged each other before, are now approach- ing a confluence which bids fair to form the one ocean-river of the collective progress of mankind. In the presence of that greater Eastern Question, with its infinite ramifications, industrial, political, moral and religious,-the international problems of the passing hour, even the gravest of them, seem dwarfed into parochial pettiness. The nearing dawn of these unmeasured possibilities only throws into clearer prominence the figure of the man whose life-story we have told. He was, if not the prophetic type, at least the precursive hint, of the change that is to come.

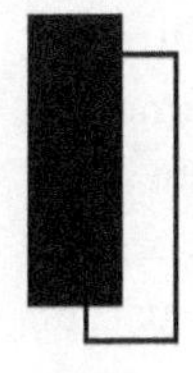

Autobiographical Image of Rammohan Roy

In conformity with the wish, you have frequently expressed, that I should give you an outline of my life, I have now the pleasure to give you the following very brief sketch.

My ancestors were Brahmins of a high order, and from time immemorial were devoted to the religious duties of their race, down to my fifth progenitor, who about one hundred and forty years ago, gave up spiritual exercises for worldly pursuits and aggrandisement. His descendents ever since follow- ed his example, and according to the usual fate of courtiers with various success, sometimes rising to honour and sometimes falling; sometimes rich and sometimes poor; some- times excelling in success, sometimes miserable through dis- appointment. But my maternal ancestors, being of the sacradotal order by profession as well as by birth, and of a family than which none holds a higher rank in that profession, have up to the present day uniformly adhered to a life of religious observances and devotion, preferring peace and tranquility of mind to the excitements of ambition and all the allurements of worldly grandeur.

In conformity with the usage of my parental race, and the wish of my father, I studied the Persian and Arabic languages, these being indispensable to those who attached themselves to the courts of the Mahommedan princes; and agreeably to the usage of my maternal relations, I devoted myself to the study of the Sanskrit and the theological works written in it, which contain the body of Hindu literature, law and religion. When about the age of sixteen, I composed a manuscript calling in question the validity of the idolatrous system of the Hindoos. This, together with my known sentiments on the subject, having produced coolness a between me and my immediate kindred, I proceeded on my travels and passed through different countries, chiefly within, but some beyond the bounds of Hindoostan, with a feeling of great aversion to the establishment of the British power in India. When I had reached the age of twenty, my father recalled me and restored me to his favour; after which I first saw and began to associate with Europeans, and soon after made myself tolerably acquainted with their laws and form of government. Finding them generally more intelligent, more steady and moderate in their conduct, I gave up my prejudice against them, and became inclined in their favour, feeling persuaded that their rule, though a foreign yoke, would lead more speedily and surely to the amelioration of the native inhabitants; and I enjoyed the confidence of several of them even in their public capacity. My continued controversies with the Brahmins on the subject of their idolatry and superstition, and my interference with their custom of burning widows, and other pernicious practices, revived and increased their animosity against me; and through their influence with my family, my father was again obliged to withdraw his countenance openly, though his limited pecuniary support was still continued to me.

After my father's death I opposed the advocates of idolatry with still greater boldness. Availing myself of the art of printing, now establishd in India, I published various works and pamphlets against their errors, in the native and foreign languages. This raised such a feeling against me, that I was at last deserted by every person except two or three Scotch friends, to whom, and the nation to which they belong, I always feel grateful.

The ground which I took in all my controversies was, not that of opposition to Brahminism, but to a perversion of it; and I endeavoured to show that the idolatry of the Brahmins was contrary to the practice of their ancestors, and the principles of the ancient books and authorities which they profess to revere and obey. Notwithstanding the violence of the opposition and resistance to my opinions several highly respectable persons, both among my own relations and others, began to adopt the same sentiments.

I now felt a strong wish to visit Europe, and obtain, by personal observation, a more thorough insight into its manners, customs, religion, and political institutions. I refrained, however, from carrying this intention into effect until the friends who coincided in my sentiments should be increased in number and strength. My expectations having been at length realized, in November 1830, I embarked for England, as the discussion of the East India company's Charter was expected to come on by which the treatment of the Natives of India, and its future government, would be determined for many years to come, and an Appeal to the King in Council, against the abolition of the practice of burning widows, was to be heard before the Privy Council; and His Majesty, the Emperor of Delhi, had likewise commissioned me to bring before the authorities in England certain encroachments on his rights by the East India Company. I accordingly arrived in England in April, 1831.

[BY MR. RAMMOHUN ROY]

*****

www.ingramcontent.com/pod-product-compliance
Lightning Source LLC
LaVergne TN
LVHW040014200726
843493LV00005B/1265